The Power of Critical Thinking 7e
Lewis Vaughn

Reasoning 101

Gonzaga University Custom Edition

OXFORD
UNIVERSITY PRESS

Contents

The Power of
Critical Thinking

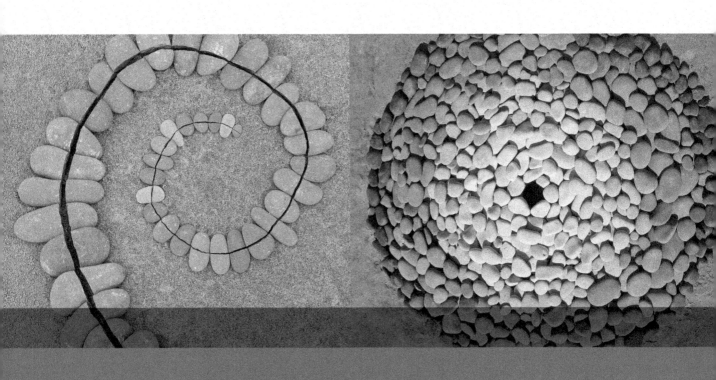

The Power of
Critical Thinking

SEVENTH EDITION

Effective Reasoning About Ordinary and Extraordinary Claims

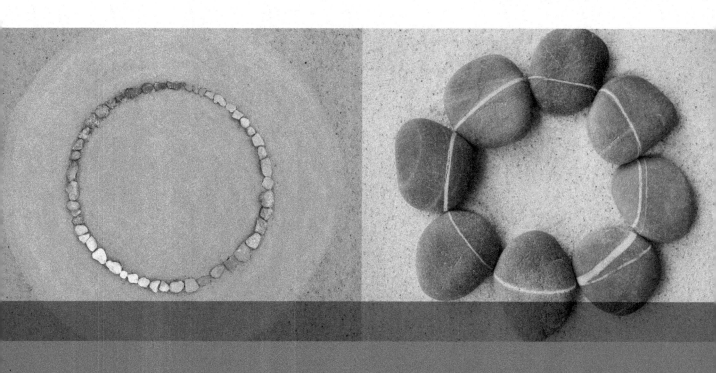

Lewis Vaughn

NEW YORK   OXFORD
OXFORD UNIVERSITY PRESS

Oxford University Press is a department of the University of Oxford.
It furthers the University's objective of excellence in research, scholarship,
and education by publishing worldwide. Oxford is a registered trade mark of
Oxford University Press in the UK and certain other countries.

Published in the United States of America by Oxford University Press
198 Madison Avenue, New York, NY 10016, United States of America.

For titles covered by Section 112 of the US Higher Education
Opportunity Act, please visit www.oup.com/us/he for the
latest information about pricing and alternate formats.

CIP data is on file at the Library of Congress.
ISBN 978-0-19-760537-0

9 8 7 6 5 4 3 2 1

Printed by Quad/Graphics, Mexico

1

The Power of Critical Thinking

CHAPTER OBJECTIVES

- Understand the definition of *critical thinking* and the importance of the definition terms "systematic," "evaluation," "formulation," and "rational standards."
- Understand how critical thinking relates to logic, the truth or falsity of statements, knowledge, and personal empowerment.

WHY IT MATTERS

- Appreciate why critical thinking is better than the passive acceptance of beliefs.
- Appreciate the relevance of the claim "The unexamined life is not worth living" to critical thinking.
- Understand why the following claims are dubious: "Critical thinking makes people too critical or cynical," "Critical thinking makes people cold and unemotional," and "Critical thinking is the enemy of creativity."
- Appreciate the pervasive use of critical thinking in all human endeavors.
- Understand how critical thinking empowers people.

HOW IT WORKS

- Distinguish between statements and nonstatements.
- Understand the basic concepts of reasons, argument, inference, premises, and conclusion.
- Know how to use indicator words to help pinpoint premises and conclusions.
- Be able to distinguish between passages that do and do not contain an argument.
- Be able to identify arguments in various contexts and distinguish between arguments and superfluous material, arguments and explanations, and premises and conclusions.

YOU CAME INTO THIS WORLD WITHOUT OPINIONS OR JUDGMENTS OR VALUES or viewpoints—and now your head is brimming with them. If you tried to write them all down, you would be busy for the rest of your life (and would probably win an award for being the world's biggest bore). They help you make your way through the world. They guide you to both failure and success, ignorance and understanding, good and bad, paralysis and empowerment. Some of your beliefs truly inform you, and some blind you. Some are true; some are not. But the question is, which ones are which? This kind of question—a question about the quality of your beliefs—is the fundamental concern of **critical thinking**.

Determining the quality or value of your beliefs is a function of thinking, and the kind of thinking that does this job best is critical thinking—a skill that higher education seeks to foster. This means that critical thinking is not about *what* you think, but *how* you think.

Notice also that the question about the quality of beliefs is not about what factors *caused* you to have the beliefs that you do. A sociologist might tell you how society has influenced some of your moral choices. A psychologist might describe how your emotions cause you to cling to certain opinions. Your best friend might allege that you have unconsciously absorbed most of your beliefs directly from your parents. But none of these speculations has much to do with the central task of critical thinking.

Critical thinking focuses not on what *causes* a belief, but on *whether it is worth believing*. A belief is worth believing, or accepting, if we have *good reasons* to accept it. The better the reasons for acceptance, the more likely the belief is to be true. Critical thinking offers us a set of standards embodied in techniques, attitudes, and principles that we can use to assess beliefs and determine if they are supported by good reasons. After all, we want our beliefs to be true, to be good guides for dealing with the world—and critical thinking is the best tool we have for achieving this goal.

Here's one way to wrap up these points in a concise definition:

CRITICAL THINKING: The systematic evaluation or formulation of beliefs, or statements, by rational standards.

Critical thinking is *systematic* because it involves distinct procedures and methods. It entails *evaluation* and *formulation* because it's used to both assess existing beliefs (yours or someone else's) and devise new ones. And it operates according to *rational standards* in that beliefs are judged by how well they are supported by reasons.

Critical thinking, of course, involves **logic**. Logic is the study of good reasoning, or inference, and the rules that govern it. Critical thinking is broader than logic because it involves not only logic but also the truth or falsity of statements, the evaluation of arguments and evidence, the use of analysis and investigation, and the application of many other skills that help us decide what to believe or do.

Ultimately, what critical thinking leads you to is knowledge, understanding, and—if you put these to work—empowerment. In addition, as you're guided by your instructor through this text, you will come to appreciate some other benefits that cannot be fully explored now: Critical thinking enables problem-solving, active learning, and intelligent self-improvement.

In Chapters 2 and 3 (the rest of Part One) you'll get a more thorough grounding in critical thinking and logical argument plus plenty of opportunities to practice your new skills. Consider this chapter an introduction to those important lessons.

Why It Matters

In large measure, our lives are defined by our actions and choices, and our actions and choices are guided by our thinking—so our thinking had better be good. Almost every day we are hit by a blizzard of assertions, opinions, arguments, and pronouncements from all directions. They all implore us to believe, to agree, to accept, to follow, to submit. If we care whether our choices are right and our beliefs true, if we want to rise above blind acceptance and arbitrary choices, we must use the tools provided by critical thinking.

We, of course, always have the option of taking the easy way out. We can simply glom onto whatever beliefs or statements come blowing by in the wind, adopting viewpoints because they are favored by others or because they make us feel good. But then we forfeit control over our lives and let the wind take us wherever it will, as if we had no more say in the outcome than a leaf in a storm.

A consequence then of going with the wind is a loss of personal freedom. If you passively accept beliefs that have been handed to you by your parents, your culture, or your teachers, then those beliefs are *not really yours*. You just happened to be in a certain place and time when they were handed out. If they are not really yours, and you let them guide your choices and actions, then they—not you—are in charge of your life. Your beliefs are yours only if you critically examine them for yourself to see if they are supported by good reasons.

To examine your beliefs in this way is to examine your life, for your beliefs in large measure define your life. To forgo such scrutiny is to abandon your chance of making your life deliberately and authentically meaningful. The great philosopher Socrates says it best: "The unexamined life is not worth living."

Thus, in the most profound sense, critical thinking is not only enlightening, but empowering. This empowerment can take several forms:

> "Are you not ashamed of caring so much for the making of money and for fame and prestige, when you neither think nor care about wisdom and truth and the improvement of your soul?"
> **—Socrates**

> **Skills for learning and exploring.** Some species of critical thinking is essential in every intellectual endeavor, every profession, and every college course. Economics, literature, philosophy, ethics, science, medicine, law—these and many other fields require you to understand and use argument, evaluation, analysis, logic, and evidence. Critical thinking is the common language of many worlds, and practicing it will help you make your way in them.

> **Defense against error, manipulation, and prejudice.** For lack of good critical thinking, many intelligent people have been taken in by clever marketers, dubious "experts," self-serving politicians, charming

demagogues, skillful propagandists, misinformed bloggers, woolly conspiracy theorists, misguided gurus, reckless alarmists, knee-jerk partisans, and smooth-talking xenophobes. For want of a little logic and careful reflection, you can easily choose the wrong career, wrong friends, wrong spouse, wrong investments, wrong religion, and wrong leaders. Without some skill in moral reasoning (critical thinking applied to ethics), you risk making bad decisions about right and wrong, about good and bad. Critical thinking is no guarantee against any of these errors, but it does provide your best possible defense.

Tools for self-discovery. A central goal of higher education is to enable students to think critically and carefully for themselves, to confront issues and problems and then devise their own warranted, defensible answers. This means you must be able not only to critically examine the arguments and assertions of others but also to apply these critical powers to your own ideas. To discover what to believe—that is, to find out which claims are worthy of belief—you must weigh them in the balance of critical reasoning. A central question of a mature intellect is, "What should I believe?" This is the fundamental query at the heart of all your conscious life choices. Only you can answer it, and ultimately only critical thinking can guide you to justified answers.

Critical thinking applies not just to some of your individual beliefs, but to all of them together. It applies to your worldview, the vast web of fundamental ideas that help you make sense of the world, what some people call a philosophy of life. We all have a worldview, and most of us want the beliefs that constitute it to be true and coherent (to fit together without internal contradictions). As you will see in Chapter 12, devising a coherent worldview is the work of a lifetime—and can only be done with the help of critical thinking.

Our choice whether to apply critical thinking skills is not an all-or-nothing decision. Each of us uses critical thinking to some degree in our lives. We often evaluate reasons for (and against) believing that someone has committed a crime, that an earnest celebrity is deluded, that one candidate in an election is better than another, that gun control laws should be strengthened or weakened, that we should buy a car, that the legendary Bigfoot does not exist, that a friend is trustworthy, that one university is superior to another, that the bill being considered in Congress would be bad for the environment, that Elvis is living the good life in a witness-protection program. But the more urgent consideration is not just whether we sometimes use critical thinking, but how well we use it.

Many people, however, will have none of this—and perhaps you are one of them. They believe that critical thinking—or what they take to be critical — thinking—makes one excessively critical or cynical, emotionally cold, and creatively constrained.

For example, there are some who view anything that smacks of logic and rationality as a negative enterprise designed to attack someone else's thinking and score points by putting people in their place. A few of these take the word *critical* here to mean "faultfinding" or "carping."

Now, no doubt some people try to use critical thinking primarily for offensive purposes, but this approach goes against critical thinking principles. The *critical* in critical thinking is used in the sense of "exercising or involving careful judgment or judicious evaluation." Critical thinking is about determining what we are justified in believing, and that involves an openness to other points of view, a tolerance for opposing perspectives, a focus on the issue at hand, and fair assessments of arguments and evidence. To paraphrase a bumper-sticker slogan: Good critical thinking does not make cynics—people make cynics.

Some people fear that if they apply critical thinking to their lives, they will become cold and unemotional—just like a computer abuzz with logic and rote functions. But this is a confused notion. Critical thinking and feelings actually complement one another. Certainly part of thinking critically is ensuring that we don't let our emotions distort our judgments. But critical thinking can also help us clarify our feelings and deal with them more effectively. Our emotions often need the guidance of reason. Likewise, our reasoning needs our emotions. It is our feelings that motivate us to action, and without motivation our reasoning would never get off the ground.

Then there's this dubious assumption: Critical thinking is the enemy of creativity. To some people, critical thinking is a sterile and rigid mode of thought that constrains the imagination, hobbles artistic vision, and prevents "thinking outside the box." But critical thinking and creative thinking are not opposed to one another. Good critical thinkers can let their imaginations run free just like anyone else. They can create and enjoy poetry, music, art, literature, and plain old fun in the same way and to the same degree as the rest of the world. Critical thinking can complement creative thinking because it is needed to assess and enhance the creation. Scientists, for example, often dream up some very fanciful theories (which are an important part of doing science). These theories pop into their heads in the same sort of ways that the ideas for a great work of art appear in the mind of its creator. But then scientists use all of their critical thinking skills to evaluate what they have produced (as artists sometimes do)—and this critical examination enables them to select the most promising theories and to weed out those that are unworkable. Critical thinking perfects the creation.

"Never, ever, think outside the box."

In a very important sense, critical thinking is thinking outside the box. When we passively absorb the ideas we encounter, when we refuse to consider any alternative explanations or theories, when we conform our ideas to the wishes of the group, when we let our thinking be controlled by bias and stereotypes and superstition and wishful thinking—we are deep, deep in the box. But we rise above all that when we have the courage to think critically. When we are willing to let our beliefs be tried in the court of critical reason, we open ourselves to new possibilities, the dormant seeds of creativity.

Why Critical Thinking Matters

- Our thinking guides our actions, so it should be of high quality.
- If you have never critically examined your beliefs, they are not truly yours.
- To examine your beliefs is to examine your life. Socrates: "The unexamined life is not worth living."
- Critical thinking involves determining what we're justified in believing, being open to new perspectives, and fairly assessing the views of others and ourselves.
- Critical thinking provides skills for learning and exploring; defense against error, manipulation, and prejudice; and tools for self-discovery.
- Critical thinking complements both our emotions and our creativity.
- Critical thinking is thinking outside the box.

Critical thinking covers a lot of territory. It's used across the board in all disciplines, all areas of public life, all the sciences, all sectors of business, and all vocations. It has played a major role in all the great endeavors of humankind—scientific discoveries, technological innovations, philosophical insights, social and political movements, literary creation and criticism, judicial and legal reasoning, democratic nation building, and more. The *lack* of critical thinking has also left its mark. The great tragedies of history—the wars, massacres, holocausts, tyrannies, bigotries, epidemics, and witch hunts—grew out of famines of the mind where clear, careful thinking was much too scarce.

How It Works

As you can see, critical thinking has extremely broad application. Principles and procedures used to evaluate beliefs in one discipline or issue can be used to assess beliefs in many other arenas. Good critical thinking is the same everywhere. Here are the common threads that make it universal.

Claims and Reasons

Critical thinking is a rational, systematic process that we apply to beliefs of all kinds. As we use the term here, *belief* is just another word for statement, or claim. A **statement** is an assertion that something is or is not the case. The following are statements:

- A triangle has three sides.
- I am cold.
- You are a liar.
- You are not a liar.

- I see blue spots before my eyes.
- 7 + 5 = 12
- You should never hit your mother with a shovel.
- The best explanation for his behavior is that he was in a trance.
- Rap music is better than punk rock.
- There are black holes in space.

So statements, or claims, are the kinds of things that are either true or false. They assert that some state of affairs is or is not actual. You may know that a specific statement is true, or you may not. There may be no way to find out at the time if the statement is true or false. There may be no one who believes the statement. But it would be a statement nonetheless.

Some sentences, though, do *not* express statements:

"What some people fail to grasp, Larry, is the difference between 'thinking outside of the box' and just being a weirdo."

© 2002 by Randy Glasbergen

- Does a triangle have three sides?
- Is God all-powerful?
- Turn that music off.
- Stop telling lies.
- Hey, dude.
- Great balls of fire!

The first two sentences are questions. The second two are commands or requests. The fifth sentence is a greeting. The sixth one is an exclamation. None asserts that something is or is not the case.

When you're engaged in critical thinking, you're mostly either evaluating statements or formulating them. In both cases your primary task is to figure out how strongly to believe them. The strength of your belief should depend on the quality of the reasons in favor of the statements. Statements backed by good reasons are worthy of strong acceptance. Statements that fall short of this standard deserve weaker acceptance.

Sometimes you may not be able to assign any substantial weight at all to the reasons for or against a statement. There simply may not be enough evidence to rationally decide. Generally when that happens, good critical thinkers don't arbitrarily choose to accept or reject a statement. They suspend judgment until there is enough evidence to make an intelligent decision.

Reasons and Arguments

Reasons provide support for a statement. That is, they provide us with grounds for believing that a statement is true. Reasons are themselves expressed as statements. So a statement expressing a reason or reasons is used to show that another statement is true or likely to be true. This combination of statements—a statement (or statements) supposedly providing reasons for accepting another statement—is known as an **argument**. Arguments are the main focus of critical thinking. They are the most important tool we have for evaluating the truth of statements (our own and those of others) and for formulating statements that are worthy of acceptance. Arguments are therefore essential for the advancement of knowledge in all fields.

Often people use the word *argument* to indicate a quarrel or heated exchange. In critical thinking, however, *argument* refers to the assertion of reasons in support of a statement.

The statements (reasons) given in support of another statement are called the **premises**. The statement that the premises are intended to support is called the **conclusion**. We can define an argument, then, like this:

ARGUMENT: A group of statements in which some of them (the premises) are intended to support another of them (the conclusion).

The following are some simple arguments:

1. Because banning assault rifles violates a constitutional right, the U.S. government should not ban assault rifles.
2. The *Wall Street Journal* says that people should invest heavily in stocks. Therefore, investing in stocks is a smart move.
3. When Judy drives her car, she's always late. Since she's driving her car now, she will be late.
4. Listen, any movie with clowns in it cannot be a good movie. Last night's movie had at least a dozen clowns in it. Consequently it was awful.
5. The war on terrorism must include a massive military strike on nation X because without this intervention, terrorists cannot be defeated. They will always be able to find safe haven and support in the X regime. Even if terrorists are scattered around the world, support from nation X will increase their chances of surviving and launching new attacks.
6. No one should buy a beer brewed in Canada. Old Guzzler beer is brewed in Canada, so no one should buy it.

Here are the same arguments where the parts are easily identified:

1. [Premise] Because banning assault rifles violates a constitutional right, [Conclusion] the U.S. government should not ban assault rifles.
2. [Premise] The *Wall Street Journal* says that people should invest heavily in stocks. [Conclusion] Therefore, investing in stocks is a smart move.
3. [Premise] When Judy drives her car, she's always late. [Premise] Since she's driving her car now, [Conclusion] she will be late.
4. [Premise] Any movie with clowns in it cannot be a good movie. [Premise] Last night's movie had at least a dozen clowns in it. [Conclusion] Consequently it was awful.
5. [Premise] Without a military intervention in nation X, terrorists cannot be defeated. [Premise] They will always be able to find safe haven and support in the X regime. [Premise] Even if terrorists are scattered around the

"What danger can ever come from ingenious reasoning and inquiry? The worst speculative skeptic ever I knew was a much better man than the best superstitious devotee and bigot."

—**David Hume**

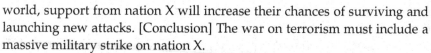

world, support from nation X will increase their chances of surviving and launching new attacks. [Conclusion] The war on terrorism must include a massive military strike on nation X.

6. [Premise] No one should buy a beer brewed in Canada. [Premise] Old Guzzler beer is brewed in Canada. [Conclusion] So no one should buy it.

What all of these arguments have in common is that reasons (the premises) are offered to support or prove a claim (the conclusion). This logical link between premises and conclusion is what distinguishes arguments from all other kinds of discourse. This process of reasoning from a premise or premises to a conclusion based on those premises is called **inference**. Being able to identify arguments, to pick them out of a block of nonargumentative prose if need be, is an important skill on which many other critical thinking skills are based.

Now consider this passage:

The cost of the new XJ fighter plane is $650 million. The cost of three AR21 fighter bombers is $1.2 billion. The administration intends to fund such projects.

Is there an argument here? No. This passage consists of several claims, but no reasons are presented to support any particular claim (conclusion), including the last sentence. This passage can be turned into an argument, though, with some minor editing:

The GAO says that any weapon that costs more than $50 million apiece will actually impair our military readiness. The cost of the new XJ fighter plane is $650 million dollars. The cost of three AR21 fighter bombers is $1.2 billion. We should never impair our readiness. Therefore, the administration should cancel both these projects.

Now we have an argument because reasons are given for accepting a conclusion.

Here's another passage:

Allisha went to the bank to get a more recent bank statement of her checking account. The teller told her that the balance was $1,725. Allisha was stunned that it was so low. She called her brother to see if he had been playing one of his twisted pranks. He wasn't. Finally, she concluded that she had been a victim of bank fraud.

Where is the conclusion? Where are the reasons? There are none. This is a little narrative hung on some descriptive claims. But it's not an argument. It could be turned into an argument if, say, some of the claims were restated as reasons for the conclusion that bank fraud had been committed.

Being able to distinguish between passages that do and do not contain arguments is a very basic skill—and an extremely important one. Many people think that if they have clearly stated their beliefs on a subject, they have presented an argument. But a mere declaration of beliefs is not an argument. Often such assertions of opinion are just a jumble of unsupported claims. Search high and low and you will not find an argument anywhere. A writer or speaker of these claims gives the readers or listeners no grounds for believing the claims. In writing courses, the absence of supporting premises is sometimes called "a lack of development."

Here are three more examples of verbiage sans argument:

Attributing alcohol abuse by children too young to buy a drink to lack of parental discipline, intense pressure to succeed, and affluence incorrectly draws attention to proximate causes while ignoring the ultimate cause: a culture that tolerates overt and covert marketing of alcohol, tobacco, and sex to these easily manipulated, voracious consumers. [Letter to the editor, *New York Times*]

[A recent column in this newspaper] deals with the living quarters of Bishop William Murphy of the Diocese of Rockville Centre. I am so disgusted with the higher-ups in the church that at times I am embarrassed to say I am Catholic. To know that my parents' hard-earned money went to lawyers and payoffs made me sick. Now I see it has also paid for a high-end kitchen. I am enraged. I will never make a donation again. [Letter to the editor, *Newsday*]

I don't understand what is happening to this country. The citizens of this country are trying to destroy the beliefs of our forefathers with their liberal views. This country was founded on Christian beliefs. This has been and I believe still is the greatest country in the world. But the issue that we cannot have prayer in public places and on public property because there has to be separation of church and state is a farce. [Letter to the editor, *Douglas County Sentinel*]

The passage on alcohol abuse in children is not an argument but an unsupported assertion about the causes of the problem. The passage from the disappointed Catholic is an expression of outrage (which may or may not be justified), but no conclusion is put forth, and no reasons supporting a conclusion are offered. Note the contentious tone in the third passage. This passage smells like an argument. But, alas, there is no argument. Each sentence is a claim presented without support.

Sometimes people also confuse **explanations** with arguments. An argument gives us reasons for believing *that something is the case*—that a claim is true or probably true. An explanation, though, tells us *why or how something is the case*. Arguments have something to prove; explanations do not. Ponder this pair of statements:

1. Adam obviously stole the money, for three people saw him do it.
2. Adam stole the money because he needed it to buy food.

Statement 1 is an argument. Statement 2 is an explanation. Statement 1 tries to show that something is the case—that Adam stole the money. And the reason offered in support of this statement is that three people saw him do it. Statement 2 does not try to prove that something is the case (that Adam stole the money). Instead, it attempts to explain why something is the case (why Adam stole the money). Statement 2 takes for granted that Adam stole the money and then tries

"He who knows only his own side of the case, knows little of that. His reasons may be good, and no one may have been able to refute them. But if he is equally unable to refute the reasons on the opposite side; if he does not so much as know what they are, he has no ground for preferring either opinion."
—**John Stuart Mill**

to explain why he did it. (Note: Explanations can be used as integral *parts* of arguments. As such, they are powerful intellectual and scientific tools that help us understand the world, which is why this text has several chapters [Part Four] devoted to explanations used in this way.)

It's not always easy to recognize an argument, to locate both premises and conclusion, but there are a few tricks that can make the job more manageable. For one, there are **indicator words** that frequently accompany arguments and signal that a premise or conclusion is present. For example, in argument 1, cited earlier in this chapter, the indicator word *because* tips us off to the presence of the premise "Because banning assault rifles violates a constitutional right." In argument 2, *therefore* points to the conclusion "Therefore, investing in stocks is a smart move."

Here are some common premise indicators:

because	due to the fact that	inasmuch as
in view of the fact	being that	as indicated by
given that	since	for
seeing that	assuming that	the reason being
as	for the reason that	

And here are some common conclusion indicators:

therefore	it follows that	it must be that
thus	we can conclude that	as a result
which implies that	so	which means that
consequently	hence	ergo

Using indicator words to spot premises and conclusions, however, is not fool-proof. They're just good clues. You will find that some of the words just listed are used when no argument is present. For example,

- I am here *because* you asked me to come.
- I haven't seen you *since* Woodstock.
- He was *so* sleepy he fell off his chair.

Note also that arguments can be put forth without the use of *any* indicator words:

We must take steps to protect ourselves from criminals. We can't rely on the government—law enforcement is already stretched thin. The police can't be everywhere at once, and they usually get involved only after a crime has been committed.

As you may have noticed from these examples, the basic structure of arguments can have several simple variations. For one thing, arguments can have any number of premises. Arguments 1 and 2 have one premise; arguments 3, 4, and 6, two premises; argument 5, three premises. In extended arguments that often appear in essays, editorials, reports, and other works, there can be many more premises. Also, the conclusion of an argument may not always appear after the premises. As in argument 5, the conclusion may be presented first.

Occasionally the conclusion of an argument can be disguised as a question—even though we would usually expect a question not to be a claim at all. (For purposes of examining such arguments, we may need to paraphrase the conclusion; in some arguments, we may also need to paraphrase premises.) Much of the time readers have little difficulty discerning what the implicit conclusion is. See for yourself:

> Do you think for one minute that liberal Democrats in Congress will support a bill that makes gun control legislation impossible? They have never voted that way. They have already declared that they will not allow such a bill. And their leadership has given them their marching orders: Don't support this bill.

Probably the best advice for anyone trying to uncover or dissect arguments is this: *Find the conclusion first.* Once you know what claim someone is trying to prove, isolating the premises becomes much easier. Ask yourself, "What claim is this writer or speaker trying to persuade me to believe?" If the writer or speaker is not trying to convince you of anything, there is no argument to examine.

Arguments in the Rough

As you've probably guessed by now, in the real world, arguments almost never appear neatly labeled as they are here. As suggested earlier, they usually come embedded in a thicket of other sentences that serve many other functions besides articulating an argument. They may be long and hard to follow. And sometimes a passage that sounds like an argument is not. Your main challenge is to identify the conclusion and premises without getting lost in all the "background noise." Ponder this passage:

> (1) A. L. Jones used flawed reasoning in his letter yesterday praising this newspaper's decision to publish announcements of same-sex unions. (2) Mr. Jones asserts that same-sex unions are a fact of life and therefore should be acknowledged by the news media as a legitimate variation on social partnerships. (3) But the news media are not in the business of endorsing or validating lifestyles. (4) They're supposed to report on lifestyles, not bless them. (5) In addition, by validating same-sex unions or any other lifestyle, the media abandon their objectivity and become political partisans—which would destroy whatever respect people have for news outlets. (6) All of this shows that the news media——including this newspaper—should never (explicitly or implicitly) endorse lifestyles by announcing those lifestyles to the world.

There's an argument here, but it's surrounded by extraneous material. The conclusion is sentence 6—"All of this shows that the news media— including this newspaper—should never (explicitly or implicitly) endorse lifestyles by announcing those lifestyles to the world." Since we know what the conclusion is, we can identify the premises and separate them from other information. Sentences 1 and 2 are not premises; they're background information about the nature of the dispute. Sentence 3 presents the first premise, and sentence 4 is essentially a restatement of that premise. Sentence 5 is the second premise.

Claims, Reasons, and Arguments

- **Statement (claim):** An assertion that something is or is not the case
- **Premise:** A statement given in support of another statement
- **Conclusion:** A statement that premises are used to support
- **Argument:** A group of statements in which some of them (the premises) are intended to support another of them (the conclusion)
- **Explanation:** A statement or statements asserting why or how something is the case
- **Indicator words:** Words that frequently accompany arguments and signal that a premise or conclusion is present

Stripped clean of nonargumentative material, the argument looks like this:

[Premise] But the news media are not in the business of endorsing or validating lifestyles. [Premise] In addition, by validating same-sex unions or any other lifestyle, the media abandon their objectivity and become political partisans—which would destroy whatever respect people have for news outlets. [Conclusion] All of this shows that the news media—including this newspaper—should never (explicitly or implicitly) endorse lifestyles by announcing those lifestyles to the world.

Now see if you can spot the conclusion and premises in this one:

(1) You have already said that you love me and that you can't imagine spending the rest of your life without me. (2) Once, you even tried to propose to me. (3) And now you claim that you need time to think about whether we should be married. (4) Well, everything that you've told me regarding our relationship has been a lie. (5) In some of your letters to a friend you admitted that you were misleading me. (6) You've been telling everyone that we are just friends, not lovers. (7) And worst of all, you've been secretly dating someone else. (8) Why are you doing this? (9) It's all been a farce, and I'm outta here.

And you thought that romantic love had nothing to do with critical thinking! In this passionate paragraph, an argument is alive and well. The conclusion is in sentence 4: "Well, everything that you've told me . . . has been a lie." Sentence 9, the concluding remark, is essentially a repetition of the conclusion. Sentences 1, 2, and 3 are background information on the current conflict. Sentences 5, 6, and 7 are the premises, the reasons that support the conclusion. And sentence 8 is an exasperated query that's not part of the argument.

You will discover that in most extended argumentative passages, premises and conclusions make up only a small portion of the total wordage. A good part of the text is background information and restatements of the premises or conclusion. Most of the rest consists of explanations, digressions, examples or illustrations, and descriptive passages.

Of all these nonargumentative elements, explanations are probably most easily confused with arguments. As we've seen, arguments try to prove or demonstrate that a statement is true. They try to show *that* something is the case. Explanations, however, do not try to prove that a statement is true. They try to show *why* or *how* something is the way it is. Consider these two statements:

- People have a respect for life because they adhere to certain ethical standards.
- People should have a respect for life because their own ethical standards endorse it.

The first statement is an explanation. It's not trying to prove anything, and no statement is in dispute. It's trying to clarify why or how people have respect for life. The second statement, though, is an argument. It's trying to prove, or provide support for, the idea that people should have a respect for life.

We discuss the basics of explanations in Chapter 10, and we deal with the other nonargumentative elements in Chapters 4 and 6. In the meantime, you should be able to locate the conclusion and premises of an argument—even when there is a lot of nonargumentative material nearby.

Finally, as you can see, learning the principles of critical thinking or logic requires at least some prior knowledge and ability. But, you may wonder (especially if this is your first course in critical or logical reasoning), where does this prior knowledge and ability come from—and do you have these prerequisites? Fortunately, the answer is yes. Since you are, as Aristotle says, a rational animal, you already have the necessary equipment, namely, a logical sense that helps you reason in everyday life and enables you to begin honing your critical reasoning.

KEY WORDS

argument	explanation	logic
conclusion	indicator words	premise
critical thinking	inference	statement

Summary

- Critical thinking is the systematic evaluation or formulation of beliefs, or statements, by rational standards. Critical thinking is *systematic* because it involves distinct procedures and methods. It entails *evaluation* and *formulation* because it's used to both assess existing beliefs (yours or someone else's) and devise new ones. And it operates according to *reasonable standards* in that beliefs are judged according to the reasons and reasoning that support them.

Why It Matters

- Critical thinking matters because our lives are defined by our actions and choices, and our actions and choices are guided by our thinking. Critical thinking helps guide us toward beliefs that are worthy of acceptance, that can us help be successful in life, however we define success.
- A consequence of not thinking critically is a loss of personal freedom. If you passively accept beliefs that have been handed to you by your family and your culture, then those beliefs are not really yours. If they are not really yours, and you let them guide your choices and actions, then they—not you—are in charge of your life. Your beliefs are yours only if you critically examine them for yourself to see if they are supported by good reasons.
- Critical thinking does not necessarily lead to cynicism. It can complement our feelings by helping us sort them out. And it doesn't limit creativity—it helps perfect it.

How It Works

- Critical thinking is a rational, systematic process that we apply to beliefs of all kinds. *Belief* is another word for statement, or claim. A *statement* is an assertion that something is or is not the case. When you're engaged in critical thinking, you are mostly either evaluating a statement or trying to formulate one. In both cases your primary task is to figure out how strongly to believe the statement (based on how likely it is to be true). The strength of your belief will depend on the strength of the reasons in favor of the statement.
- In critical thinking an argument is not a feud but a set of statements—statements supposedly providing reasons for accepting another statement. The statements given in support of another statement are called the *premises*. The statement that the premises are used to support is called the *conclusion*. An argument then is a group of statements in which some of them (the premises) are intended to support another of them (the conclusion).
- Being able to identify arguments is an important skill on which many other critical thinking skills are based. The task is made easier by indicator words that frequently accompany arguments and signal that a premise or conclusion is present. Premise indicators include *for*, *since*, and *because*. Conclusion indicators include *so*, *therefore*, and *thus*.
- Arguments almost never appear neatly labeled for identification. They usually come embedded in a lot of statements that are not part of the arguments. Arguments can be complex and lengthy. Your main challenge is to identify the conclusion and premises without getting lost in all the other verbiage.

EXERCISES

Exercises marked with * have answers in "Answers to Exercises" (Appendix C). Integrative exercises and writing assignments are not supplied with answers.

Exercise 1.1

REVIEW QUESTIONS

*1. What is critical thinking?

2. Is critical thinking primarily concerned with *what* you think or *how* you think?

3. Why is critical thinking systematic?

*4. According to the text, what does it mean to say that critical thinking is done according to rational standards?

5. According to the text, how does a lack of critical thinking cause a loss of personal freedom?

*6. What does the term *critical* refer to in critical thinking?

7. How does logic differ from critical thinking?

*8. What is a statement?

9. What is an explanation?

10. According to the text, by what standard should we always proportion our acceptance of a statement?

*11. What is an argument?

12. Give an example of an argument with two premises.

13. What is the function of a premise?

*14. What is a conclusion?

15. Why can't a mere assertion or statement of beliefs constitute an argument?

16. True or false: All disagreements contain an argument.

*17. Does the following passage contain an argument? *Sample passage:* I couldn't disagree more with Olivia. She says that video games provoke young men to violence and other insensitive acts. But that's just not true.

18. Does the following passage contain an argument? *Sample passage:* Alonzo asserts that the government should be able to arrest and imprison anyone if they are suspected of terrorist acts. But that's ridiculous. Doing that would be a violation of basic civil liberties guaranteed in the Bill of Rights.

*19. What are indicator words?

20. List three conclusion indicator words.

21. List three premise indicator words.

22. Give an example of a short argument that uses one or more indicator words.

* **23.** What is probably the best strategy for trying to find an argument in a complex passage?
   24. True or false: You can almost always find an argument in narrative writing.

Exercise 1.2

For each of the following sentences, indicate whether it is or is not a statement.

* **1.** Now that you're mayor of the city, do you still believe that the city government is a waste of time?
   2. Do not allow your emotions to distort your thinking.
   3. If someone wants to burn the American flag, they should be able to do it without interference from the police.
* **4.** Do you think that I'm guilty?
   5. Should our religious beliefs be guided by reason, emotion, or faith?
   6. Stop driving on the left side of the road!
* **7.** The Vietnam War was a terrible mistake.
   8. The Vietnam War was not a terrible mistake.
   9. I shall do my best to do my duty to God and my country.
* **10.** Are you doing your best for God and country?

Exercise 1.3

For each of the following passages, indicate whether it constitutes an argument. For each argument, specify what the conclusion is.

* **1.** Rene hates Julia, and she always upsets him, so he should avoid her.
   2. Do you think the upcoming election will change anything?
   3. I pledge allegiance to the flag of the United States of America and to the republic for which it stands, one nation under God, indivisible, with liberty and justice for all.
* **4.** Why do you think you have the right to park your car anywhere you please?
   5. Wait just a minute. Where do you think you're going?
   6. If you smoke that cigarette in here, I will leave the room.
* **7.** The *Titanic* sank, and no one came to save it.
   8. Jesus loves me, for the Bible tells me so.
   9. Spiderman is a better superhero than Superman because kryptonite can't hurt him, and he doesn't have a Lois Lane around to mess things up.
   10. "Whether our argument concerns public affairs or some other subject we must know some, if not all, of the facts about the subject on which we are to speak and argue. Otherwise, we can have no materials out of which to construct arguments." [Aristotle, *Rhetoric*]

* 11. If guns are outlawed, then only outlaws will have guns. Don't outlaw guns.

12. If someone says something that offends me, I should have the right to stop that kind of speech. After all, words can assault people just as weapons can.

13. "Citizens who so value their 'independence' that they will not enroll in a political party are really forfeiting independence, because they abandon a share in decision-making at the primary level: the choice of the candidate." [Bruce L. Felknor, *Dirty Politics*]

14. If someone says something that offends me, I cannot and should not try to stop them from speaking. After all, in America, speech—even offensive speech—is protected.

* 15. "Piercing car alarms have disturbed my walks, cafe meals or my sleep at least once during every day I have lived in the city; roughly 3,650 car alarms. Once, only once, was the wail a response to theft. . . . Silent car alarms connect immediately to a security company, while the noisy ones are a problem, not a solution. They should be banned, finally." [Letter to the editor, *New York Times*]

16. "If history is a gauge, the U.S. government cannot be trusted when it comes to sending our children to war. It seems that many years after Congress sends our children to war, we find out that the basic premise for the war was an intentional lie." [Letter to the editor, *L.A. Daily News*]

Exercise 1.4

For each of the following passages indicate whether it constitutes an argument. For each argument specify both the conclusion and the premises.

* 1. Faster-than-light travel is not possible. It would violate a law of nature.

2. You have neglected your duty on several occasions, and you have been absent from work too many times. Therefore, you are not fit to serve in your current capacity.

3. Racial profiling is not an issue for white people, but it is an issue for African Americans.

* 4. The flu epidemic on the East Coast is real. Government health officials say so. And I personally have read at least a dozen news stories that characterize the situation as a "flu epidemic."

5. The terrorist group ISIS in Syria and Iraq has killed thousands of innocent citizens. They are nothing more than fanatic murderers.

6. "Current-day Christians use violence to spread their right-to-life message. These Christians, often referred to as the religious right, are well known for violent demonstrations against Planned Parenthood and other abortion clinics. Doctors and other personnel are threatened with death, clinics have been bombed, there have even been cases of doctors being murdered." [Letter to the editor, *Arizona Daily Wildcat*]

* 7. "I am writing about the cost of concert tickets. I am outraged at how much ticket prices are increasing every year. A few years ago, one could

attend a popular concert for a decent price. Now some musicians are asking as much as $200 to $300." [Letter to the editor, *Buffalo News*]

8. "Homeland security is a cruel charade for unborn children. Some 4,000 per day are killed in their mother's womb by abortion. This American holocaust was legalized by the Supreme Court in an exercise of raw judicial power." [Letter to the editor, *Buffalo News*]

9. Witches are real. They are mentioned in the Bible. There are many people today who claim to be witches. And historical records reveal that there were witches in Salem.

* 10. Stretched upon the dark silk night, bracelets of city lights glisten brightly.

11. Vaughn's car is old. It is beat up. It is unsafe to drive. Therefore, Vaughn's car is ready for the junkyard.

Exercise 1.5

For each of the following conclusions, write at least two premises that can support it. Your proposed premises can be entirely imaginary. To concoct the premises, think of what kind of statement (if true) would convince you to believe the conclusion.

EXAMPLE

Conclusion: Pet psychics can diagnose a dog's heartburn 100 percent of the time.
Premise 1: In the past fifty years, in hundreds of scientific tests, pet psychics were able to correctly diagnose heartburn in dogs 100 percent of the time.
Premise 2: Scientists have confirmed the existence of energy waves that can carry information about the health of animals.

1. What this country needs is more family values.

2. All animals—rodents, dogs, apes, whatever—have moral rights, just as people do.

* 3. Every woman has the right to abort her fetus if she so chooses.

4. When I looked into your eyes, time stood still.

5. Repent! The end is near.

* 6. When it comes to animals, Vaughn doesn't know what he's talking about.

7. Suspicion has arisen regarding the financial dealings of Governor Spendthrift.

8. The Internet is the most dangerous tool that terrorists have in their arsenal.

* 9. The Internet is the best tool that law enforcement officials have against terrorists.

10. Pornography is good for society because it educates people about sexuality.

11. Pornography is bad for society because it misleads people about sexuality.

* 12. *The Sopranos* is the greatest series in the history of TV.

13. It is the duty of every student to prevent this arbitrary tuition increase.

14. Jill cannot hold her liquor.

Exercise 1.6

For each of the following sets of premises, write a conclusion that would be supported by the premises (your conclusion should depend on both premises). Neither the conclusion nor the premises need to be statements that are true. To formulate an appropriate conclusion, try to think of a statement (conclusion) that could reasonably be supported by the premises.

EXAMPLE

Premise 1: The price of your shares in the stock market will continue to decline for at least a year.
Premise 2: Anyone with shares whose price will continue to decline for at least a year should sell now.
Conclusion: You should sell now.

1. Premise 1: You are afraid of heights.
   Premise 2: Anyone who is afraid of heights will fall if he or she climbs a tree.

* 2. Premise 1: School vouchers are being used in thirteen states and the District of Columbia.
   Premise 2: School vouchers have decreased the quality of education in every state where they've been used.

3. Premise 1: School vouchers are being used in thirteen states and the District of Columbia.
   Premise 2: School vouchers have improved the quality of education in every state where they've been used.

* 4. Premise 1: All married people are happier than unmarried people.
   Premise 2: You are married.

5. Premise 1: If stem-cell research is banned, Edgar will be very happy.
   Premise 2: Stem-cell research is banned.

6. Premise 1: If there is no God, then there is no morality.
   Premise 2: There is no God.

7. Premise 1: There is a God.
   Premise 2: If there is a God, then life has meaning.

* 8. Premise 1: There is a great deal of pornography of all kinds on the Internet.
   Premise 2: The government has essentially established a hands-off policy toward pornography on the Internet.
   Premise 3: Kids everywhere have access to pornography of all kinds on the Internet.

9. Premise 1: People in favor of capital punishment have a complete disregard for human life.

   Premise 2: Anyone who has a complete disregard for human life cannot be trusted.

   Premise 3: Nancy favors capital punishment.

Exercise 1.7

For each of the following passages, determine if there is an argument present. If so, identify the premises and the conclusion.

* 1. "The Religious Right is *not* 'pro-family.' . . . Concerned parents realize that children are curious about how their bodies work and need accurate, age-appropriate information about the human reproductive system. Yet, thanks to Religious Right pressure, many public schools have replaced sex education with fear-based 'abstinence only' programs that insult young people's intelligence and give them virtually no useful information." [Rob Boston, *Free Inquiry Magazine*]

2. "[Francis Bacon] is the father of experimental philosophy. . . . In a word, there was not a man who had any idea of experimental philosophy before Chancellor Bacon; and of an infinity of experiments which have been made since his time, there is hardly a single one which has not been pointed out in his book. He had even made a good number of them himself." [Voltaire, *On Bacon and Newton*]

* 3. "Is there archaeological evidence for the [Biblical] Flood? If a universal Flood occurred between five and six thousand years ago, killing all humans except the eight on board the Ark, it would be abundantly clear in the archaeological record. Human history would be marked by an absolute break. We would see the devastation wrought by the catastrophe in terms of the destroyed physical remains of pre-Flood human settlements. . . . Unfortunately for the Flood enthusiasts, the destruction of all but eight of the world's people left no mark on the archaeology of human cultural evolution." [Kenneth L. Feder, *Frauds, Myths, and Mysteries*]

4. "Subjectivism claims that what makes an action [morally] right is that a person approves of it or believes that it's right. Although subjectivism may seem admirably egalitarian in that it takes everyone's moral judgments to be as good as everyone else's, it has some rather bizarre consequences. For one thing, it implies that each of us is morally infallible. As long as we approve of or believe in what we are doing, we can do no wrong. But this cannot be right. Suppose that Hitler believed that it was right to exterminate the Jews. Then it was right for Hitler to exterminate the Jews. . . . But what . . . Hitler did was wrong, even if [he] believed otherwise." [Theodore Schick Jr., *Free Inquiry Magazine*]

Field Problems

1. Obtain the "Letters to the Editor" section of any newspaper (including student newspapers and online newspapers). Select a letter that contains at least one argument. Locate the conclusion and each premise.

   Next go through the letters again to find one that contains no argument at all. Rewrite the letter so that it contains at least one argument. Try to preserve as much of the original letter as possible. Stay on the same topic.

2. Go to www.townhall.com or www.usatoday.com and select an opinion essay on any issue. Identify its premises and conclusion, and decide whether you think the argument is a good one, providing reasons for your judgment.

Self-Assessment Quiz

Answers appear in "Answers to Self-Assessment Quizzes" (Appendix D).

1. What is an argument?
2. Name at least three premise indicators and three conclusion indicators.
3. Select the sentence that is *not* a statement:

   a. When I met you, you didn't know anything about logic.
   b. Read the story and write a complete review of it.
   c. Four score and seven years ago our fathers brought forth on this continent a new nation.
   d. The best pizza in town can be had at Luigi's.

4. From the following list, select the conclusion that is supported by the premises in the following argument:

   > When conservative Pat Buchanan last spoke on this campus, he was shouted down by several people in the audience who do not approve of his politics. He tried to continue but finally had to give up and walk away. That was unfortunate, but he's not the only one. This kind of treatment has also happened to other unpopular guest speakers. How easily the students at this university forget that free speech is guaranteed by the Bill of Rights. University regulations also support free speech for all students, faculty, and visitors and strictly forbid the harassment of speakers. And this country was founded on the idea that citizens have the right to freely express their views—even when those views are unpopular.

   a. Pat Buchanan is a fascist.
   b. We should never have guest speakers on campus.
   c. Campus speakers should be allowed to speak freely without being shouted down.
   d. Some guest speakers deserve to have the right of free speech and some don't.

5. Indicate whether the following passage contains an argument. If it does, specify the conclusion.

> We live in an incredibly over-reactionary society where the mindless forces of victim demagoguery have unfortunately joined with the child-worship industry. It is obviously tragic that a few twisted kids perpetuated such carnage there in Columbine. [Letter to the editor, Salon.com]

6. Indicate whether the following passage contains an argument. If it does, specify the conclusion.

> "War doesn't solve problems; it creates them," said an Oct. 8 letter about Iraq. World War II solved problems called Nazi Germany and militaristic Japan and created alliances with the nations we crushed. . . . The Persian Gulf war solved the problem of the Iraqi invasion of Kuwait. The Civil War solved the problem of slavery. These wars created a better world. War, or the threat of it is the only way to defeat evil enemies who are a threat to us. There is no reasoning with them. There can be no peace with them . . . so it's either us or them. What creates true peace is victory. [Letter to the editor, *New York Times*]

7. Indicate whether the following passage contains an argument. If so, specify the conclusion.

> Paul Krugman will always reach the same answer, namely that President Bush is wrong about everything. This time, he asserts that the federal government is "slashing domestic spending." Really? The president's budget request for 2003 would raise domestic spending 6%. Even setting aside spending that is related to homeland security, the president's request was for more than 2% growth, or nearly $7 billion in new dollars. In total, over the last five years, domestic spending will have skyrocketed by more than 40%. [Letter to the editor, *New York Times*]

For questions 8–12, indicate which sentences or sentence fragments are likely to be conclusions and which are likely to be premises.

8. Therefore, the Everglades will be destroyed within three years.
9. Assuming that you will never reach Boston
10. This implies that you are not driving as safely as you should.
11. Given all the hoopla surrounding the football team
12. It follows that sexual harassment should be a crime.

For questions 13–15, write at least two premises for each of the numbered conclusions. You can make up the premises, but you must ensure that they support the conclusion.

13. DNA evidence should be disallowed in cases of capital murder.
14. Computers will never be able to converse with a human being well enough to be indistinguishable from humans.
15. The great prophet Nostradamus (1503–1566) predicted the September 11 terrorist attacks.

Read the following argument. Then, in questions 16–20, supply the information requested. Each question asks you to identify by number all the sentences in the argument that fulfill a particular role—conclusion, premise, background information, example or illustration, or reiteration of a premise or the conclusion. Just write down the appropriate sentence numbers.

(1) Is global warming a real threat? (2) Or is it hype propagated by tree-hugging, daft environmentalists? (3) The president apparently thinks that the idea of global climate change is bunk. (4) But recently his own administration gave the lie to his bunk theory. (5) His own administration issued a report on global warming called the *U.S. Climate Action Report 2002*. (6) It gave no support to the idea that global warming doesn't happen and we should all go back to sleep. (7) Instead, it asserted that global warming was definitely real and that it could have catastrophic consequences if ignored. (8) For example, global climate change could cause heat waves, extreme weather, and water shortages right here in the United States. (9) The report is also backed by many other reports, including a very influential one from the United Nations. (10) Yes, George, global warming is real. (11) It is as real as typhoons and ice storms.

16. Conclusion.
17. Premise or premises.
18. Background information.
19. Example or illustration.
20. Repetition of conclusion or premise.

 ## Writing Assignments

1. Select an issue from the following list and write a three-page paper defending a claim pertaining to the issue.
   - Should there be a constitutional amendment banning the desecration of the American flag?
   - Should a representation of the Ten Commandments be allowed to be displayed in a federal courtroom?
   - Should the legal drinking age be lowered?
   - Should the private ownership of fully automatic machine guns be outlawed?

2. Read Essay 1 ("Death Penalty Discriminates against Black Crime Victims") in Appendix B, specify the conclusion and premises presented in it, and outline the argument in detail.

3. Write a two-page essay in which you defend a conclusion that contradicts the one in Essay 1. Pretend that all the evidence cited in Essay 1 actually supports your argument. You may alter the description of the evidence accordingly.

4. Study the argument presented in Essay 2 ("Marine Parks"). Identify the conclusion and the premises and objections considered. Then write a two-page rebuttal to the essay. That is, show that the essay's argument is faulty. You may cite imaginary—but reasonable—evidence.

28

3

Making Sense of Arguments

 CHAPTER OBJECTIVES

ARGUMENT BASICS

- Distinguish between deductive and inductive arguments.
- Understand the terms *valid*, *invalid*, and *sound*.
- Understand the terms *strong*, *weak*, and *cogent*.

JUDGING ARGUMENTS

- Be able to follow the four-step procedure for determining whether an argument is deductive or inductive, good or bad.
- Be familiar with indicator words that suggest that an argument is deductive or inductive.

FINDING MISSING PARTS

- Know how to use the three-step procedure for uncovering implicit premises.

ARGUMENT PATTERNS

- Memorize and be able to recognize the argument patterns known as *modus ponens*, *modus tollens*, *hypothetical syllogism*, *denying the antecedent*, *affirming the consequent*, and *disjunctive syllogism*.
- Be able to use the counterexample method for determining if a deductive argument is valid or invalid.

DIAGRAMMING ARGUMENTS

- Understand the definition of *dependent* and *independent premises*.
- Be able to follow the five-step procedure to diagram arguments, both simple and complex, including those embedded in extraneous material.

ASSESSING LONG ARGUMENTS

- Understand the challenges involved in assessing long arguments.
- Be able to follow the four-step procedure for diagramming long arguments.

I N THIS CHAPTER WE RESUME OUR DISCUSSION OF ARGUMENTS BEGUN IN Chapter 1, delve deeper into the dynamics and structure of different argument types, and get a lot more practice in identifying and critiquing simple (and not so simple) arguments in their "natural habitat."

Remember, in Chapter 1 we defined an argument as a group of statements in which some of them (the premises) are intended to support another of them (the conclusion). An essential skill is the ability to identify arguments in real-life contexts and to distinguish them from nonarguments. To recognize an argument, you must be able to identify the premises and the conclusion. Indicator words such as *because* and *since* often signal the presence of premises, and words such as *therefore* and *thus* can point to a conclusion.

Argument Basics

The point of *devising* an argument is to try to show that a statement, or claim, is worthy of acceptance. The point of *evaluating* an argument is to see whether this task has been successful—whether the argument shows that the statement (the conclusion) really is worthy of acceptance. When the argument shows that the statement is worthy of acceptance, we say that the argument is *good*. When the argument fails to show that the statement is worthy of acceptance, we say that the argument is *bad*. There are different ways, however, that an argument can be good or bad. There are different ways because there are different types of arguments.

Arguments come in two forms—**deductive** and **inductive**. A deductive argument is intended to provide logically *conclusive* support for its conclusion. An inductive argument is intended to provide *probable*—not conclusive—support for its conclusion.

A deductive argument that succeeds in providing such decisive logical support is said to be **valid**; a deductive argument that fails to provide such support is said to be **invalid**. A deductively valid argument is such that if its premises are true, its conclusion *must* be true. That is, if the premises are true, there is *no way* that the conclusion can be false. In logic, *valid* is not a synonym for true. A deductively valid argument simply has the kind of logical structure that *guarantees* the truth of the conclusion *if* the premises are true. "Logical structure" refers not to the content of an argument but to its construction, the way the premises and conclusion fit together. Because of the guarantee of truth in the conclusion, deductively valid arguments are said to be **truth-preserving**.

Here's a simple deductively valid argument:

All dogs have fleas.
Bowser is a dog.
So Bowser has fleas.

And here's a golden oldie.

All men are mortal.
Socrates is a man.
Therefore, Socrates is mortal.

Persuading or Reasoning?

A fundamental distinction in critical thinking is this: Persuading someone to agree with you is not the same thing as presenting them with a good argument. You can influence people's opinions by using words to appeal to their ego, gullibility, bigotry, greed, anger, prejudice, and more. You just have to use emotional language, psychological ploys, semantic or syntactic tricks, and outright lies. But having done so, you would not have demonstrated that *any* belief is true or warranted. You would not have shown that a claim is *worthy of acceptance*. This latter task is a matter of logic and argument. The machinations of raw persuasion are not.

Certainly the presentation of a good argument (in the critical thinking sense) can sometimes be psychologically compelling. And there are times when persuasion through psychological or emotional appeals is appropriate, even necessary. You just have to keep these two functions straight in your mind.

And one in regular paragraph form:

[Premise] If abortion is the taking of a human life, then it's murder.
[Premise] It is the taking of a human life. [Conclusion] So it necessarily follows that abortion is murder.

Great persuaders aren't necessarily great critical thinkers.

In each of these arguments, if the premises are true, the conclusion must be absolutely, positively true. It is impossible for the premises to be true and the conclusions false. The conclusion *logically follows* from the premises. And the order of the premises makes no difference.

A deductively *invalid* version of these arguments might look like this:

All dogs are mammals.
All cows are mammals.
Therefore, all dogs are cows.

If Socrates has horns, he is mortal.
Socrates is mortal.
Therefore, Socrates has horns.

In each of these, the conclusion does *not* logically follow from the premises. Each is an attempt at a deductively valid argument, but the attempt fails. And, again, this would be the case regardless of the order of the premises.

An inductive argument that succeeds in providing probable—but not conclusive—logical support for its conclusion is said to be **strong**. An inductive

"In the midst of chaos, Larry is the clear voice of reason. Get him the hell out of here."

> "The most perfidious way of harming a cause consists of defending it deliberately with faulty arguments."
> —**Friedrich Nietzsche**

argument that fails to provide such support is said to be **weak**. An inductively strong argument is such that if its premises are true, its conclusion is *probably* or *likely* to be true. The structure of an inductively strong argument cannot guarantee that the conclusion is true if the premises are true—but the conclusion can be rendered probable and worthy of acceptance. (Here again, the structure and content of an argument are distinct elements.) Because the truth of the conclusion cannot be guaranteed by the truth of the premises, inductive arguments are not truth-preserving.

Let's turn our first two deductively valid arguments into inductively strong arguments:

Most dogs have fleas.
Therefore, Bowser, my dog, probably has fleas.

Ninety-eight percent of humans are mortal.
Socrates is human.
Therefore, Socrates is likely to be mortal.

Notice that in the first argument, it's entirely possible for the premise to be true and the conclusion false. After all, if only *most* dogs have fleas, there is no guarantee that Bowser has fleas. Yet the premise, if true, makes the conclusion probably true.

Likewise, in the second argument it is possible that even if 98 percent of humans are mortal and Socrates is human, the conclusion that Socrates is mortal could be false. But the premises, if true, make it likely that the conclusion is true.

Here are three more inductive arguments about some everyday concerns:

Almost every computer I've purchased at an online store has been a dud.
Therefore, the next computer I purchase at the same online store will likely be a dud.

Maria's car broke down yesterday.
When it broke down, it made the same noise and spewed the same stinky exhaust that it always does when it breaks down.
Maria's car breaks down a lot.
Her mechanic, who does excellent work, always says the same thing: The problem is the carburetor.
Therefore, Maria's car trouble yesterday was probably due to a carburetor problem.

Nine toddlers out of the thirty-two at the day care center have a cold.
Therefore, probably every child there has a cold.

Logical validity or logical strength is an essential characteristic of good arguments. But there is more to good arguments than having the proper structure. Good arguments also have *true premises*. A good argument is one that has the proper structure—*and* true premises. Take a look at this argument:

All pigs can fly.
Vaughn is a pig.
Therefore, Vaughn can fly.

The premises of this argument are false—but the conclusion follows logically from those premises. It's a deductively valid argument with all the parts in the right place—even though the premises are false. But it is not a good argument. A good argument must have true premises, and this argument doesn't. A deductively valid argument that has true premises is said to be **sound**. A sound argument is a good argument, which gives you good reasons for accepting its conclusion.

Note, however, that deductively valid arguments can have true or false premises and true or false conclusions. Specifically, deductively valid arguments can have false premises and a false conclusion, false premises and a true conclusion, and true premises and a true conclusion. A valid argument, though, cannot have true premises and a false conclusion—that's impossible. See for yourself:

False Premises, False Conclusion
All dogs have flippers.
All cats are dogs.
Therefore, all cats have flippers.

False Premises, True Conclusion
Bowser is a cat.

All cats are mammals.
Therefore, Bowser is a mammal.

True Premises, True Conclusion
Bowser is a dog.
All dogs are mammals.
Therefore, Bowser is a mammal.

 FURTHER THOUGHT

Arguments About Necessary and Sufficient Conditions

Another useful kind of argument is built on the concepts of *necessary* and *sufficient conditions*. In Chapter 9 we discuss these ideas in connection with causal arguments (inductive arguments whose conclusions contain claims about the causes of things). But here we just need to understand that the concepts can be important in an even broader range of contexts.

We sometimes speak of the conditions (or features) that a thing *must* have in order to be that thing. These are called necessary conditions. For example, being a bird is a necessary condition for being an eagle; the presence of oxygen is a necessary condition for combustion to occur; and being male is a necessary condition for being an uncle. An eagle is an eagle only if it is a bird; combustion can occur only if oxygen is present; and someone can be an uncle only if he is male. A thing often has more than one necessary condition. The necessary conditions for combustion to occur are oxygen, heat, and fuel. If even one of these conditions is absent, combustion will not occur.

Often we are also interested in the conditions that *guarantee* that something exists or is a certain kind of thing. These are known as sufficient conditions. Being a human male with a niece or nephew is a sufficient condition for being an uncle. The sufficient condition for combustion is the combination of all the necessary conditions.

Conditions can also be *both* necessary and sufficient. Fuel being heated to a certain temperature in the presence of oxygen is both a necessary and a sufficient condition for combustion.

Now suppose someone argues for the conclusion that no one ever becomes a criminal unless he or she is raised in a single-parent home. That is, she asserts that the necessary and sufficient condition for becoming a criminal is to have been raised in a household headed by just one parent. To refute this claim, all you have to do is show that this condition is *not* necessary and sufficient for becoming a criminal. You just have to produce one example of someone who is a criminal but did not come from a household headed by just one parent. And, of course, such examples abound and can be incorporated into your counterargument.

A good inductive argument must also have true premises. For example:

Scientific studies show that 99 percent of dogs have three eyes.
So it's likely that the next dog I see will have three eyes.

This is an inductively strong argument, but it's not a good argument because its premise is false. When inductively strong arguments have true premises, they are said to be **cogent**. Good inductive arguments are cogent. Bad inductive arguments are not cogent.

You may have noticed another important difference between deductive and inductive arguments. The kind of support that a deductive argument can give a conclusion is *absolute*. Either the conclusion is shown to be true, or it is not. There is no sliding scale of truth or falsity. The support that an inductive argument can provide a conclusion, however, can vary from weak to extremely strong.

Both deductive and inductive arguments can be manipulated in various ways to yield new insights. For example, let's say that you have formulated a valid deductive argument, and you know that the conclusion is false. From these facts you can infer that at least one of the premises is false. Using this tack, you can demonstrate that a premise is false because in a valid argument it leads to an absurd conclusion. Or let's say that you've fashioned a valid argument, and you know that your premises are true. Then you can infer that the conclusion must be true—even if it's contrary to your expectations. Or maybe you put forth a strong inductive argument, and you know that the premises are questionable. Then you know that the conclusion also can't be trusted.

If you don't already have a sense of the wide-ranging usefulness of deductive and inductive arguments, the coming pages will make the point clear. You will find abundant evidence that the utility of both types of arguments is *universal*.

 REVIEW NOTES

Deductive and Inductive Arguments

- A deductive argument is intended to provide conclusive support for its conclusion.
- A deductive argument that succeeds in providing conclusive support for its conclusion is said to be valid. A valid argument is such that if its premises are true, its conclusion must be true.
- A deductively valid argument with true premises is said to be sound.
- An inductive argument is intended to provide probable support for its conclusion.
- An inductive argument that succeeds in providing probable support for its conclusion is said to be strong. A strong argument is such that if its premises are true, its conclusion is probably true.
- An inductively strong argument with true premises is said to be cogent.

They apply everywhere, work everywhere, and instruct everywhere—in everyday and professional life (Chapters 4–9), in scientific and extraordinary realms (Chapters 10–11), and in moral and philosophical explorations (Chapter 12).

EXERCISE

Exercise 3.1

1. What is a deductive argument?
2. What is an inductive argument?
3. Are inductive arguments truth-preserving? Why or why not?
* 4. The terms *valid* and *invalid* apply to what types of arguments?
5. What kind of guarantee does a deductive argument provide when it is valid?
6. Can an inductive argument guarantee the truth of the conclusion if the premises are true? Why or why not?
7. What is the difference between an inductively strong argument and an inductively weak one?
* 8. What is the term for valid arguments that have true premises?
9. What is the term for strong arguments that have true premises?
10. Can a valid argument have false premises and a false conclusion? False premises and a true conclusion?
11. What logical conclusion can you draw about an argument that is valid but has a false conclusion?
* 12. Is it possible for a valid argument to have true premises and a false conclusion?
13. In what way are conclusions of deductive arguments absolute?

Judging Arguments

When it comes to deductive and inductive arguments, the most important skills you can acquire are being able to identify them and determining whether they are good or bad. Much of the rest of this text is devoted to helping you become proficient in these skills. This chapter will serve as your first lesson and give you a chance to practice what you learn.

So the obvious questions here are, when you come face to face with an argument to evaluate, (1) How can you tell whether it's deductive or inductive, and (2) How can you determine whether it gives you good reasons for accepting the conclusion (whether it's sound or cogent)? The following is a suggested four-step procedure for answering these questions. We will elaborate on it here and in later chapters.

DILBERT: © Scott Adams/Dist. By United Feature Syndicate, Inc.

Step 1. Find the argument's conclusion and then its premises. Use the techniques you learned in Chapter 1. You'll have plenty of chances to hone this skill in upcoming chapters.

Step 2. Ask: Is it the case that if the premises are true the conclusion *must* be true? If the answer is yes, treat the argument as *deductive*, for it is very likely meant to offer conclusive support for its conclusion. The argument, then, is deductively valid, and you should check to see if it's sound. If the answer is no, proceed to the next step.

Step 3. Ask: Is it the case that if the premises are true, its conclusion is *probably* true? If the answer is yes, treat the argument as *inductive*, for it is very likely meant to offer probable support for its conclusion. The argument, then, is inductively strong, and you should check to see if it's cogent. If the answer is no, proceed to the next step.

Step 4. Ask: Is the argument intended to offer conclusive or probable support for its conclusion but *fails* to do so? If you reach this step, you will have already eliminated two possibilities: a valid argument and a strong one. The remaining options are an invalid argument or a weak one. So here you must discover what type of (failed) argument is intended. These two guidelines can help you do that:

GUIDELINE 1: Generally if an argument looks deductive or inductive because of its form, assume that it is intended to be so.

Bad arguments may sometimes look like good arguments because the arrangement of their premises and conclusion—their form—is similar to that found in reliable arguments. (You saw some of these reliable argument forms in the argument examples presented earlier in this chapter.) Such argument forms are an indication of what kind of argument is intended, and that fact gives you some guidance on determining argument type.

GUIDELINE 2: Generally if an argument looks deductive or inductive because of indicator words (and its form yields no clues), assume that it is intended to be so.

"He who strikes the first blow admits he's lost the argument."
—Chinese proverb

FURTHER THOUGHT

The Smart Way to Argue Online

Suppose you go online intending to engage in some serious, honest, productive debate on an important issue. You want to argue intelligently, and you want to avoid the usual pointless, snarky, muddled back-and-forth that wastes people's time and brings out the worst in them. How do you do that? Here's how:

- Begin by avoiding people you suspect are interested only in scoring points, grandstanding, letting off steam, or trying to get a rise out of you. If halfway through the conversation you discover they are not interested in rational argument, say goodbye and leave. Gravitate toward forums where respectful, intelligent discussions are the norm.

- Keep the focus on the argument. Critique the argument's form or the truth of the premises, *not* the person. Making the debate personal sidetracks the debate, injects emotion into it, and adds nothing relevant.

- Try to understand the other person's point of view and what motivates it. By doing so you increase your chances of winning the argument, learning something you didn't know, and calming the discussion through your show of empathy. Appreciating your opponent's objections can help make your own argument stronger and demonstrate that you are serious and fair-minded.

- Show your opponent moral respect. Give her a fair hearing. Don't assume the worst about her motives, values, or background. Don't stereotype her based solely on her political leanings or affiliations. Avoid snarky comments, sarcasm, name-calling, and insults.

- Stay on point; don't veer off into irrelevant side issues or nitpicking. Pointing out your opponent's bad grammar and spelling errors does not advance your argument one bit and will likely put an end to any chance of rational discussion.

- Rein in your emotions. If you get angry, agitated, or exasperated, you won't be able to think as clearly as you should, you may start hurling insults instead of solid arguments, and your opponent will probably respond in kind.

- Know what you're talking about. Suppose you begin arguing for a position with someone only to discover that you are ignorant of the facts. But you keep insisting that you're right, because you're too embarrassed to admit you know nothing about the topic. This situation is a colossal waste of time. It's better to know the facts before you jump into the fray. Research the topic ahead of time, noting the arguments for and against the position in question.

- Think twice before trying to engage in a serious argument on Twitter. Twitter's short character limit makes conversations about complex issues and long arguments difficult or pointless. And the back-and-forth becomes even more unwieldy when a half dozen people chime in to add their two cents.

Arguments are often accompanied by words or phrases that identify them as deductive or inductive. Terms that signal a deductive argument include "It necessarily follows that," "it logically follows that," "absolutely," "necessarily," and "certainly." Words signaling an inductive argument include "likely," "probably," "chances are," "odds are," and "it is plausible that." Such indicator words, though, are not foolproof clues to argument type because they are sometimes used in misleading ways. For example, someone might end an inductively strong argument with a conclusion prefaced with "it necessarily follows that," suggesting that the argument is deductively valid. But argument-type indicators may still be useful, especially when the argument form yields no clues (when guideline 1 doesn't apply).

In step 4, once you discover which kind of argument is intended, you will know that it is either invalid or weak (because in steps 2 and 3 we eliminated the possibility of a valid or strong argument). The only remaining task is to determine whether the premises are true.[1]

Let's try out the four-step procedure on a few arguments. Consider this one:

> [Premise] Unless we do something about the massive AIDS epidemic in Africa, the whole continent will be decimated within six months. [Premise] Unfortunately we won't do anything about the AIDS epidemic in Africa. [Conclusion] It necessarily follows that the whole of Africa will be decimated within six months.

Step 1 is already done for us; the premises and conclusion are clearly labeled. In step 2, we must ask, "Is it the case that if the premises are true, the conclusion must be true?" The answer is yes: If it's true that the AIDS epidemic in Africa will decimate the population in six months unless "we do something," and it's true that "we won't do anything," then the conclusion that Africa will be decimated in six months *must* be true. So this argument is deductively valid. To determine if it's sound, we would need to check to see if the premises are true. In this case, the first premise is false because, under current conditions, it would take longer than six months for the epidemic to decimate the whole continent. The other premise ("we won't do anything") is at least dubious since we can't predict the future. So what we have here is a deductively valid argument that's unsound—a bad argument.

Now let's analyze this one:

> [Premise] This week, under pressure from the American Civil Liberties Union, the school board rescinded its policy of allowing school-sponsored public prayers at football games. [Premise] All the school board members agreed with the policy change. [Premise] And a memo from the board was circulated to all students, teachers, and coaches declaring that there will be no more public prayers at football games. [Conclusion] Let's face it, the days of public prayers at our school football games are over.

From step 2 we can see that even if this argument's three premises are all true, the conclusion can still be false. After all, even if everything described in the premises happens, there still could be a public prayer at a football game (perhaps because of some mistake or an act of protest on the part of school-prayer advocates). So the argument can't be deductively valid. But if we go through step 3, we can see that if all the premises are true, the conclusion is likely to be true, making the argument inductively strong. If the premises *are* true, the argument would be cogent.

See what you think of this one:

> [Premise] If you act like Bart Simpson, you will be respected by all your classmates. [Premise] But you don't act like Bart Simpson. [Conclusion] It follows that you will not be respected by all of your classmates.

This argument flunks the tests in steps 2 and 3: It is not deductively valid, and it is not inductively strong. But it does resemble a deductive argument in two ways. First, it displays a pattern of reasoning that can, at first glance, seem deductive. Actually, it uses an argument pattern that is always deductively *invalid* (called denying the antecedent, an argument form we will look at shortly). This alone should be evidence enough that the argument is indeed deductive but invalid. But it also contains an argument indicator phrase ("it follows that") that suggests an attempt at a deductive form.

You'll get a lot more exposure to argument forms and indicator words in the rest of this chapter (and the rest of this text). Ultimately, practice in distinguishing different types of arguments and their relative worth is the only way to gain proficiency (and confidence!) in making these judgments.

So far we've spent most of our time assessing the logical structure of arguments—that is, whether they are valid/invalid or strong/weak. We haven't focused as much attention on evaluating the truth of premises because that's a big issue best considered separately—which is what we do in Part Two of this book.

 FURTHER THOUGHT

When Reasoning Wrecks . . . Leave the Scene of the Accident

Sometimes arguments go off into a ditch and you don't know why. Here's an example of a wrecked argument from the great American satirical writer Ambrose Bierce (1842–1914?). What's wrong here?

> Sixty men can do a piece of work sixty times as quickly as one man.
> One man can dig a posthole in sixty seconds.
> Therefore, sixty men can dig a posthole in one second.

Exercise 3.2

For each of the following arguments, follow the four-step procedure to determine whether it is deductive or inductive, valid or invalid, and strong or weak. Indicate the results of applying each step.

EXAMPLE 1

Colonel Mustard did not commit the murder. Someone who had committed the murder would have dirt on his shoes and blood on his hands. Colonel Mustard has neither.

> Step 1: Conclusion: Colonel Mustard did not commit the murder. Premises: Someone who had committed the murder would have dirt on his shoes and blood on his hands. Colonel Mustard has neither.
>
> Step 2: Deductively valid.
>
> Step 3: Does not apply.
>
> Step 4: Does not apply.

EXAMPLE 2

Most people who smoke pot are irresponsible and forgetful. Looks like you smoke pot all the time. Ergo, you're irresponsible and forgetful. Can you remember that?

> Step 1: Conclusion: Ergo, you're irresponsible and forgetful. Premises: Most people who smoke pot are irresponsible and forgetful. Looks like you smoke pot all the time.
>
> Step 2: Not deductively valid.
>
> Step 3: Inductively strong.
>
> Step 4: Does not apply.

1. Either Jack is lying or he is not. If his ears turn red, he's lying. If they don't turn red, he's telling the truth. His ears are red. Jack is lying.

*2. Ethel graduated from Yale. If she graduated from Yale, she probably has a superior intellect. She has a superior intellect.

3. If you go to that party, you're completely nuts. You're going to the party. It necessarily follows that you're nuts.

4. "Good sense is of all things in the world the most equally distributed, for everybody thinks himself so abundantly provided with it, that even those most difficult to please in all other matters do not commonly desire more of it than they already possess." [Rene Descartes, *A Discourse on Method*]

41

5. All philosophers are absent-minded. All philosophers are teachers. It necessarily follows that all absent-minded people are teachers.

* 6. Every musician has had special training, and everyone with special training has a college degree. Thus, every musician has a college degree.

7. People with high IQs also have psychic abilities. People with high SAT scores—which are comparable to high IQ scores—also probably have psychic abilities.

8. If Elvis Presley's name is spelled wrong on his tombstone, there must be some kind of conspiracy surrounding the death of the King. His name is spelled wrong. Therefore, there's a conspiracy.

* 9. Some actors sing, and some play a musical instrument. So some actors who sing also play a musical instrument.

10. Anyone who is not a bigot will agree that Chris is a good fellow. Some people in this neighborhood think that he's anything but a good fellow. Some people in this neighborhood are bigots.

11. "In the actual living of life there is no logic, for life is superior to logic." [Daisetz Teitaro Suzuki, *Essays in Zen Buddhism*]

12. A vase was found broken on the floor; some money had been taken out of the safe; and there were strange scratches on the wall. It therefore follows that someone obviously burglarized the place.

13. All the evidence in this trial suggests that Lizzy Borden is guilty of murder. Let's face it: She's probably guilty.

14. If everything was all right, there would be no blood on the floor. Of course, there is plenty of blood on the floor. Therefore, everything is not all right.

* 15. If minds are identical to brains—that is, if one's mind is nothing but a brain—androids could never have minds because they wouldn't have brains. Clearly, a mind is nothing but a brain, so it's impossible for androids to have minds.

16. "From infancy, almost, the average girl is told that marriage is her ultimate goal; therefore her training and education must be directed towards that end." [Emma Goldman, "Marriage and Love"]

17. If you have scratches on your body that you can't account for, and you feel that you have been visited by space aliens, then you really have been visited by space aliens. You have such scratches, and you have experienced such feelings. Doubtless you have been visited by space aliens.

18. If bombs are falling on London, war has started. The bombs are falling now. War has begun.

Exercise 3.3

For each of the following arguments, indicate whether it is valid or invalid, strong or weak.

1. Alice says that nothing is sacred. So intolerance toward other religions is okay.

2. Social welfare is by definition a handout to people who have not worked for it. But giving people money that they have not earned through labor is not helping anyone. It follows then that social welfare does not help anyone.

* 3. If CNN reports that war has started in Iraq, then war has started in Iraq. CNN has reported exactly that. War must have started.

4. If $r = 12$, then $s = 8$; $r = 12$; therefore, $s = 8$.

5. Any sitcom that tries to imitate *The Big Bang Theory* is probably a piece of trash. All of this season's sitcoms try to ape *Big Bang*. They've gotta be trash.

6. "Poetry is finer and more philosophical than history; for poetry expresses the universal and history only the particular." [Aristotle, *Poetics*]

7. Either you're lying or you're not telling the whole story. You're obviously not lying, so you're just relating part of the story.

* 8. Either your thinking is logical or it is emotional. It's obviously not logical. It's emotional.

9. My friends say that asteroids are not real. I've never found a single asteroid or a piece of one. People claim to have found some, but I don't believe them. There are no such things as asteroids.

10. A Gallup poll says that 80 percent of Americans believe in the existence of heaven, but only 40 percent say they believe in hell. People are just too willing to engage in wishful thinking.

11. Many young black men have been shot dead by white police officers. Black people have often been harassed by white policemen. From these facts we can conclude that the recent tragic shooting in Chicago of a black teen by a white police officer was a case of first-degree murder.

12. "We say that a person behaves in a given way because he possesses a philosophy, but we infer the philosophy from the behavior and therefore cannot use it in any satisfactory way as an explanation, at least until it is in turn explained." [B. F. Skinner, *Beyond Freedom and Dignity*]

13. You flunked the last three tests. You didn't show up for the last eight classes. And you haven't written any of the essays. Looks like you don't know the material.

* 14. Bachelors are unmarried. George is a bachelor. He has never taken a wife.

15. Bachelors are unmarried, and George acts like he's not married. He's a bachelor for sure.

16. If Alicia is alone on a trip, she will be afraid. She's alone on the latest trip. She is afraid.

17. If the universe had a beginning, then it was caused to begin. We know that the universe did have a beginning in the form of the Big Bang. So it was caused to come into existence. If it was caused to come into existence, that cause must have been God. God caused the universe to come into existence.

* 18. If the United States is willing to wage war in the Middle East, it can only be because it wants the oil supplies in the region. Obviously the United States is willing to go to war there. The United States wants that oil.

19. "Someone must have been telling lies about Joseph K., for without having done anything wrong he was arrested one fine morning." [Franz Kafka, *The Trial*]

20. Anyone willing to take the lives of innocent people for a cause is a terrorist. Many Christians, Jews, and Muslims have taken innocent lives in the name of their religious cause. Many Christians, Jews, and Muslims have been terrorists.

21. If he comes back, it's probably because he wants money. There he is. He wants money.

22. If you're eighteen, you're eligible to vote. But you're only seventeen. You're not eligible to vote.

* 23. I like geometry. My geometry teacher likes me. Therefore I will pass my geometry course with flying colors.

Finding Missing Parts

Sometimes arguments not only are faulty but also have a few pieces missing. Premises (and sometimes even conclusions)—material needed to make the argument work—are often left unstated. These implicit premises, or assumptions, are essential to the argument. Of course, certain assumptions are frequently left unsaid for good reason: They are obvious and understood by all parties to the argument, and boredom would set in fast if you actually tried to mention them all. If you wish to prove that "Socrates is mortal," you normally wouldn't need to explain what *mortal* means and that the name Socrates does not refer to a type of garden tool. But many arguments do have unstated premises that are not only necessary to the chain of reasoning but also must be made explicit to fully evaluate the arguments.

For instance:

> The easy availability of assault rifles in the United States has increased the risk of death and injury for society as a whole. Therefore, assault rifles should be banned.

Notice that there is a kind of disconnect between the premise and the conclusion. The conclusion follows from the premise *only* if we assume an additional premise, perhaps something like this: "Anything that increases the risk of death and injury for society as a whole should be banned." With this additional premise, the argument becomes:

> The easy availability of assault rifles in the United States has increased the risk of death and injury for society as a whole. Anything that increases the risk of death and injury for society as a whole should be banned. Therefore, assault rifles should be banned.

Reasoning and the Law

Though arguments and critical thinking are used (and abused) everywhere, their presence is especially obvious in law. Arguments are essential parts of legal reasoning at several levels—in the making of laws, in criminal and civil

proceedings, in judicial rulings, in the weighing of evidence, and in the application of legal precedent.

- **Legislation.** The making of new laws usually involves considerable debate about the wisdom of the legislation, and reasoned argument is the presumed medium of the deliberations. For example:

  Suppose . . . that there is currently no law requiring children to wear bicycle helmets. Assume moreover that the American Medical Association (AMA), acting on the belief that we ought to prevent unnecessary injuries and/or deaths of children, convinces the legislature to hold hearings to consider the merits of adopting such a law. What would be the major content of such hearings? Obviously, *arguments* regarding the pros and cons of bicycle helmet legislation. The AMA might testify, for example, that we can save children from serious injury and even death by implementing such a law; some parents may share the concerns of the AMA, while other parents might argue that this constitutes an illegitimate intrusion by the government into what are private family matters; legal authorities might point out the difficulty they would face in enforcing such a law . . . and some might argue that the policy would place an unfair burden on the poor who cannot afford high-priced helmets.[2]

  Legal proceedings. In civil matters, litigation takes the form of opposing parties arguing the merits of their side. The point of the arguments is to show that a litigant did (or did not) legally transgress in some way. In criminal cases, prosecutors argue that the defendant did in fact commit a crime, marshaling evidence and testimony to support that conclusion. Defending attorneys argue against the conclusion, trying to cast doubt on the supporting reasons or showing why the conclusion must be false. The arguments are mainly inductive, often including the inductive pattern known as inference to the best explanation (see Chapter 10). Using this latter kind of argument, the prosecutor contends that the best explanation of the evidence is that the defendant committed the crime; the defense may then maintain that there is a better explanation (that the defendant was framed, was mistaken for someone else, etc.).

- **Judicial rulings.** The thinking involved in judicial decisions is complex, entailing judgments about the meaning and application of statutes, assessments of the relevance and implications of cases, and reasoning of both the deductive and the inductive kind. The overarching pattern is that of argument: The conclusion is the final judicial judgment, and the premises (the reasons behind the judgment) generally refer to statutes, previous cases, or other sources of judicial authority. A common argument pattern is *analogical induction*, or argument by analogy (see Chapter 9). A judge first decides that the present case is relevantly similar (analogous) to a previously decided case; then she reasons that since the earlier case was treated in a particular fashion, the present case should be treated in a similar way. In Anglo-American law, decisions in previous cases (legal precedents) carry considerable judicial weight, and arguments by analogy reflect this fact.

Now that all the premises are spelled out, you can evaluate the *full* argument just as you would any other. Not only that, but you can see that the unstated premise is questionable, which is the case with many implicit premises. Not everyone would agree that anything raising the risk of death or injury should be banned, for if that were the case we would have to outlaw automobiles, airplanes, most prescription drugs, most occupations, and who knows how many kitchen appliances! Many unstated premises are like this one: They're controversial and therefore should not be left unexamined.

Here's another one:

> Anyone who craves political power cannot be trusted to serve the public interest. Senator Blowhard can't be trusted to serve the public interest.

As stated, this argument seems like a rush to judgment because the first premise concerns *anyone* who craves power, and suddenly Senator Blowhard is denounced as untrustworthy. Something's missing. What we need is another premise connecting the first premise to the conclusion: "Senator Blowhard craves political power." Now let's plug the implicit premise into the argument:

> Anyone who craves political power cannot be trusted to serve the public interest. Senator Blowhard craves political power. He can't be trusted to serve the public interest.

So exactly when should we try to ferret out an unstated premise? The obvious answer is that we should do so when there appears to be something essential missing—an implied, logical link between premises and conclusion that is not a common-sense, generally accepted assumption. Such implicit premises should never be taken for granted because, among other things, they are often deliberately hidden or downplayed to make the argument seem stronger.

Be aware, though, that many times the problem with an argument is not unstated premises, but invalid or weak structure. Consider this:

> If Tariq works harder, he will pass his calculus course. But he will not work harder, so he will not pass calculus.

This argument is invalid; the conclusion does not follow from the premises. Like most invalid arguments, it can't be salvaged without altering it beyond what is clearly implied. It's just a bad argument. The same goes for weak arguments. They usually can't be fixed up without adding or changing premises gratuitously. Remember, the point of articulating unstated premises is to make explicit what is already implicit. Your job as a critical thinker is *not* to make bad arguments good; that task falls to the one who puts forth the argument in the first place.

To make sure that your investigation of implicit premises is thorough and reasonable, work through the following three-step process.[3]

Step 1. Search for a credible premise that would make the argument *valid*, one that would furnish the needed link between premise (or premises) and conclusion. Choose the supplied premise that

    a. is most plausible

and

    b. fits best with the author's intent.

The first stipulation (a) means that you should look for premises that are either true or, at least, not obviously false. The second stipulation (b) means that premises should fit—that is, at least not conflict—with what seems to be the author's point or purpose (which, of course, is often difficult to discern). If the premise you supply is plausible and fitting (with author's intent), use it to fill out the argument. If your supplied premise is either not plausible or not fitting, go to step 2.

Step 2. Search for a credible premise that would make the argument as *strong* as possible. Choose the supplied premise that fulfills stipulations a and b. If the premise you supply is plausible and fitting, use it to fill out the argument. If your supplied premise is either not plausible or not fitting, consider the argument beyond repair and reject it.

Step 3. Evaluate the reconstituted argument. If you're able to identify a credible implicit premise that makes the argument

I've never met anyone like you. You're just wrong about everything.

either valid or strong, assess this revised version of the argument, paying particular attention to the plausibility of the other premise or premises.

Now let's apply this procedure to a few arguments:

> If the Fed lowers interest rates one more time, there will be a deep recession. I'm telling you there's going to be a deep recession.

The first step is to see if there's a credible premise that would make the argument valid. We can see right away that one premise will do the trick: "The Fed has lowered interest rates again." Adding it to the argument will supply the needed link between the existing premise and the conclusion. We also can see that our new premise is plausible (the Fed has lowered interest rates again) and seems to fit with the point of the argument (to prove that there will be a recession). Our resulting argument, though, is probably not a good one because the premise about the effect of the Fed's lowering interest rates is dubious.

Now examine this one:

> Security officer Jones lied on her employment application about whether she had a criminal record. Security officer Jones will do a lousy job of screening passengers for weapons.

The sentence "Security officer Jones will do a lousy job of screening passengers for weapons" is the conclusion here. To try to make this argument valid, we would need a premise like "Any security officer at La Guardia airport who has lied on his or her employment application about having a criminal record will do a lousy job of screening passengers for weapons." This premise fits the point of the argument, but it isn't plausible. Surely it cannot be the case that *any* security officer who has lied will do a lousy job of screening. A more plausible premise is "Most security officers at La Guardia airport who have lied on their employment applications about having a criminal record will do a lousy job of screening passengers for weapons." This premise will do, and this is now a good argument—assuming that the other premise is true.

What about this one?

> The use of marijuana should be legal because it's an act that brings pleasure to people's lives.

To make this argument valid, we would need to add this premise (or one like it): "Any act that brings pleasure to people's lives should be legal." But this premise is hard to accept since many heinous acts—such as murder and theft—may bring pleasure to some people, yet few of us would think those acts should be legal. To try to make the argument strong, we might add this premise instead: "Some acts should be legal simply because they bring pleasure to people's lives." This premise is actually controversial in some quarters, but it at least is not obviously false. It also fits with the point of the argument. If we decide that the premise is neither plausible nor fitting, we would declare the argument beyond repair.

Exercise 3.4

I. For each of the following arguments, identify the implicit premises that will make the argument valid.

EXAMPLE

The engine is sputtering. It must be out of gas.
Implicit premise: Whenever the engine sputters, it's out of gas.

* 1. Any senator who is caught misusing campaign funds should resign his seat. Senator Greed should resign.

2. Not everyone in this country has health insurance. Therefore, healthcare is a disaster.

3. In the first week at the box office, the movie grossed over $30 million. So it's sure to win at least one Oscar.

4. The FBI doesn't have a very serious focus on stopping terrorism. Another major terrorist attack will happen in this country.

* 5. The author of the book on interventionist wars is either biased or incompetent as a journalist. So she's biased.

6. The conflict in Indonesia is a genuine war. So it can't possibly be morally justified.

7. Hillary Clinton has amazing name recognition. So she will go far.

8. The U.S. government should limit its activities to the Western Hemisphere because it doesn't have the resources to cover the whole world.

* 9. If the engine starts right away, it's because of the tune-up I gave it. Must be because of the tune-up I gave it.

10. Taslima did not criticize U.S. military action in the Gulf War or in the war in Afghanistan. She must be a hawk.

II. To each of the following arguments, change or add a premise that will make the argument strong.

1. The Republicans are more articulate about their policies and more realistic about world events than the Democrats are. They will surely win the next election.

2. Aziz regularly eats at McDonald's, so Aziz is likely to gain a few pounds.

* 3. Six out of ten of my teenage friends love rap music. So 60 percent of all teens love rap music.

4. Seventy-one percent of the faculty and staff at Goddard Community College are Democrats. So most of the students are probably Democrats.

5. Miriam was in the library when the books were stolen from the librarian's desk. She was also seen hanging around the desk. So she's probably the one who stole them.

* 6. If Assad's fingerprints are on the vase, then he's probably the one who broke it. He's probably the one who broke it.

7. If the president needs more money to balance the federal budget, he will get it from Social Security. Well, he's almost certainly going to get it from Social Security.

8. Ninety percent of students at Boston College graduate with a B.A. degree. Li Fong will probably graduate from Boston College with a B.A. degree.

* 9. The murder rates in most large American cities on the East Coast are very high. The murder rates in most large cities in the West and Midwest are very high. So the murder rate in New Orleans must be very high.

10. John has a typical American diet. His fat intake is probably excessively high.

Argument Patterns

Earlier we discussed the importance of being familiar with argument patterns, or forms, the structures on which the content is laid. The point was that knowing some common argument forms makes it easier to determine whether an argument is deductive or inductive. But being familiar with argument forms is also helpful in many other aspects of argument evaluation. Let's take a closer look at some of these forms.

Since argument forms are structures distinct from argument content, we can easily signify different forms by using letters to represent statements in the arguments. Each letter represents a different statement in much the same way that letters are used to represent values in a mathematical equation. Consider this argument:

If the job is worth doing, then it's worth doing well.

The job is worth doing.

Therefore, it's worth doing well.

We can represent this argument like this:

If p, then q.

p.

Therefore, q.

Notice that the first line in the argument is a compound statement—it's composed of at least two constituent statements, which are represented in this case by p and q. So we have three statements in this argument that are arranged into an argument form, one that is both very common and always valid. We can plug any statements we want into this form, and we will still get a valid argument. The premises may be true or false, but the form will be valid.

Some of the more common argument patterns that you encounter are like this pattern—they're deductive, and they contain one or more **conditional**, or if–then, premises. The first statement in a conditional premise (the *if* part) is known as the **antecedent**. The second statement (the *then* part) is known as the **consequent**.

The pattern shown here is called **affirming the antecedent** or, to use the Latin term, **modus ponens**. Any argument in the modus ponens form is valid—if the premises are true, the conclusion absolutely must be true. This means that if "If *p*, then *q*" and "*p*" are both true, the conclusion has to be true also. These facts, then, provide a way to quickly size up an argument. If it's in the form of modus ponens, it's valid, regardless of the content of the statements.

Another common argument form is called **denying the consequent**, or **modus tollens**:

> If Austin is happy, then Barb is happy.
>
> Barb is not happy.
>
> Therefore, Austin is not happy.

The form of modus tollens is:

> If *p*, then *q*.
>
> Not *q*.
>
> Therefore, not *p*.

Like modus ponens, modus tollens is always valid. If the premises are true, the conclusion must be true. So any argument that's in the modus tollens pattern is valid.

A third common argument form is called **hypothetical syllogism**. "Hypothetical" is just another term for conditional. A **syllogism** is a deductive argument made up of three statements—two premises and a conclusion. (Modus ponens and modus tollens are also syllogisms.) In a hypothetical syllogism, all three statements are conditional, and the argument is always valid:

> If the ball drops, the lever turns to the right.
>
> If the lever turns to the right, the engine will stop.
>
> Therefore, if the ball drops, the engine will stop.

Here's the symbolized version:

> If *p*, then *q*.
>
> If *q*, then *r*.
>
> Therefore, if *p*, then *r*.

People often use hypothetical syllogisms to reason about causal chains of events. They try to show that one event will lead inexorably to a sequence of events, finally concluding in a single event that seems far removed from the first. This linkage has prompted some to label hypothetical syllogisms "chain arguments."

Valid Argument Forms

AFFIRMING THE ANTECEDENT

(Modus Ponens)   EXAMPLE

    If p, then q.   If Spot barks, a burglar is in the house.

    p.   Spot is barking.

    Therefore, q.   Therefore, a burglar is in the house.

DENYING THE CONSEQUENT

(Modus Tollens)   EXAMPLE

    If p, then q.   If it's raining, the park is closed.

    Not q.   The park is not closed.

    Therefore, not p.   Therefore, it's not raining.

Hypothetical Syllogism   EXAMPLE

    If p, then q.   If Ajax steals the money, he will go to jail.

    If q, then r.   If Ajax goes to jail, his family will suffer.

    Therefore, if p, then r.   Therefore, if Ajax steals the money, his family will suffer.

There are two common argument forms that are *not* valid, though they strongly resemble valid forms. One is called **denying the antecedent**. For example:

> If Einstein invented the steam engine, then he's a great scientist.
>
> Einstein did not invent the steam engine.
>
> Therefore, he is not a great scientist.

Denying the antecedent is represented like this:

> If p, then q.
>
> Not p.
>
> Therefore, not q.

You can see the problem with this form in the preceding argument. Even if the antecedent is false (if Einstein did not invent the steam engine), that doesn't show that he's not a great scientist because he could be a great scientist on account of some other great achievement. Thus, denying the antecedent is clearly an invalid pattern: It's possible for the premises to be true and the conclusion false.

Here's another example of this form:

> If science can prove that God is dead, then God is dead.
>
> Science cannot prove that God is dead.
>
> Therefore, God is not dead.

Even if science cannot prove that God is dead, that in itself does not show that God is not dead. Perhaps God is dead even though science cannot prove it. In other words, it's possible for both premises to be true while the conclusion is false.

There's another common invalid form you should know about: **affirming the consequent**. Here's an instance of this form:

> If Buffalo is the capital of New York, then Buffalo is in New York.
>
> Buffalo is in New York.
>
> Therefore, Buffalo is the capital of New York.

We represent this form like this:

> If p, then q.
>
> q.
>
> Therefore, p.

Obviously, in this form it's possible for the premises to be true while the conclusion is false, as this example shows. This pattern, therefore, is invalid.

Finally, we come to a common argument form called **disjunctive syllogism**. It's valid and extremely simple:

> Either Ralph walked the dog, or he stayed home.
>
> He didn't walk the dog.
>
> Therefore, he stayed home.

The symbolized form:

> Either p or q.
>
> Not p.
>
> Therefore, q.

> "Mistakes are made on two counts: an argument is either based on error or incorrectly developed."
> —**Thomas Aquinas**

 REVIEW NOTES

Invalid Argument Forms

AFFIRMING THE CONSEQUENT	EXAMPLE
If p, then q.	If the cat is on the mat, she is asleep.
q.	She is asleep.
Therefore, p.	Therefore, she is on the mat.
DENYING THE ANTECEDENT	EXAMPLE
If p, then q.	If the cat is on the mat, she is asleep.
Not p.	She is not on the mat.
Therefore, not q.	Therefore, she is not asleep.

Keep in mind that in a disjunctive syllogism, either disjunct can be denied, not just the first one.

These six deductive argument forms (four valid ones and two invalid ones) can help you streamline the process of argument evaluation. If you want to find out quickly if a deductive argument is valid, you can use these patterns to do that. (Remember, a good deductive argument has both a valid form and true premises.) You need only to see if the argument fits one of the forms. If it fits a valid form, it's valid. If it fits an invalid form, it's invalid. If it doesn't fit any of the forms, then you need to find another way to evaluate the argument. The easiest way to regularly apply this form-comparison technique is to memorize all six forms so you can identify them whenever they arise.

Sometimes you can see right away that an argument has a valid or invalid form. At other times, you may need a little help figuring this out, or you may want to use a more explicit test of validity. In either case, the *counterexample method* can help. With this technique you check for validity by simply devising a parallel argument that has the same form as the argument you're evaluating (the test argument) but has obviously *true premises and a false conclusion*. Recall that any argument having true premises and a false conclusion cannot be valid. So if you can invent such an argument that also has the same pattern as the test argument, you've proved that the test argument is invalid.

Let's say that you are confronted with this argument:

> If crime is increasing, then our nation has abandoned God.
>
> Our nation has abandoned God.
>
> Therefore, crime is increasing.

And to check this test argument, you come up with this parallel argument:

> If George is a dog, then he is warm-blooded.
>
> George is warm-blooded.
>
> Therefore, he is a dog.

This argument has the same pattern as the previous one—but the premises are true, and the conclusion is false. So the test argument is invalid. You may have already guessed that it is an instance of affirming the consequent. The counterexample method, though, works not just for the deductive forms we've

 REVIEW NOTES

Disjunctive Syllogism

SYMBOLIZED VERSION

Either *p* or *q*.

Not *p*.

Therefore, *q*.

EXAMPLE

Either we light the fire or we will freeze.

We will not light the fire.

Therefore, we will freeze.

discussed but for all deductive forms. (We will discuss other deductive forms in upcoming chapters.)

Consider another counterexample test. The argument in question is:

> If Jackson drinks a lot of orange juice, he will get better.
>
> He didn't drink a lot of orange juice.
>
> Therefore, he will not get better.

And the parallel argument is:

> If horses could fly, they would be valuable.
>
> But horses cannot fly.
>
> Therefore, horses are not valuable.

The argument to be tested is, of course, an example of denying the antecedent, and the counterexample method shows it to be invalid.

 EXERCISES

Exercise 3.5

For each of the following arguments, determine whether it is valid or invalid and indicate the argument pattern.

* 1. If the Pilgrims built that wall, there would be archeological evidence of that. But there is no such evidence.
  So the Pilgrims did not build that wall.

2. If the butler didn't kill the master, then the maid did.
  The butler didn't kill him.
  So the maid killed him.

3. Either John drove home or he stayed late.
  He didn't drive home.
  Therefore, he stayed late.

4. If the South Africans have nuclear weapons, the South African jungle will be radioactive.
  The South African jungle is radioactive.
  Therefore, the South Africans have nuclear weapons.

5. If the *New York Times* comes out in favor of the liberal democrats, they will win the election. But the newspaper will not come out in favor of the liberal democrats, so they will not win.

* 6. If CNN News omits important news stories, then it is irresponsible. It is not irresponsible. So CNN News does not omit important news stories.

7. If ESP (extrasensory perception) were real, psychic predictions would be completely reliable.

   Psychic predictions are completely reliable.

   Therefore, ESP is real.

8. If Miley Cyrus keeps playing the role of the twisted tart on stage, she will lose all her fans. Well, she has stopped playing that role, so she will not lose all her fans.

* 9. If ESP (extrasensory perception) were real, psychic predictions would be completely reliable.

   ESP is real.

   Therefore, psychic predictions are completely reliable.

10. If laws could stop crime, there would be no crime.

    But there is crime.

    Therefore, laws cannot stop crime.

11. If I perceive what appears to be a red door, then there really is a red door there.

    There really is a red door there.

    Therefore, I perceive what appears to be a red door.

12. If it rains, Alex will get wet.

    If Alex gets wet, he will be upset.

    Therefore, if it rains, Alex will be upset.

Exercise 3.6

For each of the following premises, fill out the rest of the argument to make it valid in two different ways—modus ponens and modus tollens.

1. If God is in his heaven, then all is right with the world.

* 2. If Lino is telling the truth, he will admit to all charges.

3. If some wars are just, then pacifism is false.

4. If the new vaccine prevents the spread of the virus, the researchers who developed the vaccine should get the Nobel Prize.

* 5. If religious conflict in Nigeria continues, thousands more will die.

6. If p, then q.

7. If the glaciers are melting, global warming has increased.

8. If there is such a thing as moral progress—that is, social changes in which we judge states of affairs to be "better" now than before—then the Enlightenment ideal of moral perfection is possible.

* 9. If solar power can supply six megawatts of power in San Francisco (which is certainly not the sunniest place in the world), then solar power can transform the energy systems in places like Texas and Arizona.

10. If my honorable colleague would stop listening to only his own voice for less than sixty seconds, he would doubtless be astonished that there are other minds in the world with other ideas.

Exercise 3.7

Use the counterexample method to create a parallel argument for each of the invalid arguments in Exercise 3.5. Write out each parallel argument and represent its form using letters as discussed earlier. Answers are provided for 4, 5, 7, 8, and 11.

EXAMPLE

Test Argument:
> If the president cuts taxes again, there will be a long-term recession.
> There will be a long-term recession.
> Therefore, the president will cut taxes.

Parallel Argument:
> If Donald Trump could fly, he would be famous.
> He is famous.
> Therefore, he can fly.

> If a, then b.
> b.
> Therefore, a.

Diagramming Arguments

Most of the arguments we've looked at so far have been relatively simple. When arguments are more complex (in real life they usually are!), you may find it increasingly difficult to sort out premises from conclusions and argument parts from nonargumentative background noise. If you can visualize an argument's structure, though, the job gets much easier. That's where argument diagramming comes in.

Let's begin by diagramming the following argument:

> There is no question in my mind. I therefore maintain that Colonel Mustard is the murderer. Because if he did it, he would probably have bloodstains on the sleeve of his shirt. The bloodstains are tiny, but they are there. Any observant person could see them. Also the murder weapon was within the colonel's reach for quite a while before the crime was committed. And since of all the people in the house at the time he alone does not have an airtight alibi, he must be the killer.

The first thing we do is underline (or circle) any premise or conclusion indicator words (e.g., "therefore," "since," and "because"):

> There is no question in my mind. I <u>therefore</u> maintain that Colonel Mustard is the murderer. <u>Because</u> if he did it, he would probably have bloodstains on the sleeve of his shirt. The bloodstains are tiny, but they are there. Any observant person could see them. Also the murder weapon was within the colonel's reach for quite a while before the crime was committed. And <u>since</u> of all the people in the house at the time he alone does not have an airtight alibi, he must be the killer.

Next we number all the statements (and *only* the statements) in the passage in sequential order. (For the purposes of diagramming, an if–then statement is considered one statement, and multiple statements in a single compound sentence are to be counted as separate statements. Such statements are usually joined by "and," "or," and "but.") Then we look for the conclusion and draw a wavy line under it. Only after we've zeroed in on the conclusion should we try to locate the premises, which we can indicate by <u>underlining</u> them:

> (1) There is no question in my mind. (2) <u>I therefore maintain that Colonel Mustard is the murderer.</u> (3) <u>Because if he did it, he would probably have bloodstains on the sleeve of his shirt.</u> (4) <u>The bloodstains are tiny, but they are there.</u> (5) <u>Any observant person could see them.</u> (6) <u>Also the murder weapon was within the colonel's reach for quite a while before the crime was committed.</u> (7) <u>And since of all the people in the house at the time he alone does not have an airtight alibi,</u> he must be the killer.

And then we cross out all extraneous statements—those that are neither premises nor conclusions, those that are redundant, and those that are nothing more than background information or other logically irrelevant material.

> (1) ~~There is no question in my mind.~~ (2) <u>I therefore maintain that Colonel Mustard is the murderer.</u> (3) <u>Because if he did it, he would probably have bloodstains on the sleeve of his shirt.</u> (4) <u>The bloodstains are tiny, but they are there.</u> (5) Any observant person could see them. (6) <u>Also the murder weapon was within the colonel's reach for quite a while before the crime was committed.</u> (7) <u>And since of all the people in the house at the time he alone does not have an airtight alibi,</u> ~~he must be the killer.~~

©2008 CREATORS SYNDICATE, INC. www.creators.com

Allen is far less argumentative since Angie's introduction to falconry.

Finally, we draw the diagram. Place the numbers of the premises above the number for the conclusion. Then draw arrows from the premises to the conclusion they support. Each arrow represents a logical relationship between premise and conclusion, a relationship that we normally indicate with the word "therefore" or "is a reason or premise for."

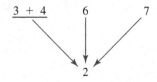

In this diagram you can see that premises 3 and 4 are handled differently from premises 6 and 7. The reason is that some premises are **independent** and some are **dependent**.

An independent premise offers support to a conclusion *without the help of any other premises*. If other premises are omitted or undermined in an argument, the support supplied by an independent premise does not change. We represent this fact in the diagram by drawing separate arrows from premises 6 and 7 to the conclusion. Premise 6 gives independent support to the conclusion, and premise 7 gives independent support to the conclusion. If we delete one of these premises, the support that the other one gives does not change.

Premises 3 and 4 are dependent premises. They do depend on each other to jointly provide support to a conclusion. If either premise 3 or 4 is removed, the support that the remaining premise supplies is undermined or completely canceled out. By itself, premise 3 ("Because if he did it, he would probably have bloodstains on the sleeve of his shirt") offers no support whatsoever to the conclusion ("Colonel Mustard is the murderer"). And by itself, premise 4 ("The bloodstains are tiny, but they are there") doesn't lend any support to the conclusion. But together, premises 3 and 4 offer a good reason to accept the conclusion. We represent dependent premises by joining them with a plus sign ("+") and underlining them, as in our diagram. Since dependent premises together act as a single premise, or reason, we draw a single arrow from the combined premises ("3 + 4") to the conclusion. With the diagram complete, we can see clearly that two independent premises and one set of dependent premises provide support for the conclusion (statement 2).

Now, consider this argument:

> (1) The famous trial lawyer Clarence Darrow (1857–1938) made a name for himself by using the "determinism defense" to get his clients acquitted of serious crimes. (2) The crux of this approach is the idea that humans are not really responsible for anything they do because they cannot choose freely—they are "determined," predestined, if you will, by nature (or God) to be the way they are. (3) So in a sense, Darrow says, humans are like wind-up toys with no control over any action or decision. (4) They have no free will. (5) Remember that Darrow was a renowned agnostic who was skeptical of all religious claims. (6) But Darrow is wrong about human free will for two reasons. (7) First, in our moral life, our own common-sense experience suggests that sometimes people are free to make moral decisions. (8) We should not abandon what our common-sense experience tells us without good reason—and (9) Darrow has given us no good reason. (10) Second, Darrow's determinism is not confirmed by science, as he claims—but actually conflicts with science. (11) Modern science says that there are many things (at the subatomic level of matter) that are not determined at all: (12) They just happen.

Indicator words are scarce in this argument, unless you count the words "first" and "second" as signifying premises. Draw a wavy line under the conclusion, underline the premises, and cross out extraneous statements, the argument looks like this:

> (1) ~~The famous trial lawyer Clarence Darrow (1857–1938) made a name for himself by using the "determinism defense" to get his clients acquitted of serious crimes.~~ (2) ~~The crux of this approach is the idea that~~

~~humans are not really responsible for anything they do because they cannot choose freely—they are "determined," predestined, if you will, by nature (or God) to be the way they are. (3) So in a sense, Darrow says, humans are like wind-up toys with no control over any action or decision. (4) They have no free will. (5) Remember that Darrow was a renowned agnostic who was skeptical of all religious claims.~~ (6) But Darrow is wrong about human free will for two reasons. (7) First, in our moral life, our own common-sense experience suggests that sometimes people are free to make moral decisions. (8) We should not abandon what our common-sense experience tells us without good reason—and (9) Darrow has given us no good reason. (10) Second, Darrow's determinism is not confirmed by science, as he claims—but actually conflicts with science. (11) Modern science says that there are many things (at the subatomic level of matter) that are not determined at all: ~~(12) They just happen.~~

To simplify things, we can eliminate several statements right away. Statements 1 through 4 are just background information on Darrow's views. Statement 5 is irrelevant to the argument; his agnosticism has no logical connection to the premises or conclusion. Statement 12 is a rewording of statement 11.

After this elimination process, only the following premises and conclusion (statement 6) remain:

(6) But Darrow is wrong about human free will for two reasons.
(7) First, in our moral life, our common-sense experience suggests that sometimes people are free to make moral decisions.
(8) We should not abandon what our common-sense experience tells us without good reason.
(9) Darrow has given us no good reason.
(10) Darrow's determinism is not confirmed by science, as he claims—but actually conflicts with science.
(11) Modern science says that there are many things (mostly at the subatomic level of matter) that are not determined at all.

REVIEW NOTES

Diagramming Arguments: Step by Step

1. Underline all premise or conclusion indicator words, such as "since," "therefore," and "because." Then number the statements.
2. Find the conclusion and draw a wavy line under it.
3. Locate the premises and underline them.
4. Cross out all extraneous material—redundancies, irrelevant sentences, questions, exclamations.
5. Draw the diagram, connecting premises and conclusions with arrows showing logical connections. Include both dependent and independent premises.

The question is, how are these premises related to the conclusion? Well, premises 7, 8, and 9 are dependent premises supporting the conclusion. Taken separately, these premises are weak, but together they constitute a plausible reason for accepting statement 6. Premise 10 directly supports the conclusion, and it in turn is supported by premise 11. These logical relationships can be diagrammed like this:

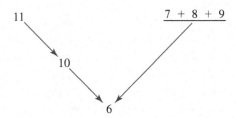

Now read this one:

As the Islamic clerics cling to power in Iran, students there are agitating for greater freedom and less suppression of views that the clerics dislike. Even though ultimate power in Iran rests with the mullahs, it is not at all certain where the nation is headed. Here's a radical suggestion: The Islamic republic in Iran will fall within the next five years. Why do I say this? Because the majority of Iranians are in favor of democratic reforms, and no regime can stand for very long when citizens are demanding access to the political process. Also, Iran today is a mirror image of the Soviet Union before it broke apart—there's widespread dissatisfaction and dissent at a time when the regime seems to be trying to hold the people's loyalty. Every nation that has taken such a path has imploded within five years. Finally, the old Iranian trick of gaining support for the government by fomenting hatred of America will not work anymore because Iran is now trying to be friends with the United States.

When we number the statements and underline the indicators, we get this:

(1) As the Islamic clerics cling to power in Iran, students there are agitating for greater freedom and less suppression of views that the clerics dislike. (2) Even though ultimate power in Iran rests with the mullahs, it is not at all certain where the nation is headed. Here's a radical suggestion: (3) The Islamic republic in Iran will fall within the next five years. Why do I say this? (4) <u>Because</u> the majority of Iranians are in favor of democratic reforms, (5) and no regime can stand for very long when citizens are demanding access to the political process. (6) Also, Iran today is a mirror image of the Soviet Union before it broke apart—there's widespread dissatisfaction and dissent at a time when the regime seems to be trying to hold the people's loyalty. (7) Every nation that has taken such a path has

imploded within five years. (8) Finally, the old Iranian trick of gaining support for the government by fomenting hatred of America will not work anymore (9) <u>because</u> Iran is now trying to be friends with the United States.

And here's the passage with the premises and conclusion underlined and the extraneous material crossed out:

~~(1) As the Islamic clerics cling to power in Iran, students there are agitating for greater freedom and less suppression of views that the clerics dislike. (2) Even though ultimate power in Iran rests with the mullahs, it is not at all certain where the nation is headed. Here's a radical suggestion:~~ (3) <u>The Islamic republic in Iran will fall within the next five years.</u> Why do I say this? (4) <u>Because the majority of Iranians are in favor of democratic reforms,</u> (5) <u>and no regime can stand for very long when citizens are demanding access to the political process.</u> (6) Also, <u>Iran today is a mirror image of the Soviet Union before it broke apart—there's widespread dissatisfaction and dissent at a time when the regime seems to be trying to hold the people's loyalty.</u> (7) <u>Every nation that has taken such a path has imploded within five years.</u> (8) <u>Finally, the old Iranian trick of gaining support for the government by fomenting hatred of America will not work anymore</u> (9) <u>because Iran is now trying to be friends with the United States.</u>

The conclusion is statement 3, and the premises are statements 4 through 9. The first two statements are extraneous. Statements 4 and 5 are dependent premises, and so are statements 6 and 7. Statements 8 and 9 constitute an argument that gives support to the passage's conclusion. Statement 8 is the conclusion; statement 9, the premise. Notice also that the sentence "Why do I say this?" is not diagrammed at all because it's not a statement. The diagram of this argument is as follows:

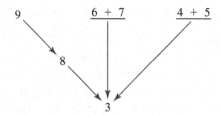

By the time you work through the diagramming exercises in this chapter, you will probably be fairly proficient in diagramming arguments of all kinds. Just as important, you will have a better appreciation of how arguments are built, how they're dissected, and how you can judge their value in a penetrating, systematic way.

Exercise 3.8

For each of the following diagrams, devise an argument whose premises and conclusion can be accurately depicted in the diagram. Write out the argument, number each statement, and insert the numbers into the diagram at the appropriate places.

* 1.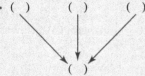

2.

3.

* 4.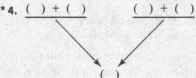

5.
( ) + ( )
      |
      ↓
    ( )
      |
      ↓
    ( )

6.

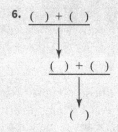

7.

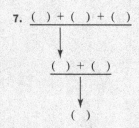

Exercise 3.9

Diagram the following arguments using the procedure discussed in the text.

1. I shouldn't take physics this semester. My course load is already too heavy. There's no room for the course in my schedule. And I don't like physics.

2. The president is soft on the environment. He has weakened clean-air regulations and lifted restrictions on logging in the West.

3. Congressman Porkbarrel is either dishonest or incompetent. He's not incompetent, though, because he's expert at getting self-serving legislation through Congress. I guess he's just dishonest.

4. If an individual in a coma is no longer a person, then giving him a drug to kill him is not murder. Such an individual is in fact not a person. Therefore, giving him the drug is not murder.

5. "The City Council deserves the gratitude of all New Yorkers for introducing a bill to ban the use of cell phones in places of public performance. . . . These rules may be hard to enforce, but so are bans on littering, auto horn honking and other quality-of-life offenses. By changing the law, the city will send a clear message that cell phone abuse is not just an etiquette issue but robs audience members of their right to enjoy the performance they paid for." [Letter to the editor, *New York Times*, November 28, 2002]

* 6. If Marla buys the house in the suburbs, she will be happier and healthier. She is buying the house in the suburbs. So she will be happier and healthier.

7. If you gain too much weight, your blood pressure will increase. If your blood pressure increases, your risk of stroke or heart attack rises. Therefore, gaining too much weight can increase your risk of stroke and heart attack.

8. "Grow accustomed to the belief that death is nothing to us, since every good and evil lie in sensation. However, death is the deprivation of sensation. Therefore . . . death is nothing to us." [Epicurus]

9. "A cause-and-effect relationship is drawn [by those opposed to pornography] between men viewing pornography and men attacking women, especially in the form of rape. But studies and experts disagree as to whether any relationship exists between pornography and violence, between images and behavior. Even the pro-censorship Meese Commission Report admitted that the data connecting pornography to violence was unreliable." [*Free Inquiry*, Fall 1997]

* 10. The existence of planets outside our solar system is a myth. There is no reliable empirical evidence at all showing that planets exist outside our solar system.

11. If Li Yang gets a high score on her test, she will have a perfect grade point average. If she gets a low score, she will drop out of school. She will get a high score on the test, so she will have a perfect grade point average.

12. Most atheists are liberals, and George is an atheist. Therefore, George is probably a liberal. Therefore, George is probably in favor of increased welfare benefits because most liberals are in favor of increased welfare benefits.

13. Bill is a student at Yale. No student at Yale has won the Nobel Prize. Therefore, Bill has not won the Nobel Prize.

14. "An international agreement proscribes the use of gas and so germ warfare must be developed." [Germaine Greer, *The Female Eunuch*]

15. The only valid reasons for dishonorably discharging someone from the Army are health problems and violations of Army regulations. So if Amal says that he was dishonorably discharged for simply being gay, he is lying or is mistaken. He is not lying. So he is mistaken.

16. "It is clear that archaeologists have not yet come to terms with dowsing [the alleged ability to detect underground water or treasure by paranormal means]. Where it has been the subject of tests, the tests have been so poorly designed and executed that any conclusion whatsoever could have been drawn from them. The fact that such tests are usually carried out only by researchers with a prior positive view of dowsing means that the conclusions will likely also be positive. The normal processes of peer review and scholarly discussion have also failed to uncover the lack of properly controlled test conditions in such studies as those of Bailey et al. and Locock, causing a generation of students and general readers in the United Kingdom, at least, to remain under the impression that the reality of archaeological dowsing had been all but confirmed by science." [*Skeptical Inquirer*, March/April 1999]

* 17. There are at least two main views regarding the morality of war. Pacifism is the view that no war is ever justified because it involves the taking of human life. Just-war theory is the view that *some* wars are justified for various reasons—mostly because they help prevent great evils (such as

massacres, "ethnic cleansing," or world domination by a madman like Hitler) or because they are a means of self-defense. I think that our own moral sense tells us that sometimes (in the case of World War II, for example) violence is occasionally morally justified. It would be hard for anyone to deny that a war to prevent something like the Holocaust is morally right.

18. Some say that those without strong religious beliefs—nonbelievers in one form or another—cannot be moral. But millions upon millions of people have been nonbelievers or nontheists and yet have produced some of the most noble and most morally principled civilizations in history. Consider the Buddhists of Asia and the Confucianists of China. Consider also the great secular philosophers from the ancient Greeks to the likes of Bertrand Russell and John Searle of the twentieth century.

19. Either Maggie, Jose, or Ling broke the window. Jose couldn't have done it because he was studying in his room and was observed the whole time. Maggie couldn't have done it because she was out of town at the time and has witnesses to prove it. So the perpetrator had to be Ling.

*20. The picnic will probably be spoiled because there is a 90 percent probability of rain.

21. The Golden Gate Bridge will probably be attacked by terrorists within the next two years. The latest intelligence reports from the Justice Department confirm this prediction. Plus terrorists have already stated publicly that they intend to destroy various symbolic structures or monuments in the United States, including Mount Rushmore and the Golden Gate.

22. We shouldn't pay Edward an allowance because he never does any work around the house, and he will probably just waste the money because he has no conception of the value of anything.

Assessing Long Arguments

The general principles of diagramming can help you when you have to evaluate arguments that are much longer and more complicated than most of those in this chapter. Some arguments are embedded in extended passages, persuasive essays, long reports, even whole books. In such cases, the kind of *detailed* argument diagramming we use to analyze short passages won't help you much. In very lengthy works, our five-step diagramming procedure would be tedious and time-consuming—if not maddening. But the *general approach* used in the procedure is relevant to longer arguments.

When you have to evaluate a very long passage, you're almost always faced with three obstacles:

1. Only a small portion of the prose may contain statements that serve as the premises and conclusion. (The rest is background information, reiterations of ideas, descriptions, examples, illustrations, asides, irrelevancies, and more.)

2. The premises or conclusion may be implicit.
3. Many longer works purporting to be filled with arguments contain very few arguments or none at all. (It's common for many books—even bestsellers—to pretend to make a case for something but to be devoid of genuine arguments.)

Fortunately, you can usually overcome these impediments if you're willing to put in some extra effort. The following is a four-step procedure that can help.

Step 1. Study the text until you thoroughly understand it. You can't locate the conclusion or premises until you know what you're looking for—and that requires having a clear idea of what the author is driving at. Don't attempt to find the conclusion or premises until you "get it." This understanding entails having an overview of a great deal of text, a bird's-eye view of the whole work.

Step 2. Find the conclusion. When you evaluate extended arguments, your first task, as in shorter writings, is to find the conclusion. There may be several main conclusions or one primary conclusion with several subconclusions (as depicted in some of the previous argument diagrams). Or the conclusion may be nowhere explicitly stated but embodied in metaphorical language or implied by large tracts of prose. In any case, your job is to come up with a single conclusion statement for each conclusion—even if you have to paraphrase large sections of text to do it.

Step 3. Identify the premises. Like the hunt for a conclusion, unearthing the premises may involve condensing large sections of text into manageable form—namely, single premise statements. To do this, you need to disregard extraneous material and keep your eye on the "big picture." Just as in shorter arguments, premises in longer pieces may be implicit. At this stage you shouldn't try to incorporate the details of evidence into the premises, though you must take them into account to fully understand the argument.

Step 4. Diagram the argument. After you identify the premises and conclusion, diagram them just as you would a much shorter argument.

Let's see how this procedure works on the following selection:

The Case for Discrimination

Edgardo Cureg was about to catch a Continental Airlines flight home on New Year's Eve when he ran into a former professor of his. Cureg lent the professor his cell phone and, once on board, went to the professor's seat to retrieve it. Another passenger saw the two "brown-skinned men" (Cureg is of Filipino descent, the professor Sri Lankan) conferring and became alarmed that they, and another man, were "behaving suspiciously." The three men were taken off the plane and forced to get later flights. The incident is now the subject of a lawsuit by the ACLU.

Several features of Cureg's story are worth noting. First, he was treated unfairly, in that he was embarrassed and inconvenienced because he was wrongly suspected of being a terrorist. Second, he was not treated unfairly, because he was not wrongly suspected. A fellow passenger, taking account of his apparent ethnicity, his sex and age, and his behavior, could reasonably

No Arguments, Just Fluff

Once you get really good at spotting arguments in a variety of passages, you may be shocked to see that a massive amount of persuasive writing contains no arguments at all. Apparently many people—including some very good writers—think that if they clearly express their opinions, then they have given an argument. You could look at this state of affairs as evidence that people are irrational—or you could view it as a time-saver: No need to waste your time on a bunch of unsupported opinions.

Unsupported opinions are everywhere, but they seem to permeate political writing, letters to the editor, and anything that's labeled "spiritual." Sometimes opinions are so weakly supported that they're almost indistinguishable from completely unsupported ones. Here's a taste:

> My family and friends have season tickets for the Buffalo Bandits. The disrespect that is shown to America by this team is appalling, particularly in this time of war. As both the Canadian and American national anthems are sung before each game, members of the team are hopping around, tugging at their uniforms, talking and carrying on amongst themselves. The players can't even wait for the national anthem to finish before they run off to their respective field positions. Whether one is for or against the war is irrelevant. Have some respect for America and what it stands for. [Letter to the editor, *Buffalo News* website]

No argument here, just indignation.

> So after a decade of progress, we have our smog problem back (as if it ever left). Another problem overlooked? Couldn't be because of all the giant behemoths (SUVs) on the road, could it? Nah. Or letting all the trucks from south of the border into our country without safety and smog inspections could it? Nah. It couldn't be because the government needs to have control of all it surveys? Nah. It must be something simpler, you think? Nah. [Letter to the editor, *Daily News* (Los Angeles) website]

No argument here either.

> How little is said of the soul-life and its complete identification with the human being! To most men the soul is something apart from themselves that is only to be talked of and trusted in on special occasions: There is no real companionship, no intimate affiliation, between men's minds and souls in their everyday existence. Now there is in every man a divine power, and when that divinity, which is real self, is acknowledged and understood by the mind, it takes a very active part in man's life—indeed, it could fill at the very least one-half of his thought-life. [Theosophy website]

Nope.

come to the conclusion that he was suspicious. Third, passengers' anxieties, and their inclination to take security matters into their own hands, increase when they have good reason to worry that the authorities are not taking all reasonable steps to look into suspicious characters themselves. . . .

Racial profiling of passengers at check-in is not a panacea. John Walker Lindh could have a ticket; a weapon could be planted on an unwitting 73-year-old nun. But profiling is a way of allocating sufficiently the resources devoted to security. A security system has to, yes, discriminate—among levels of threat. [*National Review*, July 1, 2002]

In this example, the author has given us a break by alluding to the conclusion in the title: Discrimination by racial profiling is a justified security measure. Notice that this conclusion is not explicitly stated in the text but is implied by various remarks, including "A security system has to, yes, discriminate." Given this conclusion, we can see that the entire first paragraph is background information—specifically, an example of racial profiling. The first premise is implicit. We glean it from the comments in the second paragraph: Racial profiling is a reasonable response in light of our legitimate concerns about security. The second premise is explicit: Profiling is a way of allocating sufficiently the resources devoted to security.

Laid out in neat order, this argument looks like this:

(1) Racial profiling is a reasonable response in light of our legitimate concerns about security.
(2) Profiling is a way of allocating sufficiently the resources devoted to security.
(3) Therefore, discrimination by racial profiling is a justified security measure.

The diagram of this argument looks like this:

A fact that can further complicate the argument structure of a long passage is that complex arguments can sometimes be made up of simpler arguments (subarguments). For example, the conclusion of a simple argument can serve as a premise in another simple argument, with the resulting chain of arguments constituting a larger complex argument. Such a chain can be long. The complex argument can also be a mix of both deductive and inductive arguments. Fortunately, all you need to successfully analyze these complex arguments is mastery of the elementary skills discussed earlier.

Let's take a look at another long passage:

Contemporary debates about torture usually concern its use in getting information from suspects (often suspected terrorists) regarding future attacks, the identity of the suspects' associates, the operations of terrorist cells, and the like.

"Our minds anywhere, when left to themselves, are always thus busily drawing conclusions from false premises."
—**Henry David Thoreau**

How effective torture is for this purpose is in dispute, mostly because of a lack of scientific evidence on the question. We are left with a lot of anecdotal accounts, some of which suggest that torture works, and some that it doesn't. People who are tortured often lie, saying anything that will make the torturers stop. On the other hand, in a few instances torture seems to have gleaned from the tortured some intelligence that helped thwart a terrorist attack.

Is torture sometimes the right thing to do? The answer is yes: In rare situations torture is indeed justified. Sometimes torturing a terrorist is the only way to prevent the deaths of hundreds or thousands of people. Consider: In Washington, D.C., a terrorist has planted a bomb set to detonate soon and kill a half million people. FBI agents capture him and realize that the only way to disarm the bomb in time is for the terrorist to tell them where it is, and the only way to get him to talk is to torture him. Is it morally permissible then to stick needles under his fingernails or waterboard him? The consequences of not torturing the terrorist would be a thousand times worse than torturing him. And according to many plausible moral theories, the action resulting in the best consequences for all concerned is the morally correct action. When we weigh the temporary agony of a terrorist against the deaths of thousands of innocents, the ethical answer seems obvious.

The length of this passage might suggest to you that the argument within it is long and tangled. But that's not the case here. The conclusion is this: In rare situations torture is morally justified. The first paragraph just provides background information; the second contains two premises. A paraphrase of the first premise would go something like this: In a ticking-bomb scenario, the consequences of not torturing a terrorist would be far worse than those of torturing him. The second premise says that the morally right action is the one that results in the best consequences for all concerned. Notice that these premises are dependent ones.

The argument then looks like this:

(1) In a ticking-bomb scenario, the consequences of not torturing a terrorist would be far worse than those of torturing him.
(2) The morally right action is the one that results in the best consequences for all concerned.
(3) Therefore, in rare situations torture is morally justified.

And the diagram looks like this:

The best way to learn how to assess long passages is to practice, which you can do in the following exercises. Be forewarned, however, that this skill depends heavily on your ability to understand the passage in question. If you do grasp the author's purpose, then you can more easily paraphrase the premises and conclusion and uncover implicit statements. You will also be better at telling extraneous stuff from the real meat of the argument. (Also see Appendix E: Critical Thinking and Writing.)

Exercise 3.10

For each of the following passages, (1) list the conclusion and premises and (2) diagram the argument.

* 1. "There are those who maintain . . . that even if God is not required as the author of the moral law, he is nevertheless required as the enforcer of it, for without the threat of divine punishment, people will not act morally. But this position is [not plausible]. In the first place, as an empirical hypothesis about the psychology of human beings, it is questionable. There is no unambiguous evidence that theists are more moral than non-theists. Not only have psychological studies failed to find a significant correlation between frequency of religious worship and moral conduct, but convicted criminals are much more likely to be theists than atheists. Second, the threat of divine punishment cannot impose a moral obligation, for might does not make right. Threats extort; they do not create a moral duty." [*Free Inquiry*, Summer 1997]

2. "I love *Reason* [magazine], but [regarding a previous article by Nick Gillespie] I'm wondering if all the illegal drugs that Nick Gillespie used to take are finally getting to him. He has a right to speak out against President Bush, but when he refers to him as 'the millionaire president who waited out the Vietnam War in the Texas Air National Guard,' it reminds me of the garbage rhetoric that I might see if I were reading Ted Rall, or Susan Sontag, or one of the other hate-mongering, America-bashing, leftist whiners. That kind of ad hominem attack is not only disrespectful to a man who is doing a damned good job as commander-in-chief (with approval ratings of more than 80%); it detracts from the whole point of the article." [Letter to the editor, *Reason*, July 2002]

3. "The fifth way [of proving that God exists] is taken from the governance of the world. We see that things which lack knowledge, such as natural bodies, act for an end, and this is evident from their acting always, or nearly always, in the same way, so as to obtain the best result. Hence it is plain that they achieve their end, not fortuitously, but designedly. Now whatever lacks knowledge cannot move towards an end, unless it be directed by some being endowed with knowledge and intelligence; as the arrow is directed by the archer. Therefore some intelligent being exists by whom all natural things are directed to their end; and this being we call God." [Thomas Aquinas, *Summa Theologica*]

4. "The first thing that must occur to anyone studying moral subjectivism [the view that the rightness or wrongness of an action depends on the beliefs of an individual or group] seriously is that the view allows the possibility that an action can be both right and not right, or wrong and not wrong, etc. This possibility exists because, as we have seen, the subjectivist claims that the moral character of an action is determined by individual subjective states; and these states can vary from person to person, even when directed toward the same action on the same occasion. Hence one and the same action can evidently be determined to have—simultaneously—radically different moral characters . . . . [If] subjectivism . . . does generate such contradictory conclusions, the position is certainly untenable." [Phillip Montague, *Reason and Responsibility*]

5. A Florida judge dismissed a lawsuit that accused the Vatican of hiding instances of sexual abuse by priests. The suit was thrown out because Florida's statute of limitations had run out on the case. I submit that the dismissal was proper and ethical considering the community stature and function of priests and the benefits that accrue to society in the aftermath of the decision. Let's consider community stature first. The community stature of priests must always be taken into account in these abuse cases. A priest is not just anybody; he performs a special role in society—namely, to provide spiritual guidance and to remind people that there is both a moral order and a divine order in the world. The priest's role is special because it helps to underpin and secure society itself. Anything that could undermine this role must be neutralized as soon as possible. Among those things that can weaken the priestly role are publicity, public debate, and legal actions. Abuse cases are better handled in private by those who are keenly aware of the importance of a positive public image of priests. And what of the benefits of curtailing the legal proceedings? The benefits to society of dismissing the legal case outweigh all the alleged disadvantages of continuing with public hearings. The primary benefit is the continued nurturing of the community's faith, without which the community would cease to function effectively.

🔑 KEY WORDS

affirming the antecedent

affirming the consequent

antecedent

cogent argument

conditional statement

consequent

deductive argument

denying the antecedent

denying the consequent

dependent premise

disjunctive syllogism

hypothetical syllogism

independent premise

inductive argument

invalid argument

modus ponens

modus tollens

sound argument

strong argument

syllogism

truth-preserving

valid argument

weak argument

Summary
Argument Basics

- Arguments come in two forms: deductive and inductive. A deductive argument is intended to provide logically conclusive support for a conclusion; an inductive one, probable support for a conclusion. Deductive arguments can be valid or invalid; inductive arguments, strong or weak. A valid argument with true premises is said to be sound. A strong argument with true premises is said to be cogent.

Judging Arguments

- Evaluating an argument is the most important skill of critical thinking. It involves finding the conclusion and premises, checking to see if the argument is deductive or inductive, determining its validity or strength, and discovering if the premises are true or false.

Finding Missing Parts

- Sometimes you also have to ferret out implicit, or unstated, premises. Finding implicit premises is a three-step process.

Argument Patterns

- Arguments can come in certain common patterns, or forms. Two valid forms that you will often run into are modus ponens (affirming the antecedent) and modus tollens (denying the consequent). Two common invalid forms are denying the antecedent and affirming the consequent.
- Using the counterexample method can help you determine whether a deductive argument is valid or invalid.

Diagramming Arguments

- Analyzing the structure of arguments is easier if you diagram them. Argument diagrams can help you visualize the function of premises and conclusions and the relationships among complex arguments with several subarguments.

Assessing Long Arguments

- Assessing very long arguments can be challenging because they may contain lots of verbiage but few or no arguments, and many premises can be implicit. Evaluating long arguments, though, requires the same basic steps as assessing short ones: (1) Ensure that you understand the argument, (2) locate the conclusion, (3) find the premises, and (4) diagram it to clarify logical relationships.

 Field Problems

1. Find a 150- to 200-word passage purporting to present an argument for a particular view but actually being devoid of arguments. Look in magazine or newspaper letters to the editor or on advocacy or political websites. Then rewrite the passage and include an argument for the original view.

2. Visit a website intended to support a particular view on a social or political issue. Using the information on the website, write a 100-word passage containing an argument for a view that the website might endorse.

3. Visit www.townhall.com, www.usatoday.com, or www.csmonitor.com. Find an essay arguing for a particular view, and identify the premises and the conclusion. Decide whether you think the argument is a good one. Be prepared to explain why.

 Self-Assessment Quiz

Answers appear in "Answers to Self-Assessment Quizzes" (Appendix D).

1. What is a deductive argument? An inductive argument?
2. What is a valid argument? An invalid one? What is a strong inductive argument?
3. What is a sound argument?

    Indicate whether the following arguments are deductive or inductive.

4. If you refuse to surrender, then you will be arrested. You refuse to surrender. Prepare yourself: You will be arrested.
5. There's an 80 percent chance that the hurricane will veer northward tomorrow and hit Tampa. So Tampa will probably feel the force of the hurricane tomorrow.
6. Ethel is reckless. She is going to have an accident sooner or later.
7. Whatever Hillary Clinton says is true. She says that the Republicans are weak. So the Republicans are weak.

In each of the following arguments, identify the implicit premise that will make the argument either valid or strong.

8. Jones has never openly criticized any military action against any Middle Eastern nation. He is a warmonger.
9. Maria failed her driving test three times. She's probably not paying attention.
10. If 60 percent of people believe in astrology or tarot cards, the future of the country does not look bright. Grades in college science courses will probably drop dramatically.

For each of the following exercises, provide an example of the argument pattern indicated.

11. Modus ponens
12. Modus tollens
13. Denying the antecedent
14. Affirming the consequent

Diagram the following arguments.

15. Cole is up to no good. He's been acting suspiciously for days, and he told Rachel that he was going to steal something valuable.

16. The sitcom *Friends* is becoming really lame. The writing is predictable and plodding. The acting is worse than ever.

17. If dolphins have minds comparable to ours, then these creatures are self-conscious, intelligent, and creative. If they are self-conscious, then they should react appropriately when they see their reflections in a mirror. They do react appropriately. If they're intelligent, they should be able to solve complex problems. They can solve such problems. If they're creative, they should be able to create some form of art. In a rudimentary way, they do create art. They are definitely self-conscious, intelligent, and creative.

18. If the dictum to always tell the truth in all circumstances is a valid moral principle, then it should fit well with our considered moral judgments. But it does not fit well with our considered moral judgments because there are times when lying is actually the right thing to do, as when we lie to save a life. So the dictum to always tell the truth is not a valid moral principle.

19. I don't think that I should vote for any independent candidate in the next election. Independents never win, and I want the person I vote for to win. Also, independents have a tendency to be a little wacky. And we definitely don't need any more wacky politicians in power.

20. Creationism is an inadequate theory about the origins of life. It conflicts with science, and it is incapable of predicting any new facts.

 Integrative Exercises

These exercises pertain to material in Chapters 1–3.

For each of the following passages, indicate whether it contains an argument. If it does, specify the conclusion and premises, any argument indicator words, whether the argument is deductive or inductive, and whether it contains an example of face-saving or group-pressure thinking. Also identify any implicit premises and diagram the argument.

1. If Anne is in town, then she's staying at the Barbary Hotel. She's in town. Therefore, she's staying at the Barbary Hotel.

2. If the death penalty deterred anyone from crime, then there would be a lower crime rate in countries that have the death penalty than in countries

that do not. But crime rates are often higher in countries with the death penalty. So the death penalty is really no crime deterrent.

3. "In the wake of the attacks of September 11th, 2001, the governments of Canada and the United States have passed sweeping anti-terrorism bills that effectively lay the groundwork for the criminalization of ideas. One consequence has been . . . the policing of freedom of expression. In Canada, a post–September 11th exhibit of contemporary Arab-Canadian art at the National Museum in Ottawa was abruptly cancelled by the organizers to allow the curators to 'reconsider' the political works on display: The exhibition did go ahead as scheduled, but only after a determined public campaign challenging the museum's actions." [*Alternative Press Review*, Spring 2002]

4. "[Is] there scientific evidence that prayer really works? . . . The problem with . . . any so-called controlled experiment regarding prayer is that *there can be no such thing as a controlled experiment concerning prayer*. You can never divide people into groups that received prayer and those that did not. The main reason is that there is no way to know that someone did not receive prayer. How would anyone know that some distant relative was not praying for a member of the group . . . identified as having received no prayer?" [*Free Inquiry*, Summer 1997]

5. "Going hand in hand with the fundamental dishonesty of America's news media is the second problem: hypocrisy. The news media claims to disdain capitalism and profit, yet most media outlets are part of huge for-profit corporations that engage in fierce, often cutthroat, competition." [Accuracy in Media, www.aim.org, October 28, 2002]

6. "Current-day Christians use violence to spread their right-to-life message. These Christians, often referred to as the religious right, are well known for violent demonstrations against Planned Parenthood and other abortion clinics. Doctors and other personnel are threatened with death, clinics have been bombed, there have even been cases of doctors being murdered." [Letter to the editor, *Daily Wildcat*, September 17, 2002]

7. Everyone knows how beneficial an operating casino can be to a city of this size. But since establishing a casino here is prohibitively expensive, we need to try to institute gambling on a smaller scale—by placing a few slot machines in government buildings.

8. The financial health of the banking industry will improve dramatically in the next few months. This improvement will immediately lead to more lenient loan terms for individuals. So it's better to wait a few months to ask a bank for a loan.

9. We evaluated the accuracy of recent news reports on a wide range of news topics. We focused on reports aired or published by three major media outlets. We found that 40 percent of their news reports were highly inaccurate. So, though it's hard to believe, 40 percent of all the news reports that people are exposed to are questionable.

10. A recent poll shows that 76 percent of Americans believe in life after death. In addition, there are thousands of first-person reports of either contacting dead people or seeing their spirits. Life after death is a reality.

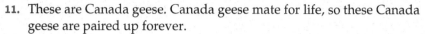

11. These are Canada geese. Canada geese mate for life, so these Canada geese are paired up forever.

12. If sex education in the schools can reduce the teen pregnancy rate or help delay the onset of teen sexual activity, I'm all for it. A recent study of several hundred teens showed that sex education in school lowered the incidence of teen pregnancy. We should have sex ed in all public schools.

13. The worst calamity that will befall the world in the next twenty years will be the use of small nuclear weapons by terrorists or rogue states. The death toll from such a state of affairs is likely to be higher than that of any other kind of human devastation. The United Nations just issued a report that comes to the same conclusion. We should act now to prevent the proliferation of nuclear weapons and nuclear-weapons-grade material from falling into the wrong hands.

14. Many surveys show that most people not only believe in "remote viewing" (the ability to observe distant locations without using the physical senses) but also think that science has already proved its existence. This demonstrates that the majority of people are scientifically illiterate. If they understood the least bit about the methods of science and how it reaches conclusions, they would denounce silly ideas like remote viewing—or at least not accept them blindly.

15. Magazines regularly publish articles on "the sexiest man alive" or "the most beautiful woman in the world." All you have to do to see that these claims of superior attractiveness are bunk is to stroll down any main thoroughfare in any nation's capital. There you will see people—male and female—who make the magazines' favorite personifications of beauty or sexiness look like dogs.

16. The biblical story of Noah and the ark is immediately shown to be a fraud or fantasy by one fact: The volume of dung produced by the ark's animals (one pair of everything!) would fill a hundred arks, and shoveling all that stuff overboard would have taken scores of laborers working round the clock for two years.

17. Peanuts are good for you. A million little monkeys can't be wrong.

18. "There is no justice in the world. Amelia Earhart's plane went down, and despite fifty years of looking, no one has ever been able to find her. But Yasser Arafat's plane goes down, and he's rescued in fifteen minutes." [Jay Leno, *The Tonight Show*]

19. "The following is in response to the letter, 'Let the Middle East fight its own wars.' I can understand the writer's concern about not wanting to start a war with Iraq. However, if Saddam Hussein poses a threat to the whole world—be it with nuclear or germ warfare—shouldn't we Americans take it upon ourselves to help protect the world? Or should we sit back and wait until Saddam is triumphant in developing his nuclear arsenal? Our intervention is considered necessary for all the present turmoil that's been taking place in the Middle East. We are the most intelligent and developed country in the world. We owe it to the lesser-developed countries to be peacekeepers. I ask the writer this: Where would the world be today if the United States had sat back and watched

as Adolf Hitler rained terror on Europe?" [Letter to the editor, *Buffalo News*, November 29, 2002]

20. Freedom is a necessary component of the good life. The good life is something that every human being has a right to. Everything that humans have a right to should be acquired by any means necessary. Therefore, any war conducted to secure freedom for any of us is justified.

 ## Writing Assignments

1. Study the argument presented in Essay 3 ("A Feminist Defense of Pornography") in Appendix B. Identify the conclusion and the premises and objections considered. Then write a two-page critique of the essay's argument.

2. Write a three-page essay arguing for a position that directly contradicts the conclusion defended in Essay 3. You may cite imaginary but reasonable evidence.

3. Select an issue from the following list and write a three-page paper defending a claim pertaining to the issue. Follow the procedures discussed in Appendix E for outlining the essay and identifying a thesis.

   • Should the U.S. government be permitted to kill American citizens overseas who have been identified as terrorists?
   • Should the federal government permit same-sex marriages?
   • Does pornography lead to violence against women?
   • Should the police or other security officers be permitted to use racial profiling to prevent terrorist attacks?

4

Reasons for Belief and Doubt

 CHAPTER OBJECTIVES

WHEN CLAIMS CONFLICT

- Understand that when a claim conflicts with other claims we have good reason to accept, we have good grounds for doubting it.
- Recognize that if a claim conflicts with our background information, we have good reason to doubt it.
- Appreciate that when we are confronted with a claim that is neither completely dubious nor fully credible, we should proportion our belief to the evidence.
- Realize that it's not reasonable to believe a claim when there is no good reason for doing so.

EXPERTS AND NONEXPERTS

- Understand what makes someone an expert and what does not.
- Understand that if a claim conflicts with expert opinion, we have good reason to doubt it.
- Realize that when the experts disagree about a claim, we have good reason to doubt it.
- Be able to recognize fallacious appeals to authority.
- Be able to distinguish true experts from nonexperts by using the four indicators of expertise.

PERSONAL EXPERIENCE

- Understand that it's reasonable to accept the evidence provided by personal experience only if there's no good reason to doubt it.
- Appreciate the importance of the common factors that can give us good reason to doubt the reliability of personal experience—impairment, expectation, and innumeracy.

LET'S REMIND OURSELVES ONCE AGAIN WHY WE'VE COME THIS WAY. IF WE CARE whether our beliefs are true or reliable, whether we can safely use them to guide our steps and inform our choices, then we must care about the reasons for accepting those beliefs. The better the reasons for acceptance, the more likely are the beliefs, or statements, to be true. Inadequate reasons, no reasons, or fake reasons (discussed in the next two chapters) should lead us not to accept a statement, but to doubt it.

As we saw in earlier chapters, the reasons for accepting a statement are often spelled out in the form of an argument, with the statement being the conclusion. The reasons and conclusion together might compose a deductive argument or an inductive argument. In such cases, the reasons are normally there in plain sight. But in our daily lives, statements, or claims, usually confront us alone without any accompanying stated reasons. An unsupported claim may be the premise of an argument (and its truth value may then determine whether the argument is sound or cogent). Or it may simply be a stand-alone assertion of fact. Either way, if we care whether the claim is acceptable, we must try to evaluate the claim as it stands.

Of course, it helps to be knowledgeable about the subject matter of a claim. But understanding and applying some critical thinking principles for assessing unsupported claims can be even more useful. Let's take a close look at these.

When Claims Conflict

Suppose you come across this claim in a reputable local newspaper:

[Claim 1] The historic Sullivan Building at the corner of Fifth and Main Streets was demolished yesterday to make way for a parking lot.

But say you have very good reasons to believe this claim:

[Claim 2] The historic Sullivan Building at the corner of Fifth and Main Streets was NOT demolished yesterday to make way for a parking lot.

What do you make of such a conflict between claims? Well, as a good critical thinker, you can know at least this: You have good reason to doubt claim 1 and therefore have no good grounds for accepting it. You have good reason to doubt it because it conflicts with another claim you have good reason to believe (claim 2). When two claims conflict, they simply cannot *both* be true; at least one of them has to be false. So this principle comes into play:

If a claim conflicts with other claims we have good reason to accept, we have good grounds for doubting it.

With conflicting claims, you are not justified in believing either one of them until you resolve the conflict. Sometimes this job is easy. If, for example, the competing claims are reports of personal observations, you can often decide

Favorite Unsupported Claims

In the information age, you don't have to look far for unsupported claims. They jump out at you from all directions. Many of them are a joy to behold because they're so imaginative, unusual, or provocative. They don't offer much of a challenge for critical thinkers, but they sure are fun. The following is a little sampling from cyberspace.

- "Become INVISIBLE! This is not a toy, a magic trick or a scam. This is not an illusion, a rip-off or a Ninja technique. The Secret of Invisibility renders you completely invisible. This method is currently used by the CIA and foreign intelligence agencies. Don't Scoff! You can go anywhere, at anytime, without being seen."

- "Is it strange how, when we are in the middle of summer, it can be raining out, and one day it is very 'hot,' the next day it is 15 degrees cooler, and two days later, it is 'hot' again? Does this seem strange? How about earthquakes in parts of the world, that are so devastating, that if they were to happen here, our whole economy could be ruined. Do you think it is 'odd' that people would suggest that the government can and does control the weather? I know it sounds a little paranoid, but if you do the research to investigate, you will undoubtedly arrive at the same conclusions. Our weather is controlled!"

- "Some of you may be wondering what Aliens and UFO stuff have to do with the Bible. The truth is Aliens and UFOs ARE a BIG part of the Bible, New World Order, and last days deception. Yes they exist, they are the fallen angels who rebelled with Lucifer before and even after the flood, and they are coming back with Lucifer to dominate and control the earth in the last days. To be forewarned, is to be prepared. The Lord has called me forth to inform and warn His people about what is coming."

- "Contrary to all reports about a lone drifter named Mark David Chapman who allegedly shot John Lennon in the back December 8, 1980, you'll find ample evidence in the back issues of *Time*, *Newsweek*, and *U.S. News & World Report* magazines to suggest otherwise. Namely, that John Lennon was not only politically assassinated, but that Richard Nixon, Ronald Reagan and, you'd better sit down, horror novelist Stephen King are the three people who can be proven guilty of the crime."

- "The thought screen helmet blocks telepathic communication between aliens and humans. Aliens cannot immobilize people wearing thought screens nor can they control their minds or communicate with them. Results of the thought screen helmet are preliminary. As of June 2000, aliens have not taken any abductees while they were wearing thought screen helmets using Velostat shielding."

- "Conclusions: 1. Life forms exist on the surface of the moon. 2. Lunar-surface life forms can grow into large forms and shapes. Some shapes assume cylindrical, linear and curved profiles. Others are complicated and entangled. 3. Lunar-surface life forms have the capability of attaching to equipment with a potential ability to cause equipment malfunction. 4. Lunar-surface life forms can change size and shape, and can do so quickly. 5. Pressure of the MET wheels on the surface appears to arouse lunar life forms to a state of luminescence. 6. Some 'rocks' which in macro view appear to be like earth-like rocks really are not but, rather, are a build-up of an accumulation of growing life forms. 7. Apollo 14 did land on the moon."

between them by making further observations. If your friend says that your dog is sleeping atop your car, and you say that your dog is not sleeping atop your car (because you checked a short time ago), you can see who's right by simply looking at the roof of your car. (Remember, though, that even personal observations can sometimes mislead us, as we'll soon see.)

Many times, however, sorting out conflicting claims requires a deeper inquiry. You may need to do some research to see what evidence exists for each of the claims. In the best-case scenario, you may quickly discover that one of the claims is not credible because it comes from an unreliable source (a subject taken up in the next few pages).

Now suppose that you're confronted with another type of conflict—this time a conflict between a claim and your background information. **Background information** is that huge collection of very well supported beliefs that we all rely on to inform our actions and choices. A great deal of this lore consists of basic facts about everyday things, beliefs based on overwhelming evidence (including our own reliable personal observations and the statements of excellent authorities), and strongly justified claims that we would regard as "common sense" or

Fact and Opinion

When we evaluate claims, we often are concerned with making a distinction between facts and opinions. But just what is the difference? We normally use the term *fact* in two senses. First, we may use it to refer to a state of affairs—as in, "Examine the evidence and find out the facts." Second, and more commonly, we use *fact* to refer to *true statements*—as in, "John smashed the dinnerware— that's a fact." Thus, we say that some claims, or statements, are facts (or factual) and some are not. We use the word *opinion*, however, to refer to a *belief*—as in, "It's John's opinion that he did not smash the dinnerware." Some opinions are true, so they are facts. Some opinions are not true, so they are not facts.

Sometimes we may hear somebody say, "That's a matter of opinion." What does this mean? Often it's equivalent to something like, "Opinions differ on this issue" or "There are many different opinions on this." But it also frequently means that the issue is not a matter of objective fact but is entirely subjective, a matter of individual taste. Statements expressing matters of opinion in this latter sense are not the kinds of things that people can disagree on, just as two people cannot sensibly disagree about whether they like chocolate ice cream.

"common knowledge." Background beliefs include obvious claims such as "the sun is hot," "the Easter bunny is not real," "humans are mortal," "fire burns," and "George Washington lived in the eighteenth century." Suppose then that you're asked to accept this unsupported claim:

Some babies can bench-press a five-hundred-pound weight.

You are not likely to give much credence to this claim for the simple reason that it conflicts with an enormous number of your background beliefs concerning human physiology, gravity, weight lifting, and who knows what else.

Or how about this claim:

The U.S. president is entirely under the control of the chief justice of the United States.

This claim is not as outlandish as the previous one, but it too conflicts with our background beliefs, specifically those having to do with the structure and workings of the U.S. government. So we would have good reason to doubt this one also.

The principle exemplified here is:

If a claim conflicts with our background information, we have good reason to doubt it.

Other things being equal, the more background information the claim conflicts with, the more reason we have to doubt it. We would normally—and rightfully—assign a low probability to any claim that conflicts with a great deal of our background information.

You would be entitled, for example, to have some doubt about the claim that Joan is late for work if it conflicts with your background information that Joan has never been late for work in the ten years you've known her. But you are entitled to have very strong doubts about, and to assign very low credibility to, the claim that Luis can turn a stone into gold just by touching it. You could even reasonably dismiss the claim out of hand. Such a claim conflicts with too much of what we know about the physical world.

It's always possible, of course, that a conflicting claim is true and some of our background information is unfounded. So many times it's reasonable for us to examine a conflicting claim more closely. If we find that it has no good reasons in its favor, that it is not credible, we may reject it. If, on the other hand, we discover that there are strong reasons for accepting the new claim, we may need to revise our background information. For example, we may be forced to accept the claim about Luis's golden touch (and to rethink some of our background information) if it is backed by strong supporting evidence. Our background information would be in need of some serious revision if Luis could produce this stone-to-gold transformation repeatedly under scientifically controlled conditions that rule out error, fraud, and trickery.

We need to keep in mind that although our background information is generally trustworthy, it is not infallible. What we assume is a strongly justified belief may be nothing more than prejudice or dogma. We should therefore be willing to re-examine background beliefs that we have doubts about—and to be open to reasonable doubts when they arise.

So it is not reasonable to accept a claim if there is good reason to doubt it. And sometimes, if the claim is dubious enough, we may be justified in dismissing a claim out of hand. But what should we believe about a claim that is not quite dubious enough to summarily discard yet not worthy of complete acceptance? We should measure out our belief according to the strength of reasons. That is,

We should proportion our belief to the evidence.

The more evidence a claim has in its favor, the stronger our belief in it should be. Weak evidence for a claim warrants weak belief; strong evidence warrants strong belief. And the strength of our beliefs should vary across this spectrum as the evidence dictates.

Implicit in all of the foregoing is a principle that deserves to be explicit because it's so often ignored:

It's not reasonable to believe a claim when there is no good reason for doing so.

The famous twentieth-century philosopher Bertrand Russell tried hard to drive this idea home. As he put it, "It is undesirable to believe a proposition when there is no ground whatever for supposing it true."[1] Russell claimed that if the use of this principle became widespread, social life and political systems would be transformed.

Experts and Nonexperts

Attitudes toward experts and expertise are changing. Many people, for example, seem to confidently believe the following:

- If you read a book, do a Google search, and see what people are saying on social media, you will be an expert.
- Experts have been wrong so often that they have no credibility.
- Experts can't be trusted, because they contradict my beliefs.
- On the Internet, there are no experts: Everyone's opinion on any issue is equal to everyone else's.

"None of my friends could diagnose the symptoms, Doctor. You're my last hope!"

This chapter (combined with the preceding ones) shows that these beliefs are in fact false. The probability of becoming an instant expert is pretty low, and experts are not—and never have been—infallible, but neither are they clueless. Nonexperts can come to know a lot about some complex issues if they respect evidence, expertise, and critical thinking. And the insight and know-how of experts—when approached critically and used wisely—can help us live more intelligently and avoid mistakes.

An **expert** is someone who is more knowledgeable in a particular subject area or field than most others are. Experts in professions and fields of knowledge provide us with reasons for believing a claim because, in their specialty areas, they are more likely to be right than we are. They are more likely to be right because (1) they have mastered particular skills or bodies of knowledge, and (2) they practice those skills or use that knowledge as their main occupation in life.[2] Experts make mistakes, but in general they are much less likely to err than nonexperts are. True experts are familiar with the established facts and existing data in their field, understand how to properly evaluate that information, and know how to apply it. Essentially, this means that they know how to assess the evidence and arguments for particular claims involving that information. They are true authorities on a specified subject. Someone who knows the lore of a field but can't evaluate the reliability of a claim is no expert.

Now, when a claim runs counter to a consensus among experts, this principle holds:

If a claim conflicts with expert opinion, we have good reason to doubt it.

This tenet follows from our definition of experts. If they really are more likely to be right than nonexperts about claims in their field, then any claim that conflicts with expert opinion is at least initially dubious.

Here's the companion principle:

When the experts disagree about a claim, we have good reason to doubt it.

If a claim is in dispute among experts, then nonexperts can have no good reason for accepting (or rejecting) it. Throwing up your hands and arbitrarily deciding to believe or disbelieve the claim is not a reasonable response. The claim must remain in doubt until the experts resolve the conflict or you resolve the conflict yourself by becoming informed enough to competently decide on the issues and evidence involved—a course that's possible but usually not feasible for nonexperts.

But when is a claim considered in dispute among experts? It's in dispute when *substantial* numbers of experts disagree with one another—but not when a mere handful of dissidents disagree with almost all of the others. We cannot reasonably consider a claim in dispute when, say, three experts disagree with five thousand of their fellows. It is disingenuous and misleading to declare that an issue is undecided when a few experts disagree with the opinions of the overwhelming majority—which was the case in 2019 when 97 percent of climate scientists agreed that climate-warming trends are extremely likely to be caused by human activities.[3]

Sometimes we may have good reason to be suspicious of unsupported claims even when they are purportedly derived from expert opinion. Our doubt is justified when a claim comes from someone deemed to be an expert who in fact is *not* an expert. When we rely on such bogus expert opinion, we make the mistake known as the **fallacious appeal to authority**.

The fallacious appeal to authority usually happens in one of two ways. First, we may find ourselves disregarding this important rule of thumb: *Just because someone is an expert in one field, he or she is not necessarily an expert in another.* The opinion of experts generally carries more weight than our own—but only in their areas of expertise. Any opinions that they proffer outside their fields are no more authoritative than those of nonexperts. Outside their fields, they are not experts.

We needn't look far for real-life examples of such skewed appeals to authority. Any day of the week we may be urged to accept claims in one field based on the opinion of an expert from an unrelated field. An electrical engineer or Nobel Prize–winning chemist may assert that herbs can cure cancer. A radio talk-show host with a degree in physiology may give advice in psychology. A former astronaut may declare that archeological evidence shows that Noah's ark now rests on a mountain in Turkey. A botanist may say that the evidence for the existence of ESP is conclusive. The point is not that these experts can't be right, but that their expertise in a particular field doesn't give us reason to believe their pronouncements in another. There is no such thing as a general expert, only experts in specific subject areas.

Second, we may fall into a fallacious appeal to authority by regarding a nonexpert as an expert. We forget that a nonexpert—even one with prestige, status, or sex appeal—is still a nonexpert. Movie stars, famous actors, YouTube celebs,

Are Doctors Experts?

Yes and no. Physicians are certainly experts in the healing arts, in diagnosing and treating disease and injury. They know and understand the relevant facts, and they have the wherewithal to make good judgments regarding those facts. But are physicians experts in determining whether a particular treatment is safe and effective? Contrary to what many believe, the answer is, in general, no. Determining the safety and efficacy of treatments is a job for scientists (who may also be physicians). Medical scientists conduct controlled studies to try to ascertain whether Treatment X can safely alleviate Disease A—something that usually cannot be determined by a doctor interacting with her patients in a clinical setting. Medical studies are designed to control all kinds of extraneous variables that can skew the study results, the same extraneous variables that are often present in the doctor's office.

Critical thinkers should keep this distinction in mind because they will often hear people assert that Treatment Y works just because Dr. Wonderful says so.

renowned athletes, and well-known politicians endorse products of all kinds in online, TV, and print advertising. But when they speak outside their areas of expertise—when they back their claims by nothing more than their own opinion—they give us no good reason for believing that the products are as advertised. Advertisers, of course, know this, but they hope that we will buy the products anyway because of the appeal or attractiveness of the celebrity endorsers.

Historically the regarding of a nonexpert as an expert has probably been the most prevalent form of the fallacious appeal to authority—with disastrous results. Political, religious, tribal, and cultural leaders often have been designated as authorities not because they knew the facts and could correctly judge the evidence but because culture, tradition, or whim dictated that they be regarded as authorities. When these "authorities" spoke, people listened and believed—then went to war, persecuted unbelievers, or undertook countless other ill-conceived projects. If we are to avoid this trap, we must look beyond mere labels and titles and ask, *"Does this person provide us with any good reasons or evidence?"*

This question about good reasons, of course, is just another way of asking if someone is a true expert. How can we tell? To be considered an expert, someone must have shown that he or she has the knowledge, judgment, and competence required in a particular field. What are the indicators that someone has this essential kind of expertise? There are several that provide clues to someone's ability but *do not guarantee* the possession of true expertise.

In most professional fields, the following two indicators are considered minimal prerequisites for being considered an expert:

1. **Education and training from reputable institutions or programs** in the relevant field (usually evidenced by degrees or certificates). Teachers, airline pilots, plumbers, electricians, and many others are required to have credentials to show that they have met standards of knowledge and competence.
2. **Experience in the field.** Long experience (generally the more years the better) suggests that the expert is good enough to have outlasted others who are unsuited to, or unskilled in, the work. They have had chances to learn from their mistakes and to handle challenges that less experienced practitioners may have yet to encounter.

But, unfortunately, people can have the requisite education and experience and still not know what they're talking about in the field in question. Woe be to us, for in the real world there are well-trained, experienced auto mechanics who do terrible work—and tenured Ph.D.'s whose professional judgment is shaky. Two additional indicators, though, are more revealing:

1. **Reputation among peers** (as reflected in the opinions of others in the same field, relevant prestigious awards, and positions of authority).
2. **Professional accomplishments.**

These two indicators are more helpful because they are very likely to be correlated with the intellectual qualities expected in true experts. People with excellent reputations among their professional peers and with significant accomplishments to their credit usually are true experts.

As we've seen, we are often justified in believing an unsupported claim because it's based on expert opinion. But if we have reason to doubt the opinion of the experts, then we are not justified in believing the claim based on that opinion. And chief among possible reasons for doubt (aside from conflicting expert opinion) is bias. When experts are biased, they are motivated by something other than the search for the truth—perhaps financial gain, loyalty to a cause, professional ambition, emotional needs, political outlook, sectarian dogma, personal ideology, or some other judgment-distorting factor. Therefore, if we have reason to believe that an expert is biased, we are not justified in accepting the expert's opinion.

But how can we tell when experts are biased? There are no hard-and-fast rules here. In the more obvious cases, we often suspect bias when an expert is being paid by special-interest groups or companies to render an opinion, or when the expert expresses very strong belief in a claim even though there is no evidence to support it, or when the expert stands to gain financially from the actions or policies that he or she supports.

It's true that many experts can render unbiased opinions and do high-quality research even when they have a conflict of interest. Nevertheless, in such situations we have reasonable grounds to suspect bias—unless we have good reason to believe that the suspicion is unwarranted. These good reasons might include the fact that the expert's previous opinions in similar circumstances have been reliable or that he or she has a solid reputation for always offering unbiased assessments.

There are, of course, many other possible reasons to doubt the opinion of experts. Any blatant violation of the critical thinking principles discussed in this text, for example, would give us good reason to question an authority's reliability. Among the more common tip-offs of dubious authority are these:

- The expert is guilty of simple factual or formal errors.
- The expert's claims conflict with what you have good reason to believe.
- The expert does not adequately support his or her assertions.
- The expert's writing contains logical contradictions or inconsistent statements.
- The expert does not treat opposing views fairly.
- The expert is strongly biased, dogmatic, dismissive, or intolerant.
- The expert relies on information you know is out of date.
- The expert cherry-picks data to support his or her claims.
- Most other experts in the same field disagree.

The amount of weight you give to any one of these factors—and the subsequent degree of doubt you attach to an expert's opinion—will vary in each case.

 FURTHER THOUGHT

Do Nonexperts Know Best?

Some people have a bias against experts—*all* experts. Their thoughts on the subject might run something like this: "It's the uneducated ones, the simple seekers of knowledge who are the truly wise, for their thinking has not yet been corrupted by ivory-tower learning and highbrow theorizing that's out of touch with the real world. Thus the wisdom of the nonexpert is to be preferred over the expert whenever possible." This attitude is, oddly enough, sometimes embraced by very educated people.

This nonexpertism is related to the appeal to ignorance discussed in Chapter 6. (A variation of the appeal to ignorance says that since there's no evidence refuting a position, it must be true.) The problem is that both tacks, though psychologically compelling, are fallacious. A lack of good reasons— evidence or expert testimony—does not constitute proof of a claim. In addition, when we as nonexperts try to judge scientific and medical claims using only our personal experience, we are likely to reach conclusions that are wrong (as explained in the next section).

The history of science shows that virtually all notable scientific discoveries have been made by true experts—men and women who were fully knowledgeable about their subject matter. There have been many more instances, however, of cocksure nonexperts who proposed theories, cures, and solutions to problems that turned out to be worthless.

In general, a single minor error of fact or style does not justify dismissing an expert's entire article that is otherwise excellent. But doubt is cumulative, and as reasons for doubt are added, you may rightfully decide that you are not justified in believing any part of an expert's testimony, regardless of his or her credentials. Depending on your aims, you may decide to check the expert's assertions against other sources or to consult an authority with much less evidential or rhetorical baggage.

Keep in mind that there are certain kinds of issues that we probably don't want experts to settle for us. Indeed, in most cases the experts *cannot* settle them for us. These issues usually involve moral, social, or political questions. If we're intellectually conscientious, we want to provide our own final answers to such questions, though we may draw heavily on the analyses and arguments provided by experts. We may study what the experts have to say and the conclusions they draw. But we want ultimately to come to our own conclusions. We prefer this approach in large part because the questions are so important and because the answers we give help define who we are. What's more, the experts typically disagree on these issues. So even if we wanted the experts to settle one of these questions for us, they probably couldn't.

Here's an obvious truth that's easy to forget: Even qualified, unbiased, honest experts can be wrong. In fact, they are often wrong. Error is in the nature of expertise, especially in attempts at prediction. Experts were wrong when they predicted that

- fast-moving trains would kill passengers by asphyxiation.
- rockets will never be able to leave Earth's atmosphere.
- flying cars will soon become common.
- the Soviet Union is in no danger of collapsing.
- we will find weapons of mass destruction in Iraq.
- people will never want a computer in their homes.
- the Internet will be a spectacular flop.
- the iPhone will be a market failure.
- the American economy is basically healthy (it collapsed in 2008).
- Donald Trump will not win the presidential election of 2016.
- An artificial intelligence computer program will not be able to beat a human player at the board game Go until around 2025 (it happened in 2016).

But the mistakes of experts do not invalidate our earlier premise that, in general, genuine experts are more likely to be right about things in their fields than we are. When errors do occur, they usually happen because experts depart from investigating and explaining the facts and jump to trying to predict the facts. Prediction in any field is hard, and most experts aren't very good at it, although some are better at it than others. Prediction is notoriously iffy in the social sciences (notably economics, history, and political science) and in public policy. The natural sciences have a much better track record.

In *The Death of Expertise*, Tom Nichols reminds us that

Predictive failure, however, does not retroactively strip experts of their claim to know more than laypeople. Laypeople should not jump to the assumption that a missed call by the experts therefore means all opinions are equally valid (or equally worthless). The polling expert Nate Silver, who made his reputation with remarkably accurate forecasts in the 2008 and 2012 presidential elections, has since admitted that his predictions about Republican presidential nominee Donald Trump in 2016 were based on flawed assumptions. But Silver's insights into the other races remain solid, even if the Trump phenomenon surprised him and others.[4]

 NEWSMAKERS

Fallacious Appeal to (Questionable) Authority

Why do so many people listen to the advice and endorsements of famous people who may be no more knowledgeable than the least informed among us? If you have ever fallen for the celebrity version of the fallacious appeal to authority, maybe the following quotes will do you good. They prove that some really famous people can say some really stupid things—and knowing that might help you think twice before getting stung by this fallacy.

I love them. Love them. I think the more positive approach you have to smoking, the less harmful it is.
—Sienna Miller

What is my talent? Well, a bear can juggle and stand on a ball and he's talented, but he's not famous.
—Kim Kardashian

Would you not be so much more interested in finding out that Bigfoot existed than in watching a really good movie? I believe in aliens. I am childlike in my spirit, and I want to believe in fairy tales. Loch Ness monster . . . the Bell Witch. What distracts me from my reality is Bigfoot. They are my celebrities.
—Megan Fox

Sorry losers and haters, but my I.Q. is one of the highest—and you all know it! Please don't feel so stupid or insecure, it's not your fault.
—Donald Trump

I've been noticing gravity since I was very young.
—Cameron Diaz

It's okay to have beliefs, just don't believe in them.
—Guy Ritchie

So where's the Cannes Film Festival being held this year?
—Christina Aguilera

I think that gay marriage is something that should be between a man and a woman.
—Arnold Schwarzenegger

Rarely is the question asked: Is our children learning?
—George W. Bush

 REVIEW NOTES

Conflicting Claims

- If a claim conflicts with other claims we have good reason to accept, we have good grounds for doubting it.
- If a claim conflicts with our background information, we have good reason to doubt it.
- We should proportion our belief to the evidence.
- It's not reasonable to believe a claim when there is no good reason for doing so.
- If a claim conflicts with expert opinion, we have good reason to doubt it.
- When the experts disagree about a claim, we have good reason to doubt it.

Personal Experience

We accept a great many claims because they are based on personal experience—our own or someone else's. Personal experience, broadly defined, arises from our senses, our memory, and our judgment involved in those faculties. In countless cases, personal experience is our evidence (or part of the evidence) that something is or is not the case. You believe that Jack caused the traffic accident because you, or someone else, witnessed it. You think that the herbal tea cured your headache because the pain went away after you drank it. You believe that your friend can bend spoons with her mind because you saw her do it at a party. You're sure that the other guy threw the first punch, not you, because that's how you remember the incident. Or you vote to convict the defendant because eyewitness testimony puts him at the scene of the crime with a gun in his hand. But can you trust personal experience to reveal the truth?

The answer is a *qualified* yes. And here's the qualification in the form of an important principle:

> It's reasonable to accept the evidence provided by personal experience only if there's no good reason to doubt it.

If we have no good reason to doubt what our personal experience reveals to us, then we're justified in believing it. This means that if our faculties are working properly and our use of them is unimpeded by anything in our environment, we're entitled to accept what our personal experience tells us. If we seem to see a cat on the mat under good viewing conditions—that is, we have no reason to believe that our observations are impaired by, say, poor lighting, cracked glasses, or too many beers—then we're justified in believing that there's a cat on the mat.

The problem is that personal experience, though generally reliable, is not infallible. Under certain circumstances, our senses, memory, and judgment can't be trusted. It's easy enough to identify these circumstances in an abstract way, as you'll see later. The harder job is (1) determining when they actually occur in real-life situations and (2) avoiding them or taking them into account.

The rest of this section is a rundown of some of the more common factors that can give us good reason to doubt the reliability of personal experience.

Impairment

This should be obvious: If our perceptual powers are somehow impaired or impeded, we have reason to doubt them. The unambiguous cases are those in which our senses are debilitated because we are ill, injured, tired, stressed out, excited, drugged, drunk, distracted, or disoriented. And just as clear are the situations that interfere with sensory input—when our environment is, say, too dark, too bright, too noisy, or too hazy. If any of these factors are in play, the risk of misperception is high, which gives us reason to doubt the trustworthiness of what we experience.

Memories can be affected by many of the same factors that interfere with accurate perception. They are especially susceptible to distortion if they are formed during times of stress—which helps explain why the memories of people who witness crimes or alleged ghosts are so often unreliable. These situations are understandably stressful.

The impairment of our faculties is complicated by the peculiar way they operate. Contrary to what many believe, they are not like recording devices that make exact mental copies of objects and events in the world. Research suggests that they are more like artists who use bits of sensory data or memory fragments to concoct creative representations of things, not exact replicas. Our perception and memory are constructive, which means that what we perceive and remember is to some degree fabricated by our minds. Some of the more blatant

> "Besides learning to see, there is another art to be learned—not to see what is not."
> **—Maria Mitchell**

Tinkering with Your Memory

The memories of eyewitnesses are notoriously unreliable. One reason is that your memory of an event can be altered if you later receive new information regarding the event. Research shows that your memory can be changed in this way, but you won't know it. You will be sincerely convinced that your altered memory is the original memory. Research studies have uncovered this phenomenon again and again. Here's a description of the classic case:

> Once upon a time, a man (whom we'll call Mike) stumbled upon an armed robbery in a hardware store. The robber rummaged around the cluttered store brandishing a silver weapon; finally, he stole all the money. Then, almost as an afterthought, he grabbed a hand calculator and a hammer, placing these in his satchel as he left the store. The police were summoned immediately, but before they arrived, Mike talked to another customer about the robbery. We'll call her Maria. Maria told Mike that she saw the robber grab a calculator and a screwdriver, stuffing them in his satchel as he left the store. The police arrived, and when they questioned Mike, he recounted the robbery at some length: He described in detail the silver weapon, the money, and the calculator. When the police asked him about a tool that they heard had been taken, "Did you see if it was a hammer or a screwdriver?," he said, "Screwdriver."[5]

examples: You see a man standing in the shadows by the road—then discover when you get closer that the man is a tree stump. You anxiously await a phone call from Aunt Mary, and when the call comes and you hear the person's voice, you're sure it's her—then realize that it's some guy asking for a charitable donation. While in the shower you hear the phone ring—but no one is calling, and the ringing is something your mind is making up.

The constructive workings of our minds help us solve problems and deal effectively with our environment. But they can also hinder us by manufacturing too much of our experiences using too little data. Unfortunately, the constructive tendency is most likely to lead us astray precisely when our powers of perception and memory are impaired or impeded. Competent investigators of alleged paranormal phenomena understand this and are rightfully skeptical of paranormal claims based on observations made under dubious conditions like those mentioned here. Under the right conditions, the mind is very good at showing us UFOs and midnight ghosts that aren't there. Likewise, juries are expected to be suspicious of the testimony of eyewitnesses who swear they plainly saw the dirty deed committed but were frightened, enraged, or a little tipsy at the time.

Look! Martian Canals

How easy it is for even trained observers to see what isn't there! This famous example, one of many, is explained by psychologist Terence Hines:

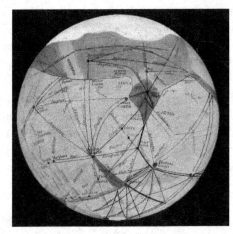

Lowell's drawings of Martian canals.

> The constructive nature of perception accounts for a famous astronomical illusion—the canals of Mars. These were first reported in 1877 by the Italian astronomer Schiaparelli. They were popularized in the early twentieth century by the American astronomer Percival Lowell. . . . Lowell argued that the canals were constructed by an advanced Martian civilization. It turns out, however, that the canals of Mars don't exist. [Carl Sagan and P. Fox (1975)] have compared the photos taken by *Mariner 9*, which photographed the entire Martian surface, with maps of the canals. When the actual Martian surface is examined, there are no canals and no other physical features that could account for what Schiaparelli and Lowell reported. So, where did the canals come from? Sagan and Fox state that "the vast majority of the canals appear to be largely self-generated by the visual observers of the canal school, and stand as monuments to the imprecision of the human eye–brain–hand system under difficult observing conditions."[6]

Expectation

A tricky thing about perception is that we often perceive exactly what we expect to perceive—regardless of whether there's anything there to detect. Ever watch the second hand on an electric clock move—then suddenly realize that the clock is not running at all? Ever been walking through a crowd looking for a friend and hear her call your name—then find out later that she was ten blocks away at the time? Such experiences—the result again of the constructive tendencies of mind—are common examples of how expectation can distort your perceptions.

Scientific research shows that expectation can have a more powerful effect on our experiences than most people think. In numerous studies, subjects who expected to see a flash of light, smell a certain odor, or feel an electric shock did indeed experience these things—even though the appropriate stimuli were never present. The mere suggestion that the stimuli would occur was enough to cause the subjects to perceive, or apparently perceive, things that did not exist.

Our tendency to sometimes perceive things that are not really there is especially pronounced when the stimuli are vague or ambiguous. For example, we may perceive completely formless stimuli—clouds, smoke, "white noise," garbled voices, random-patterned wallpaper, blurry photos, lights in the night sky, stains on the ceiling—yet think we observe very distinct images or sounds. In the formlessness we may see ghosts, faces, and words and hear songs, screams, or verbal warnings. We may see or hear exactly what we expect to see or hear. Or the mere suggestion of what we should perceive helps us perceive it. This phenomenon is a kind of illusion known as *pareidolia*. It's the reason some people claim to hear satanic messages when rock music is played backward, or to observe a giant stone face in fuzzy pictures of the surface of Mars, or to see the perfect likeness of Jesus in the skillet burns on a tortilla.

 NEWSMAKERS

Eyewitness Testimony and Injustice

Eyewitness testimony is unreliable. So says a raft of scientific evidence, including this study that made headlines in 2007:

Because of a misidentification, Jerry Miller was convicted of a crime he did not commit and spent twenty-five years in prison. In 2007 he became the two hundredth prisoner in the United States to be exonerated by DNA evidence.

> Brandon L. Garrett, a law professor at the University of Virginia, has, for the first time, systematically examined . . . 200 cases, in which innocent people served an average of 12 years in prison. In each case, of course, the evidence used to convict them was at least flawed and often false—yet juries, trial judges and appellate courts failed to notice.
>
> "A few types of unreliable trial evidence predictably supported wrongful convictions," Professor Garrett concluded in his study, "Judging Innocence," to be published in *The Columbia Law Review* in January.

The leading cause of the wrongful convictions was erroneous identification by eyewitnesses, which occurred 79% of the time. In a quarter of the cases, such testimony was the only direct evidence against the defendant.[7]

Scientists are keenly aware of the possible distorting influence of expectancy, so they try to design experiments that minimize it. We too need to minimize it as much as possible. Our strong expectations are a signal that we should double-check our sensory information and be careful about the conclusions we draw from it.

Innumeracy and Probability

When we make an off-the-cuff judgment about the chances of something happening (whether an event in the past or one in the future), we should be extra careful. Why? Because, generally, we humans are terrible at figuring probabilities.

Here's a classic example. Imagine that your classroom has twenty-three students present, including yourself. What are the chances that at least two of the students have exactly the same birthday? (Not the same *date of birth*, but the same birthday out of the 365 possible ones.) The answer is neither 1 chance in 365 (1/365) nor 1 in 52 (1/52). It's *1 chance in 2* (1/2, or 50/50)—a completely counterintuitive result.

A common error is the misjudging of coincidences. Many of us often believe that an event is simply too improbable to be a mere coincidence, that something else surely must be going on—such as paranormal or supernatural activity. But we mustn't forget that amazing coincidences occur all the time and, in fact, *must* occur according to elementary laws of statistics. The probability that a particular strange event will occur—say, that an ice cube tossed out of an airplane will hit the roof of a barn—may be extremely low, maybe one in a billion. But that same event given enough opportunities to occur may be highly probable over the long haul. It may be unlikely in any given instance for you to flip a coin and get tails seven times in a row. But this "streak" is virtually certain to happen if you flip the coin enough times.

What are the odds that someone will be thinking of a person she knew, or knew of, from the past twenty-five years then suddenly learn that the person is seriously ill or dead? Believe it or not, such a strange event is likely to occur several times a day. If we make the reasonable assumption that someone would recognize the names of a few thousand people (both famous and not so famous) from the past twenty-five years and that a person would learn of the illness or death of each of those few thousand people in the twenty-five years, then the chances of our eerie coincidence happening to someone somewhere are pretty good. We could reasonably expect that each day several people would have this experience.[8]

Another error is to think that previous events can affect the probabilities in the random event at hand. This mistake is known as the **gambler's fallacy**. Let's say you toss an unbiased coin six times in a row. On the first toss, the odds are, of course, one in two, or 50/50, that it will land tails. It lands tails. Astoundingly, on the other five tosses the coin also lands tails. That's six tails in a row. So what are the odds that the coin will land tails on the seventh toss? Answer: 50/50. Each toss has exactly the same probability of landing tails (or heads): 50/50. The coin does not remember previous tosses. To think otherwise is to commit the gambler's fallacy. You see it a lot in casinos, sporting events, and—alas—everyday decision-making.

The lesson here is not that we should mistrust all judgment about probabilities, but that we shouldn't rely solely on our intuitive sense in evaluating them. Relying entirely on intuition, or "gut feeling," in assessing probabilities is usually not a reason to trust the assessment, but to doubt it.

If we require greater precision in judging probabilities, we're in luck because mathematicians have worked out how to quantify and evaluate them. In the simplest case, calculating the probability of the occurrence of an event or outcome is a matter of division. For example, the probability of getting heads in the toss of an unbiased coin is one chance in two—1/2 or 0.50. There is one toss and only two possible outcomes, heads or tails. Likewise, the probability of randomly drawing the jack of spades out of a standard deck of fifty-two cards is one chance in fifty-two—1/52, or 0.192. And the probability of drawing one of the hearts out of the deck is thirteen in fifty-two, or 0.25 (because there are thirteen cards in each suit).

But suppose we want to know the probability of getting a 10 by throwing two dice (two unbiased, six-sided dice). Here we are talking about two events that are *independent* of each other—the event of the first die showing a 5 and the event of the second die showing a 5. The one event has no effect on the other. The probability of the first event occurring is one chance in six—1/6, and the other event has the same probability, 1/6. To determine the probability of *both* events happening in one throw of the dice, we find the mathematical product of the two: 1/6 × 1/6 = 1/36. Just as you would expect, the chances of these dual events happening (1/36) are much lower than that of just one of them happening (1/6). So to calculate the probability of two independent events happening together,

 REVIEW NOTES

Personal Experience

- It's reasonable to accept the evidence provided by personal experience only if there's no good reason to doubt it.
- If our perceptual powers are impaired or impeded, we have reason to doubt them.
- Our perception and memory are *constructive*, which means that our minds are capable of manufacturing what we experience.
- We often perceive exactly what we expect to perceive, and this tendency is enhanced when stimuli are vague or ambiguous.
- The gambler's fallacy is the mistake of thinking that previous events can affect the probabilities in the random event at hand.

we *multiply* the probability of the first event occurring by the probability of the second event occurring.

Now let's say the events in question are *not independent* of one another—each event can affect the other. Suppose we want to know the probability of drawing two hearts one after another from one standard (shuffled) deck of

I Just *Know!*

Suppose you make a claim that you have neither evidence nor argument to back up, and someone asks, "How do you know?" And you say, "I just know," or "My gut (or intuition) tells me it's true." In such situations, do you really know—do you really possess knowledge? Many epistemologists (philosophers who study knowledge) would

argue that you do not, unless your ordinary means of acquiring knowledge (reason and observation) have validated the reliability of your intuition or gut. Nevertheless, many people believe that their gut is a reliable way of knowing. Here's a famous case of "gut knowing" that has been criticized by several authors, including the philosopher Stephen Law:

> Notoriously, during George W. Bush's presidency, Bush's gut became the oracle of the state. Bush was distrustful of book learning and those with established expertise in a given area. When he made the decision to invade Iraq, and was subsequently confronted by a skeptical audience, Bush said that ultimately, he just *knew in his gut* that invading was the right thing to do. . . .
>
> The invasion went ahead. A few months later, Senator Joe Biden told Bush of his growing worries about the aftermath. In response, Bush again appealed to the reliability of his "instincts. . . ."
>
> How did Bush suppose his gut was able to steer the ship of state? He supposed it was functioning as a *sort of God-sensing faculty.* Bush believed that by means of his gut he could sense what God wanted of him. . . . Those who, like George W. Bush, place a simple trusting faith in their gut, or wherever else they think their *sensus divinitatis* is located, are being irresponsible and foolish.[9]

Assuming this account of George Bush's thinking is accurate, do you think he really *knew* that invading Iraq was the right thing to do? If so, how does this kind of intuitive knowing work? Exactly how is knowledge gained this way? If not, where do you think Bush's error lies? What is wrong with "knowing in your gut"?

cards. Note that the deck will be light by one card after the first draw, thereby giving the second draw slightly different odds. The probability of drawing the first heart is 13/52 (thirteen hearts in the deck of fifty-two), and the probability of drawing the next one is 12/51. To determine the probability of drawing two hearts in a row, we multiply: $13/52 \times 12/51 = 1/17$. So even when two events *are* affected by each other, to figure the odds of joint occurrence, we still *multiply* the probability of the first event occurring by the probability of the second event occurring.

Sometimes we may want to know the chances of *either* one of two events happening. Here we are not looking merely for two events to occur jointly, as in the previous examples. We are interested in the odds of either one happening when they are mutually exclusive (if one occurs, the other cannot). Say we want to know the probability of pulling either a diamond or a club from a fifty-two-card deck in one draw. The odds of drawing a diamond is one chance in four (1/4), and the odds of drawing a club is also one in four (1/4). To figure the odds of drawing either one, we *add* the two probabilities: $1/4 + 1/4 = 1/2$.

🔑 KEY WORDS

background information	fallacious	gambler's fallacy
expert	fallacious appeal to authority	

Summary
When Claims Conflict

- Many times we need to be able to evaluate an unsupported claim—a claim that isn't backed by an argument. There are several critical thinking principles that can help us do this. An important one is: *If a claim conflicts with other claims we have good reason to accept, we have good grounds for doubting it.*
- Sometimes there is a conflict between a claim and your background information. Background information is the large collection of very well supported beliefs that we rely on to inform our actions and choices. The relevant principle is: *If a claim conflicts with our background information, we have good reason to doubt the claim.*
- It's not reasonable to accept a claim if there is good reason to doubt it. In the case of claims that we can neither accept nor reject outright: *We should proportion our belief to the evidence.*

Experts and Nonexperts

- An expert is someone who is more knowledgeable in a particular subject area than most others are. The important principle is: *If a claim conflicts with expert opinion, we have good reason to doubt it.*
- We must couple this principle with another one: *When the experts disagree about a claim, we have good reason to doubt it.* When we rely on bogus expert opinion, we commit the fallacy known as the fallacious appeal to authority.

Personal Experience

- Many claims are based on nothing more than personal experience, ours or someone else's. We can trust our personal experience—to a point. The guiding principle is: *It's reasonable to accept the evidence provided by personal experience only if there's no reason to doubt it.*
- Some common factors that can raise such doubts are impairment (stress, injury, distraction, emotional upset, and the like), expectation, and our limited abilities in judging probabilities.

 EXERCISES

Exercise 4.1

REVIEW QUESTIONS

1. What kinds of beliefs are part of a person's background information?
2. What is the most reasonable attitude toward a claim that conflicts with other claims you have good reason to believe?
3. What degree of probability should we assign to a claim that conflicts with our background information?
* 4. What is the most reasonable attitude toward a claim that is neither worthy of acceptance nor deserving of outright rejection?
5. What is an expert?
6. What should be our attitude toward a claim that conflicts with expert opinion?
7. What should be our attitude toward a claim when experts disagree about it?
8. What is the fallacious appeal to authority?
9. According to the text, in most fields, what are the two minimal prerequisites for being considered an expert?

*10. According to the text, beyond the minimal prerequisites, what are two more telling indicators that someone is an expert?

11. Under what three circumstances should we suspect that an expert may be biased?

12. When is it reasonable to accept the evidence provided by personal experience?

13. What are two factors that can give us good reason to doubt the reliability of personal experience?

14. In what ways are our perception and memory constructive?

15. Are doctors experts? Why or why not?

16. What are three good reasons for doubting the opinion of experts?

*17. In what two ways does the fallacious appeal to authority usually happen?

Exercise 4.2

Based on claims you already have good reason to believe, your background information, and your assessment of the credibility of any cited experts, indicate for each of the following claims whether you would accept it, reject it, or proportion your belief to the evidence. Give reasons for your answers. If you decide to proportion your belief to the evidence, indicate generally what degree of plausibility you would assign to the claim.

1. Israeli psychic Uri Geller can bend spoons with his mind.

2. In Russia, some people live to be 150 years old.

3. Every year in the United States over three hundred people die of leprosy.

*4. According to Dr. Feelgood, the spokesperson for Acme Mattresses, the Easy-Rest 2000 from Acme is the best mattress in the world for back-pain sufferers.

5. Some bars in the suburbs of Chicago have been entertaining their nightly patrons with pygmy hippo tossing.

*6. Every person has innate psychic ability that, when properly cultivated, can enable him or her to read another person's mind.

7. The prime minister of Canada works with the government of the United States to suppress the economic power of French Canadians.

8. Molly, a thirty-four-year-old bank manager, says that stock prices will plummet dramatically in two months and will trigger another deep, year-long recession.

9. Humans use only about 10 percent of the brain's capacity for thinking and creating.

*10. Fifteen women have died after smelling a free perfume sample that they received in the mail.

11. A chain letter describing the struggles of a nine-year-old girl with incurable cancer is circulating on the Internet. The more people who receive the letter, the better the little girl's chances of survival.

102

12. A report from the National Institutes of Health says that there is no evidence that high doses of the herb ephedra can cure cancer.

13. Giant albino alligators crawl through the underground sewers of New York City.

* 14. Crop circles—large-scale geometric patterns pressed into crop fields—are the work of space aliens.

15. Crop circles are the work of human hoaxers.

16. North Korea is a communist paradise where everyone prospers and human rights are respected.

* 17. Dr. Xavier, a world-famous astrologer, says that the position of the sun, planets, and stars at your birth influences your choice of careers and your marital status.

18. Eleanor Morgan, a Nobel Prize–winning economist, says that modern democratic systems (including developed nations) are not viable.

19. Eating meat rots your colon.

20. The highway speed limit in New York is 65 mph.

Exercise 4.3

For each of the following situations and the claim associated with it, indicate whether there may be good reasons to doubt the claim and, if so, specify the reasons.

* 1. Standing on a street corner in heavy fog, Eve thinks she sees an old friend walking away from her on the other side of the street. She says to herself, "That's Julio Sanchez."

* 2. While playing an old rock tune backward, Elton thinks that he hears a sentence on the tape. It's almost inaudible, but he thinks it says, "Hello, Elton, long time no see."

3. Detective Jones views the videotape of the robbery at the 7-Eleven, which occurred last night. He sees the robber look into the camera. "I know that guy," he says. "I put him away last year on a similar charge."

Exercise 4.4

For each of the following claims, indicate whether it is: (a) probably true, (b) probably false, (c) almost certainly true, (d) almost certainly false, or (e) none of the above.

* 1. "Most people are not aware that the cartoonish 'Bigfoot' figure is a distorted product of ancient and modem stories describing a real but unacknowledged species that is still occasionally observed today in North American forests." [The Bigfoot Field Researchers Organization]

2. "The actual risk of falling ill from a bioterrorist attack is extremely small." [American Council on Science and Health]

3. Nobody in the world is truly altruistic. Everyone is out for himself alone.

4. School violence is caused mainly by hypocrisy on the part of teachers and school administrators.

* 5. "The world shadow government behind the U.S. government is at it again, destroying U.S. buildings and killing people with staged acts of terrorism [on 9/11/01], the intent of which being—among other things—to start WW III." [website devoted to 9/11 theories]

* 6. "What is Pre-Birth Communication? It's something that many people experience, yet very few talk about—the sense that somehow we are in contact with a being who is not yet born! It may be a vivid dream, the touch of an invisible presence, a telepathic message announcing pregnancy, or many other types of encounter. It is a mystery, one that challenges our ideas about ourselves and our children." [website on "pre-birth communication"]

* 7. Physicians, drug companies, the food industry, the National Cancer Institute, and the American Cancer Society are all fighting to prevent "natural" cancer cures such as vitamin supplements and herbs from being used by cancer patients.

8. Medieval history is a lie—or, rather, it doesn't exist. Monks made it up based on a corrupt copy of ancient history.

 Field Problems

1. On the Internet, find a controversial claim on a topic having to do with science or economics. Indicate whether it is: (a) probably true, (b) probably false, (c) almost certainly true, (d) almost certainly false, or (e) none of the above. Give reasons for your answer.

2. Write down a claim in which you strongly believe. Select one that pertains to an important social, religious, or political issue. Then indicate what evidence would persuade you to change your mind about the claim.

3. Select a news item or press release from a pro-life website (such as www.covenantnews.com or www.prolifeamerica.com) and a pro-choice one (such as www.choiceusa.org or www.prochoiceamerica.org). Analyze each selection, looking for evidence of bias or slanting—loaded or biased language, unsupported opinion, emotional appeals, omission of relevant but opposing information, and undeserved emphasis on aspects of the story.

 Self-Assessment Quiz

Answers appear in "Answers to Self-Assessment Quizzes" (Appendix D).

1. How should a critical thinker regard an unsupported claim that conflicts with a great deal of her background information?

2. State in your own words Bertrand Russell's principle regarding unsupported claims.

3. Name four factors to consider in deciding whether someone should be considered an expert.

4. According to the text, what are some telltale signs that an expert may be biased?

5. Name three types of perceptual impairment that can give us good reason to doubt the reliability of our personal experience.

For each of the following situations and the claim associated with it, indicate whether there may be good reasons to doubt the claim and, if so, specify the reasons.

6. Standing on a street corner in heavy fog, Eve thinks that she sees an old friend walking away from her on the other side of the street. She says to herself, "That's Julio Sanchez."

7. While playing an old rock tune backward, Elton thinks that he hears a sentence on the tape. It's almost inaudible, but he thinks it says, "Hello, Elton, long time no see."

8. Detective Jones views the videotape of the robbery at the 7-Eleven, which occurred last night. He sees the robber look into the camera. "I know that guy," he says. "I put him away last year on a similar charge."

Drawing on your understanding of the relevant opinion of experts, indicate whether each of the following claims is: (a) probably true, (b) probably false, (c) almost certainly true, (d) almost certainly false, or (e) none of the above.

9. "Most people are not aware that the cartoonish 'Bigfoot' figure is a distorted product of ancient and modern stories describing a real but unacknowledged species that is still occasionally observed today in North American forests." [The Bigfoot Field Researchers Organization]

10. "The actual risk of falling ill from a bioterrorist attack is extremely small." [American Council on Science and Health]

11. Nobody in the world is truly altruistic. Everyone is out for himself alone.

12. School violence is caused mainly by hypocrisy on the part of teachers and school administrators.

13. "The world shadow government behind the U.S. government is at it again, destroying U.S. buildings and killing people with staged acts of terrorism [on 9/11/01], the intent of which being—among other things—to start WW III." [website devoted to 9/11 theories]

14. "What is Pre-Birth Communication? It's something that many people experience, yet very few talk about—the sense that somehow we are in contact with a being who is not yet born! It may be a vivid dream, the touch of an invisible presence, a telepathic message announcing pregnancy, or many other types of encounter. It is a mystery, one that challenges our ideas about ourselves and our children." [website on "pre-birth communication"]

15. Physicians, drug companies, the food industry, the National Cancer Institute, and the American Cancer Society are all fighting to prevent

"natural" cancer cures such as vitamin supplements and herbs from being used by cancer patients.

16. Medieval history is a lie—or, rather, it doesn't exist. Monks made it up based on a corrupt copy of ancient history.

17. Global warming is real, and its major cause is human activity.

18. The U.S. government is covertly controlled by a cabal of satanic pedophiles coordinated by the Democratic party.

19. COVID-19 is a hoax.

20. Vaccines for the COVID-19 virus are dangerous.

 ## Integrative Exercises

These exercises pertain to material in Chapters 1–4.

1. What is a deductive argument? An inductive one?

2. What is a valid argument? A strong one?

3. What is an expert?

4. What is the appeal to authority?

For each of the following arguments, specify the conclusion and premises and indicate whether it is deductive or inductive. If it's inductive, indicate whether it's strong or weak; if deductive, indicate whether it's valid or invalid. If necessary, add implicit premises and conclusions.

5. "Sentencing reforms have produced some perverse results. For example, the primary goal of sentencing guidelines was to reduce the disparity among criminals who committed the same crime. Yet, by equalizing only prison sentences, the guidelines make it impossible for judges to equalize the 'total' penalty, which can include fines and restitution. How these are imposed can vary dramatically among criminals." [Opinion, John Lott, *USA Today*]

6. "We believe that affirmative action has been good for the country because it creates diverse student populations that give everyone a shot at the top—the American promise." [Editorial, *Times Herald–Record*, Middletown, NY]

7. If the United States attacks Syria, it will lose the support of every nation in the world. Fortunately, it will not attack Syria. So it will not lose worldwide support.

8. No one is going to support the prime minister if he backs the United States again in a war. But it looks like he is going to back the Americans. Thus, no one will support him.

9. For years, the grass simply would not grow, no matter how much watering or fertilizing she did. But after adding Miracle Sprout, the grass started to grow and spread throughout the property. Miracle Sprout did the trick.

10. "Of course, Banzhaf's argument—that so-called 'fast food' fare, like cigarettes, is addictive and causes illness and death—is ludicrous. Food supports life and only contributes to obesity when it is overused, that is, when we consume more calories (regardless of the source) than are expended in exercise. You will become overweight whether your excess calories come from beer, butter, beans, or burgers." [Editorial, *New York Post*]

11. "The dueling arguments about protecting the flag are familiar. One side says, 'Yes, the flag is a revered symbol, and those who insult it are vulgar fools. But in the end it is freedom that the flag represents, even the freedom to denigrate the nation. To limit free expression would dishonor the meaning of the stars and stripes in a way that flag burners never can.'" [Opinion, *Miami Herald*]

12. "'Yes, replies the other side, freedom is what the flag stands for. But the flag is special. It is sacred, consecrated with the blood of patriots recent and remote. America's detractors can say whatever they please about the nation—only not in this one indefensible way.'" [Opinion, *Miami Herald*]

13. If God be for us, no one can stand against us. If God be against us, we will know only defeat. We continue to see only defeat. God is against us.

14. Vitamin X can lower blood pressure in middle-aged adults. At least four well-controlled scientific studies of nearly three thousand people prove it.

15. Franklin is either evil or crazy. He's definitely not crazy, so he must be evil.

16. If Julio doesn't pay his bills, he will be bankrupt. He will pay his bills. Therefore, he will not be bankrupt.

For each of the following unsupported claims, specify whether it seems worthy of acceptance, rejection, or a degree of belief in between.

17. I saw a ghost last night. I awoke in the middle of the night, looked up, and saw the figure of a woman at the foot of my bed. But I was too drowsy to pay much attention then. I fell back into a deep sleep.

18. My doctor says that drinking ten glasses of water every day can prevent heart disease, diabetes, and high blood pressure.

19. Wearing an evil grin on his face when he was captured, the goon had to be the guy who committed the recent Central Park mugging.

20. The contractor for the giant high-rise says that constructing it makes good economic sense.

 ## Writing Assignments

1. Write an outline for Essay 6 ("What's Wrong with Adultery?") in Appendix B. Include a thesis statement, each premise, conclusion, and points supporting each premise.

2. Write a three-page assessment of the argument in Essay 6, touching on the premises and the evidence supporting them.

3. Select one of the following topics and extract an issue from it that you can write about. Investigate arguments on both sides of the issue, and write a three-page paper defending your chosen thesis.

immigration
the morning-after pill
the federal deficit
textbook censorship
media bias
cloning humans
American drone strikes of reputed terrorists in foreign countries
North Korea and nuclear weapons
endangered species
animal rights
date rape
school prayer

5

Media Manipulation: Fake News, Bias, and Advertising

CHAPTER OBJECTIVES

FAKE NEWS

- Appreciate the importance of *reasonable skepticism* in evaluating claims and countering fake news.
- Distinguish between legitimate and illegitimate reasons for accepting a claim.
- Know how to assess the reliability of online information by reading laterally, reading critically, using Google and Wikipedia carefully, and checking your own biases.
- Understand that it is reasonable to (1) accept claims that are supported independently by reliable authorities, evidence, or other claims that you know to be true; (2) accept claims that are adequately supported by the source itself through citations to other credible sources; (3) reject claims when there is good reason for believing them false; and (4) suspend judgment on claims that you are unsure of.
- Take seriously the ethical questions concerning the sharing of fake news.

MEDIA BIAS

- Know that in news reporting, *accuracy* entails faithfulness to the evidence, and *incompleteness* refers to leaving out important parts of a story (context, for example) and thereby distorting the presentation of the facts.
- Understand that objectivity in journalism is ensuring that the story exhibits no explicit or implicit preference for one set of values over another.
- Understand that bias is a distorted and unfair perspective caused by the values of the writer or editor. A biased news story contains a distorted and unfair presentation of facts, *and* the distortion and unfairness is caused by the writer's or editor's values, not merely by error or oversight.
- Be aware that (1) a partisan reporter does not necessarily produce biased stories (she may control her bias while writing and reporting), (2) a nonpartisan reporter may produce biased stories, and (3) a story defending a partisan view is biased only if it contains distortions caused by the reporter's values.

- Distinguish between *denotation* and *connotation* and know how evaluative terms can be used to express judgments about something, but that not all evaluative language expresses bias.
- Learn the differences between *news*, *opinion*, and *analysis*.
- Know that opinions in the news business are expressions of views that cannot be verified in the same way that news can. They are explanations, interpretations, judgments, speculations, and the like, and in newspapers, magazines, and other publications, opinion articles are frequently labeled as such or as "editorial," "op-ed," or "commentary."
- Understand that news becomes biased when it introduces inaccuracies and unfairness caused by the writer's values. Opinions can be biased for the same reason, but they need not be. When opinions are well supported by evidence, they can be free of distortions and actually enhance the audience's understanding and awareness of complex social and political issues.
- Know that two common conservative and liberal arguments about news bias are unsound. (Conservatives argue that surveys consistently show that most American journalists are liberals; thus, the media has a liberal slant, for liberal journalists cannot help but insert their worldview into their work. Liberals argue that large conglomerates own all large national news organizations, and their heads (who are often conservatives) are thought to skew media coverage toward conservative positions that benefit the corporations financially and economically; therefore, the news media has an overall conservative bias.)
- Know that the sweeping accusation that mainstream news outlets consistently lean left or right is harder to prove than many realize.

ADVERTISING

- Realize that although advertising can be both truthful and helpful, its primary function is *not* to provide objective and accurate information to consumers; its purpose is *not* to help consumers make fully informed, rational choices about available options.
- Be aware that behind every ad you see online, data scientists and computer programmers are using statistics and linear algebra to optimize the impact of the ad by microtargeting you as a potential prospect.
- Understand how advertising messages are communicated through paid search ads, social media ads, and display ads.
- Be able to distinguish between editorial content and native advertising.
- Understand the factors that can make political videos so powerful.
- Appreciate some of the ways that manipulated political videos can lie, mislead, and obfuscate.

O N THE INTERNET OUR ABILITY TO FIND INFORMATION ON JUST ABOUT ANY-thing is nearly limitless. But—as you surely know by now—a massive share of that information is suspect, false, misleading, self-serving, biased, and crazy. A vast trove of it is generated by seriously uninformed people, malicious trolls, unscrupulous organizations, partisan zealots, and bots and sock puppets. (A bot is a computer program cleverly pretending to be a person; a sock puppet is a real person assuming fake identities.)

Social media, blogs, and websites have made every person a potential publisher who can say almost anything online. But unlike traditional publishers, these writers typically have no one—no fact-checkers, no editors, no peer reviewers—to help ensure factual accuracy and to question their version of the facts. Too many of them are well-meaning but unaware, passionate but vile, interesting but unhinged. New media has given us tools to unify the world through open and respectful discussions about shared values and cultural differences. But too much of cyberspace is fragmented into a multitude of competing voices and factions, each talking past the other, each shouting its own opinions and claiming its own private set of facts. And too often there seems to be not a square inch of common ground anywhere and no plausible way to bridge the gaps among competing narratives.

Among the most influential—and potentially most harmful—of these are fake news, media bias, and commercial and political advertising. Can we possibly wade through all this to uncover the facts, detect the nonsense, and think our way to reasonable conclusions and intelligent solutions?

The answer is yes, and critical thinking shows us how.

Fake News

Fake news is deliberately false or misleading news stories that masquerade as truthful reporting. In modern media, the term has been used as a warning about misinformation, as an accusation against adversaries, and as an incantation that's supposed to make objective truth disappear. Liberals have used it to accuse conservatives of promoting misinformation and half-truths, while conservatives have wielded it to charge liberals with trying to unfairly discredit views on the right. Some conservatives have claimed that fact-checking, which has often resulted in a charge of fake news against them, is a left-wing conspiracy, and some liberals have argued that conservatives undermine legitimate journalism by falsely labeling real news as fake. We can see these crosscurrents of skepticism in two extreme modes of thinking: the acceptance of claims coming only from one's own partisan tribe or the rejection of all claims from all other partisan tribes. As one observer puts it,

> fake news, and the proliferation of raw opinion that passes for news, is creating confusion, punching holes in what is true, causing a kind of fun-house effect that leaves the reader doubting everything, including real news.
>
> That has pushed up the political temperature and increased polarization. No longer burdened with wrestling with the possibility that they might be wrong, people on the right and the left have become more entrenched in their positions, experts say. In interviews, people said they felt more empowered, more attached to their own side and less inclined to listen to the other. Polarization is fun, like cheering a goal for the home team.[1]

Yet the fact remains: Fake news, whether real or imagined, whether soothing or vexing, is bad for intelligent discourse, bad for the pursuit of knowledge, bad for sane politics, and bad for democracy. Critical thinking, whether pleasing or upsetting, offers a necessary corrective.

Much of the fake news we see is LOL funny or ridiculous, but a great deal of it is harmful, destructive, and dangerous. Fake news has sown distrust among people, pushed political conflict to the boiling point, exaggerated disagreements and social conflicts, and incited confrontation and violence by proclaiming the reality of imaginary events. Conspiracy theorists and their accomplices have, in the aftermath of mass shootings and other tragedies, posted fake news designed to incite fear, suspicion, and hate. Even before the flames are extinguished and the victims are counted, conspiracy theories fly around the Internet to blame the innocent, point fingers randomly, or declare that the innocent victims were really actors.

One of the most unsettling recent examples of the damage that fake news can do to a democracy is the 2016 fake news attack orchestrated by the Russian government. According to the Center for Information Technology and Society at University of California, Santa Barbara,

> during and after the 2016 election, Russian agents created social media accounts to spread fake news that stirred protests and favored presidential candidate Donald Trump while discrediting candidate Hillary Clinton and her associates. They paid Facebook for advertisements that appeared on that site to spread fake news and turn Americans against one another. The U.S. Congressional Intelligence committees responsible for investigating fake news have released 3,500 of these advertisements to the public.
>
> Ads focused on controversial social issues such as race, the Black Lives Matter movement, the 2nd Amendment, immigration, and other issues. The Russians even went so far as to instigate protests and counter protests about a given issue, literally having Americans fight one another . . . Facebook messages created "events" out of thin air, in an effort to get people to believe them, show up, and make trouble.[2]

Fake news has also harmed innocent people by falsely accusing them of immoral or criminal acts, arousing unjustified anger or hatred against them, and causing them to be the targets of relentless trolling. The classic example of fake news leading to harassment and violence is the so-called Pizzagate incident. In 2016, a twenty-nine-year-old North Carolina man carrying three guns showed up at a Washington, D.C., pizzeria and fired off a military-style assault rifle, frightening employees and customers who ran terrified out of the restaurant. Why did he do such a thing? He read some fake news. He saw a tweet from a white supremacist account claiming, falsely, that the restaurant housed a child sex-trafficking ring tied somehow to Democratic presidential candidate Hillary Clinton. So he went to the pizzeria to rescue the enslaved children. But there were none. He was arrested, convicted, and sentenced to four years in prison and three years of probation. Before the shooting, the false tweet had been appearing in other news feeds, prompting many people to harass those who worked at the pizzeria.

Such dramatic episodes overshadow the countless bomblets of familiar fake news that are quietly and potentially hazardous, for example, the myriad websites, emails, and blogs that promote "miracle" cures and novel treatments for both minor and serious diseases. Typically the products are unproven, disproven, or seriously harmful. Just as bad are online campaigns against medical treatments proven through rigorous research to work.

Research on fake news shows that it spreads much faster and farther through social media than true stories can. Why? Researchers speculate that part of the answer is that false stories win the race because they are political, anger-provoking, surprising, strange, or sensational. This fact fits with the old witticism (often attributed to Mark Twain but actually traced back to Jonathan Swift in 1710) that a lie can travel halfway around the world before the truth can put on its boots. And of course, thanks to digital technology, lies really can travel halfway around the world in a blink.

Fake news overlaps, or is distinct from, other kinds of messages and misinformation:

Lies: Because fake news involves *deliberate* deception, it is a lie—a falsehood intended to deceive. But false statements that arise because of mistakes, errors, or misunderstandings are not lies and do not constitute fake news.

Propaganda: Propaganda is deliberately biased or misleading information designed to promote a political cause or point of view. Propaganda and fake news are distinct, but the latter can be used in the former. In contemporary public relations work and political lobbying, propaganda is a common tool.

Opinions: Writing that expresses opinions or advocates change (advocacy journalism) is not fake news unless there is a deliberate attempt to deceive. The same goes for inept reporting and sloppy writing. The information may be false, unclear, or controversial, but that alone does not make it fake news.

Bias: Biased reporting is not necessarily fake news, but it can easily become fake news with the addition of intentional deception. A writer who cherry-picks facts to support her arguments, ignores contrary evidence, and mischaracterizes her opponents' views may or may not be churning out fake news (because she may not be trying to deliberately deceive), but she is, at the very least, practicing bad journalism and dishonest reporting.

Hoaxes: A hoax is a lie intentionally fabricated to appear truthful and to gain an advantage (financial or otherwise) or to provoke a reaction. Many hoaxes propagated through the media are rightly considered fake news, but others are better known as financial or health scams, computer virus hoaxes, urban legends, email hoaxes, and art-world hoaxes.

Satire: Satirical news is intended to be funny or outrageous and is definitely fake—but is not necessarily fake news. It is often mistaken for real news, even though websites and stories are frequently

identified plainly (or not so plainly) as satirical. In the world of satirical reporting, President Trump has sold California to Mexico, the
pope has declared all religions true fiction and satire, and the Clinton
Foundation has smuggled refugees. The distinction between satire
and intentional misinformation is often lost on readers. (Satire sites
include the Onion, Daily World Update, the Daily Mire, Clickhole,
and many others.)

Telling Fake from Real

If you've already concluded that fake news is so widespread and treacherous
that there's nothing much you can do to protect yourself from it, your conclusion is premature. Many Internet-savvy people who have thought a lot about
the problem say there is indeed an effective defense against fake news, and it
is—you guessed it—critical thinking. But although applying the tools of critical
thinking to media fallacies and fictions is crucial, something even more important is required, something without which critical thinking is not possible: an
attitude of **reasonable skepticism**.

This attitude entails that we give up the habit of automatically accepting
claims in the media, that we reject the questionable assumption that most of
what's said online is true, that we stop taking the word of online sources on faith.
Above all, reasonable skepticism means that we *do not believe a claim unless there
are legitimate reasons for doing so*. Legitimate reasons are those that increase the
likelihood of a claim being true. Such reasons come from reliable evidence, trustworthy sources, and critical reasoning. The problem is that we too often reach
for illegitimate reasons, those that are *irrelevant* to the truth of a claim. Here are
some illegitimate reasons for accepting or rejecting claims from a media source:

- My group (political faction, fans of politician X or pundit Y, online community, etc.) trusts this source. (So I will too.)
- This source contradicts my beliefs. (If I disagree with it, it must be fake
  news.)
- An opposing group rejects this source. (So I will accept it because I hate the
  opposing group.)
- This source reinforces what I'd like to believe. (So I will believe it without
  question.)
- I reject any claim that comes from sources I don't like. (Because nothing
  they say can be right.)
- I feel strongly that the claims made by this source are true; therefore they
  are true. (Because my feelings alone can certify claims.)
- I have faith in my leader, and he or she hates this source. (So I will hate it
  too, because I believe whatever he or she says.)
- Believing this claim or source makes me feel good. (And feeling good is
  what matters.)
- I let my intuition or gut tell me whether to trust a source. (It saves time and
  energy.)

There are times when it's perfectly rational to believe a claim just because a source says it's true. But that attitude is appropriate only when you have previously verified the reliability of the source by checking for legitimate reasons supporting the source's claims.

Maybe you're already a skeptic: You mistrust *all sources* in the mainstream media. Perhaps you're right to do so. Or not. In any case, the crucial question to ask is, again, What are the legitimate reasons for your view? Just saying that the mainstream media is untrustworthy does not relieve you of the duty to apply critical thinking to the claim.

When critically evaluating media (mainstream or otherwise) for trustworthiness, there is no way around the hard work of checking for good reasons to believe or disbelieve. And there is no denying that doing this often takes tremendous courage. Remember, *a good critical thinker is prepared to believe almost anything—given enough good reasons.*

So in overcoming the menace of fake news, cultivating a reasonable skepticism is essential. Fortunately even in the Wild West of the infosphere, there are also helpful strategies we can employ to discern what's real, what's fake, and what's worth our time. Here are the most important ones.

Read laterally. When professional fact-checkers want to know whether a website is a reliable source of information, they read *laterally*—they leave the site after a quick look and see what other sources have to say about the person or organization behind the site. They don't just read *vertically*—they don't stay within the site and let themselves be distracted by features that are not sure indicators of reliability (like the site's layout, design, and authoritative-sounding name). Thus good fact-checkers are more likely than others to reach accurate conclusions about a site's reliability and to do so quicker.

That's the upshot of recent research that examined how ten historians, twenty-five Stanford undergraduates, and ten professional fact-checkers evaluated digital information.[3] The study looked at how these participants evaluated the credibility of online sources covering six different social and political issues. For one of these issues, participants were asked to evaluate articles about bullying on the websites of the American Academy of Pediatrics ("the Academy") and the American College of Pediatricians ("the College").

Despite the similar names, the organizations differed dramatically in their goals and in their reliability. According to the researchers,

> the Academy, established in 1932, is the largest professional organization of pediatricians in the world, with 64,000 members and a paid staff of 450. The Academy

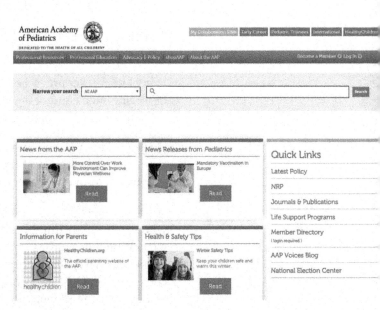

Website for the American Academy of Pediatrics.

Website for the American College of Pediatricians.

publishes *Pediatrics*, the field's flagship journal, and offers continuing education on everything from Sudden Infant Death Syndrome to the importance of wearing bicycle helmets during adolescence.

By comparison, the College is a splinter group that in 2002 broke from its parent organization over the issue of adoption by same-sex couples. It is estimated to have between 200–500 members, one full-time employee, and publishes no journal. The group has come under withering criticism for its virulently anti-gay stance, its advocacy of "reparative therapy" (currently outlawed for minors in nine U.S. states), and incendiary posts (one advocates adding P for pedophile to the acronym LGBT, since pedophilia is "intrinsically woven into their agenda") (American College of Pediatricians, 2015). The Southern Poverty Law Center has labeled the College a hate group that is "deceptively named" and acts to "vilify gay people." The College's portrayal of research findings on LGBT youth has provoked the ire of the nation's leading scientists, including Francis Collins, the former director of National Institutes of Health, who wrote that "the American College of Pediatricians pulled language out of context from a book I wrote . . . to support an ideology that can cause unnecessary anguish and encourage prejudice. The information they present is misleading and incorrect."[4]

Participants were asked which website was most reliable, and their answers differed in surprising ways:

Every fact checker unreservedly viewed the Academy's site as the more reliable; historians often equivocated, expressing the belief that both sites were reliable; and students overwhelmingly judged the College's site the more reliable.[5]

The fact-checkers reached accurate conclusions about each website's credibility because they looked beyond the confines of the website. They did lateral reading. For example, one fact-checker (Checker C)

spent a mere eight seconds on the College's landing page before going elsewhere. "The first thing I would do is see if I can find anything on the organization," he said as he typed the organization's name into Google. He clicked on Wikipedia's entry about the College and read that it is a "socially conservative association of pediatricians . . . founded in 2002 . . . as a protest against the [American Academy's] support for adoption by gay couples." Wikipedia's entry linked to sources including a Boston Globe story

("Beliefs drive research agenda of new think tanks," Kranish, 2005), a report from the Southern Poverty Law Center ("American College of Pediatricians Defames Gays and Lesbians in the Name of Protecting Children," Lenz, 2012), and a brief from the American Civil Liberties Union ("Misinformation from Doctors . . . Out to Hurt Students?," Coleman, 2010). . . .

Rendered in under two minutes, Checker C's conclusion was not only an accurate evaluation of the bullying article but also of the rest of the College's website, which presents an anti-gay stance throughout.[6]

Most of the historians did not read laterally, relying instead on the more superficial and less telling features of the site. They were impressed by the College's name and logo, the site's pleasing aesthetics, the layout of the information, and the "scientific" appearance signaled by abstracts, footnotes, and degrees after authors' names.

Most of the students did not read laterally either, and 60 percent of them thought the College's site was the more reliable one. The researchers cite this typical response:

Student 19, who planned to major in either ancient Greek or bioengineering, based her evaluation almost exclusively on features like the organization's name ("sounds pretty legitimate"); the site's layout, which included bullet points ("nice to understand quickly") and section headings ("that's really smart"); and the absence of banner ads ("makes you focus on the article"). Largely on the basis of graphic design, she concluded that the College's page was the more reliable of the two: "What struck me was how [the College's site] was laid out." Student 19's approach was representative of how the majority of students conducted their evaluations.[7]

So by reading laterally, you can quickly do at least three things:

(1) Determine who is really behind the information you're seeing,
(2) Uncover the purpose or motivation behind the information (is it to sell you something, persuade you to support a cause, push political views, report the news, or entertain you?), and
(3) Find out how credible the source of the information is.

Reading laterally is about comparing sources, and that's especially important in debates about political or social questions. Consulting a variety of sources helps you put the information in proper perspective, uncover errors and bias, pinpoint consensus and disagreement among experts, and find out where the preponderance of evidence points. Certainly your hunt for sources should be carefully planned and limited, but examining too few of them can lead to views that are one-sided, incomplete, and wrong.

How can you tell if the news you're getting is incomplete, if there's important news or facts you're not seeing? You can't, unless you check alternative news sources for any missing stories. Reading a variety of newspapers, news magazines, blogs, websites, and journals of opinion is the best way to ensure that you're getting the big picture.

The Ethics of Sharing Fake News

Like many of our actions and choices, how we handle fake news—whether we create it, disseminate it, or change our lives because of it—has moral implications. For example, since fake news is a lie (an intentionally told falsehood), communicating it is morally problematic. A common argument in ethics goes like this: A lie is wrong because it violates or undermines people's autonomy, their rational capacity for self-governance or self-determination, their ability to direct their own lives and choose for themselves. When we lie to people, we violate their autonomy by interfering with or thwarting their ability to choose their own paths and make their own judgments.

Autonomy involves the capacity to make personal choices, but choices cannot be considered entirely autonomous unless they are fully informed. When we make decisions in ignorance—without relevant information or blinded by misinformation—our autonomy is diminished just as surely as if someone physically manipulated us.

If this is correct, then concocting fake news or sharing it after receiving it is, in most cases, morally wrong. (This judgment, of course, would not apply to jokes, satire, and any other obviously unserious content.) This means that when the fake news we share causes harm (by, for example, provoking violence, harassment, or emotional distress), we would bear some responsibility for that harm. If we share it only with friends, we still may not be off the hook because they may also share it—and who knows where the sharing will end? Sharing information that we *know* is fake news is worse than sharing it when we are not sure, but most ethicists would probably condemn both actions.

A useful aid in comparing perspectives is the website AllSides.com. Using reasonable criteria, it rates the political biases of hundreds of media outlets and writers and then, for particular news stories, provides articles that cover those stories from multiple political perspectives, ranging from left to center to right. Another reliable site that also covers multiple perspectives on controversial issues is ProCon.org.

Read critically. Ultimately, the credibility of websites, social media, and other sources of information comes down to the truth of the claims. Critical thinking tells us that it is reasonable to

(1) accept claims that are supported independently by reliable authorities, evidence, or other claims that you know to be true;

(2) accept claims that are adequately supported by the source itself through citations to other credible sources (experts, research, reports, etc.) or through references to supporting facts;

(3) reject claims when there is good reason for believing them false; and

(4) suspend judgment on claims that you are unsure of, for it is unreasonable to accept a claim without good reasons, and the only cure for uncertainty about a source's claims is further research and reflection.

Here are the key questions to ask:

- *Are the claims plausible?* Do the claims make sense on their face? Did the U.S. Immigration and Customs Enforcement throw a pregnant woman over a border wall so she wouldn't have her baby on U.S. soil, as reported by the satirical site the Onion? Definitely not plausible. The feat would be almost physically impossible, and it is reported by a satirical website famous for just such wacky stories. (See the Snopes.com debunking of this claim.)

  If a post or website announces that a UFO landed on the White House lawn yesterday, you would be right to doubt the claim because, among other things, such outrageous assertions are common on the Internet, no UFO claims have ever been proven, no major news organization has ever reported an actual UFO landing, and scientists and competent investigators have never authenticated even one UFO case, etc.

  If a claim doesn't seem plausible to you, don't believe it, unless you have verified it.

- *What is the support for the claims?* Check if they are supported by references to trustworthy websites or news organizations, scientific research, legitimate experts, or polls by reputable organizations. See if the arguments are solid—that is, whether the supporting premises are true and the conclusions follow logically from the premises. If photos are offered as evidence, check them out: Do a reverse-image search on images.google.com or TinEye.com (more on this later).

- *Have reliable fact-checking organizations examined the claims?* Viral stories are often fact-checked by at least one of the top fact-checkers—including Snopes.com, FactCheck.org, PolitiFact.com, TruthorFiction.com, Hoax-Slayer.com, and *Washington Post*'s Fact Checker. (See the box "Trustworthy Fact-Checkers.")

Use Google and Wikipedia carefully. Skilled researchers use Google and Wikipedia—but they do so sensibly. When you type questions or key words into Google, the first sources listed will almost certainly be sponsored sources—ads—which are likely to be biased or misleading. Other results at the top of the list will be chosen by Google's algorithms or by others who want their websites listed first. Thus the first results will not necessarily be reliable or relevant.

But Google can still be a useful research tool if you know how to employ it. Try these tips:

- Search with Google Scholar (scholar.google.com). It will retrieve links only to trustworthy scholarly journals, papers, and books.

- Narrow your searches to domains most likely to yield reliable information—that is, to domains ending in .edu (educational sites), .gov (official governmental agencies at national, state, and local levels), and .org (nonprofit and for-profit entities including schools and communities).

- To better zero in on your topic and to avoid getting a lot of extraneous hits, use quotation marks around words that should be searched as a unit:

  Type: "John Carson" novelist Chicago
  Instead of: John Carson novelist Chicago

- Search *inside* specific websites with the syntax "site:"; for example, to find an article in *USA Today* on refugees, type: site:usatoday.com refugees.
- Search for websites similar to one you're interested in with the syntax "related:"; for example, type: related:artvoice.com.my.

Wikipedia articles are user created and thus considered by scholars and journalists to be not as consistently accurate or dependable as reference works from well-known reputable publishers. This is why citing a Wikipedia article as a source in an academic paper is so often frowned on. Nevertheless, Wikipedia is a very useful place to *start* a research project. The extensive lists of resources at the end of articles can point you to huge troves of authoritative books, essays, reference materials, experts, and websites. Starting at these resource lists, you can follow where your research leads, checking out the reliability and suitability of the resources as you go.

Check your own biases. As you know by now, confirmation bias—the tendency to seek out and trust only information that confirms our existing beliefs—is a common human weakness. It is rampant in all media and in public and private life. (It seems to reign supreme in politics.) But when we go out of our way to find only confirming evidence, we can end up accepting a claim that's not true, seeing relationships that aren't there, and finding confirmation that isn't genuine.

The best cure is to look for *disconfirming as well as confirming evidence*. We naturally gravitate to people and policies we agree with, to the books that support our views, to the magazines and newspapers that echo our political outlook. Acquiring a broader, smarter, more critical perspective takes effort and courage.

Media Bias

We seem to be of two minds about what we want from the news media. On one hand, we like news that echoes our beliefs, reinforces our prejudices, and validates our membership in a union of like-minded believers. On the other hand, we want (or say we want) the objective truth, the real news unslanted and unobscured by partisan bias, unwarped and undiluted by commercial and financial interests. The former is a detour into self-interest, and the challenge is to contend with our own biases as we wrestle with reality. The latter is a concern about the biases and objectivity of others, about the view of the world constructed for us

Trustworthy Fact-Checkers

Fact-checking websites rate the reliability of sources and the truth of claims, but who rates the trustworthiness of the fact-checkers? Fortunately the best, most reliable fact-checker organizations share certain characteristics that we can readily identify: (1) They are nonpartisan, and their funding is fully disclosed; (2) they explain their fact-checking methodology and disclose their sources; (3) they use nonpartisan and primary sources whenever possible and are appropriately skeptical of strongly biased information; (4) they employ neutral wording and minimize appeals to emotions, stereotypes, and logical fallacies; (5) they avoid partisan considerations in selecting topics to cover; (6) they promptly correct errors after publication; and (7) they have a solid track record in accurate reporting. Here are five top sites that meet all or almost all of these criteria.*

Snopes.com: One of the oldest and possibly the most trusted of fact-checking sites. For years it has been rendering definitive verdicts on urban legends, rumors, myths, and fake news. Factual accuracy: high.

PolitiFact.com: The best site for checking the accuracy of political claims. Won the Pulitzer Prize. Factual accuracy: high.

FactCheck.org: Like PolitiFact, this site strives to decrease deception and misinformation in American politics. Checks the accuracy of political statements in speeches, TV ads, news releases, interviews, and more. Factual accuracy: very high.

TruthOrFiction.com: Similar to Snopes, this site fact-checks urban legends, myths, Internet rumors, and other questionable claims but typically focuses on recurring stories rather than on those arising from current events. Factual accuracy: very high.

Hoax-Slayer.com: A reliable site that mainly debunks Internet hoaxes, especially those that crop up on Facebook. Factual accuracy: very high.

Other recommended sites: Fact Checker at the *Washington Post*, AP Fact Check (https://www.apnews.com/APFactCheck), NPR Fact Check (npr.org), the Sunlight Foundation (sunlightfoundation.com), the Poynter Institute (poynter.org), AllSides.com, FlackCheck.org, and OpenSecrets.org.

* The source for these judgments is MediaBiasFactCheck.com, the authoritative rater of bias and accuracy in traditional and online news sources. MediaBiasFactCheck.com itself meets all seven criteria noted here. Some recommended fact-checkers such as Snopes.com and FactCheck.org are also signatories to the International Fact-Checking Network code of principles (https://www.poynter.org/ifcn-fact-checkers-code-of-principles/).

by purveyors of news. So understanding what media bias really is, how it affects us, and what we can and should do about it is a taller order than many might think. Let's see what progress we can make.

Objectivity and Bias

As news consumers, we expect responsible journalists to be truthful, or at least to strive to be. And most of them do aim at truthfulness, as they understand this value. Truthfulness in the news, however, is not a straightforward concept; it contains several elements, some of which are not widely understood. Truth-telling involves, among other things, *accuracy*, *completeness*, *objectivity*, and *lack of bias*. Accuracy entails faithfulness to the evidence. Stephen Klaidman and Tom L. Beauchamp, who have written about the ethics of journalism, say that "to be as accurate as possible requires reporting as facts only information for which there is good and sufficient evidence, and no reasonable doubt about the preponderance of the evidence."[8] Incompleteness refers to leaving out important parts of a story (context, for example) and thereby distorting the presentation of the facts. A story can also be rendered incomplete by telling it from only one perspective when several perspectives are needed to fully understand it. As Klaidman and Beauchamp say,

> If we view the concept of completeness as a continuum with "no truth" at one end and "the whole truth" as the other, the threshold standard that journalists should satisfy is *substantial completeness*, the point at which a reasonable reader's requirements for information are satisfied. . . . By providing substantially complete coverage, we mean that . . . a news organization would, over the course of its coverage, publish enough information to satisfy the needs of an intelligent nonspecialist who wants to evaluate the situation.[9]

For over a century, journalists have thought of objectivity as their defining aspiration, the journalistic standard that separates them from the work of the world's marketers, hacks, partisans, and propagandists. But the traditional concept of objectivity has proven itself problematic. For a long time, journalists thought objectivity demanded reporting that had as little input from them as possible, a journalism of "just the facts," without the intrusion of the journalist's opinions, judgments, explanations, and interpretations. But this objective "view from nowhere" is impossible to achieve. There is indeed a way the world is—an objective reality—but journalists, like the rest of humanity, are forced to view it from where they are and who they are, influenced by their emotions, evaluations, reasons, and personal prejudices. The nothing-but-the-facts approach, says award-winning journalist John McManus, has caused the profession nothing but trouble:

> First, [the traditional concept of] objectivity conveys false assurance that journalists see the world as it is—without any biases of their own. . . .

Second, objectivity creates the misperception that news media "reflect" the world like a mirror. In actuality, a few fallible humans assemble a partial description of a tiny percentage of current events with carefully selected, words, sounds, and images. . . . Even the very best reporting is an incomplete and rough first draft of history. . . .

Third . . . even journalists who have sworn allegiance to objectivity can't agree on its definition. . . .

Fourth, objectivity encourages reliance on official sources, even when reporters believe they are being spun or deceived. That's because it's much easier to report and defend the accuracy of *quotes* from designated authorities than to seek and defend the best version of the *truth* a journalist can obtain.[10]

Fortunately, journalists have adopted a more reasonable notion of objectivity. Klaidman and Beauchamp explain:

To present a story objectively entails writing and organizing the material so as not to express or suggest a preference for one set of values over another (even though, of course, there are reasons for covering the story that are themselves evaluative judgments of what is newsworthy).[11]

So objectivity is about fairness, which involves a particular kind of balance:

Fairness does not always entail giving equal weight to the views of those on either side of an issue; some views might be absurd, uninformed, framed and calculated to political ends, and so on. If the preponderance of thoroughly assembled evidence overwhelmingly supports the conclusion that the earth is an oblate spheroid, this view deserves more weight than the tenuously supported opinion that the earth is flat. . . . Balance entails more than a mechanistic measuring of words so that each partisan position is given an equal number of inches, minutes, or representation.[12]

Also, some partisan views may be more complicated or nuanced than others and thus may require more explanation or analysis. So a news story that pays more attention to one side in a dispute than another is not necessarily violating the principle of objectivity. **Objectivity** in journalism, then, is ensuring that the story exhibits no explicit or implicit preference for one set of values over another.

Bias is a charge often leveled at the news media, sometimes by readers and viewers who are confused about what bias is. Conservatives see liberal bias, liberals see conservative bias, and some see bias in any expression of opinion whatsoever. The dictionary meaning of *bias* is an inclination or prejudice for or against a person or group. But a better definition relating to journalism and the media is this: **bias**—a distorted and unfair perspective caused by the values of the writer or editor. A biased news story contains a distorted and unfair presentation of facts, *and* the distortion and unfairness is caused by the writer's or editor's values, not merely by error or oversight. A news story inadvertently containing factual errors is not necessarily biased. But note: (1) a partisan reporter does not necessarily produce biased stories (she may control her bias while writing and reporting), (2) a nonpartisan reporter may produce biased stories, and (3) a story defending a partisan view is biased only if it contains distortions caused by the reporter's values.[13]

Bias can manifest itself in the selection of information contained in a news story or in the selection of topics that a site or publication chooses to cover or not cover. By omitting unflattering or incriminating information about a presidential candidate, for example, a story can paint a picture of the candidate that is inaccurate and one-sided. By including these negative facts and downplaying positive ones, the opposite picture can emerge. Many news sites have been guilty of bias not because they publish inaccurate information, but because when they write about a partisan group they don't like, they include only stories that make the group look bad and ignore the stories that do the opposite. The work of the bias-monitoring group mediabiasfactcheck.com shows that many news sites report the facts accurately but still exhibit a strong bias as a result of the misleading and unfair selection of stories they cover.

This caution about introducing bias through selection of information also applies to selection of sources. It's easy to spin an essay or post in a particular direction by quoting or citing only the sources that agree with your view of things, or using better-quality sources to support your side, or supporting only your view with sources and omitting sources for the opposing side.

A very potent kind of news bias occurs when a story is presented without the context from which the reported events arose. W. James Potter, author of *Media Literacy*, explains the problem like this:

> Context is what helps audiences understand the meaning of the event in the news stories. For example, a story could report that Mr. Jones was arrested for murder this morning. That fact can convey very different meanings if we vary the context. Let's say that the journalist put in some historical context that Mr. Jones had murdered several people a decade ago, was caught and convicted, served time in prison, but was recently let go because of a ruling of an inexperienced and liberal judge. In contrast, let's say that Mr. Jones, one of the candidates running for mayor, was arrested despite the fact that police had in custody another man who possessed the probable murder weapon and who had confessed. The fact of the arrest takes on a very different meaning within different contexts.[14]

Probably the most obvious indicators of bias are rhetorical—specifically, the use of emotional and evaluative words to skew the audience's view. This skewing is achieved mainly by manipulating the connotation of words. *Denotation* refers to the literal or primary meaning of words (sometimes called the dictionary meaning), but *connotation* is the feelings and attitudes associated with words, associations beyond the literal meanings of a term. People use connotations to put an argument or view in a negative or positive light, one that may be misleading or partisan and not justified by any evidence or argument.

For example, some people might call a politician with strong views "resolute" and "principled," while others might call the same politician "stubborn" and "pigheaded." The connotations change, and the emotional associations change with them. A capable business executive might be characterized as "self-confident" and "decisive" by some and "bossy" and "overbearing" by others. An American president may be called "strong and decisive" by his supporters but "cruel and impulsive" by his political opponents. In debates about abortion, those who oppose abortion may refer to their position as "pro-life" or "pro-child." Those opposed to this view may call it "anti-choice" or even "anti-woman." In disputes about guns, those who want to restrict gun ownership may label their position "anti–assault weapon." Those opposed to this position may call it "anti–self defense."

Consider this faux news report about the aftermath of a mass shooting:

After the October 5 shooting of ten students at Logan High School in Ames, Iowa, *anti-gun forces went on the attack against the Second Amendment* and demanded more restrictions on the *right to own guns* and to protect one's *family against criminals*. Editorials in the *New York Times* and the *Washington Post* played up the loss of life at the school, without mentioning the *many lives saved by armed shopkeepers and homeowners who have successfully defended themselves against murderous thieves and intruders*. Yesterday at the school, a *left-wing mob threw* insults at the NRA and at members of Congress who *believe in constitutional rights*.

The connotations of the italicized words in this passage paint gun regulation supporters in a uniformly negative (and distorted) way—as unreasonable, aggressive, callous, and extremist. A more neutral version might go like this:

After the October 5 shooting of ten students at Logan High School in Ames, Iowa, advocates of gun restrictions criticized the unrestricted private ownership of guns and called for some reasonable regulations to help reduce the risk of gun of violence. Editorials in the *New York Times* and the *Washington Post* decried the loss of life at the school and urged the passage of new legislation that would deny gun ownership and possession to the psychologically impaired and to people convicted of violent crimes and violations of protection orders. The columnists argued that such legislation would save lives. Yesterday at the school, about a hundred people gathered to peacefully protest current gun policies. They denounced the NRA and criticized members of Congress who regularly vote against gun regulation.

Evaluative terms are words that imply value judgments about something. Of course the connotations of words do this, but other value-laden words do too, and they can easily convey bias. Consider this headline: "President sends Congress $4.4 trillion budget that features *excessively high* deficits." The value-laden term here is *excessively high*. The headline may be biased—but only if the deficits cannot be realistically described in such a troubling way. And look at this headline: "*Erratic* President of Philippines *starves* population by preventing imports of food." The evaluative words *erratic* and *starves* convey the message that the Philippine president is mentally unstable and that the people are in the midst of an extreme humanitarian crisis. If these alarming words don't accurately describe the situation—if the president is actually just *unpredictable* and the people are simply *dissatisfied* with the kind of food available to them—then this headline is unacceptably biased.

So not all evaluative language indicates bias. Suppose a journalist writes a news piece about a large oil spill in the Gulf of Mexico, and to describe the situation she uses the evaluative (and prejudicial) words "disaster," horrific," "terrified," "infuriatingly," "disheartening," "disregard," and "recklessness." Are such adjectives proof of bias in the report? Look:

> Today in the Gulf of Mexico, in an oil rig accident that has become a greater commercial and environmental *disaster* than the *Deepwater Horizon* spill in 2011, the Sunsea Point oil rig exploded into flames, killing three rig workers, and spilling thousands of barrels of crude oil into the Gulf. The fire itself was *horrific*, forcing over one hundred workers to abandon the rig. Several ships arrived quickly on the scene to help evacuate the *terrified* survivors, but rescue ships from Sunsea, which should have come immediately, were seen later *infuriatingly* idle on shore. Documents show a *disheartening* history of safety violations and preventable accidents in Sunsea's history. Survivors from the rig blamed the deaths on Sunsea for its *disregard* of the safety of its employees. They did not seem surprised that Sunsea's *recklessness* had finally led to a tragedy.

This is a damning news report that describes the actions of the oil company critically and unfavorably. But is there bias here? Evaluative words introduce bias only when they create a distorted and unfair account. The question is whether there is good evidence to support the evaluative assessments. In the Sunsea case, does it seem there are good reasons to believe that the spill is more accurately described as a "disaster" than merely as an "accident"? Does the evidence suggest that Sunsea's history of safety violations really is "disheartening" and that the company really is "reckless"? If the answer to such questions is yes, then the evaluative language does not constitute bias. In that case, *omitting* the language might be a distortion.

Opinion, Analysis, Advocacy

According to a recent Pew Research Center study, people are bad at telling the difference between news and opinion—a finding that may help explain why news stories are so often *incorrectly* accused of bias (and fake news).[15] The idea behind the accusations is that the presence of an opinion in a piece of writing is a sure sign of bias. But this assumption is false.

Most major news organizations try to make a distinction between *news*, *opinion*, and *analysis*. In general, news is an account of events or situations that can be verified through objective evidence. Oil spills, traffic accidents, deaths, hurricanes, speeches, discoveries, jury verdicts, interviews—these and an infinite number of other happenings are considered news.

Opinions, in the news business, are expressions of views that often cannot be verified entirely in this way—they are explanations, interpretations, judgments, speculations, and the like. In newspapers, magazines, and other publications, opinion articles are frequently labeled as such or as "editorial," "op-ed," or "commentary." "Analysis" (or news analysis) is a kind of opinion writing consisting of examinations, interpretations, or explanations of news events. It includes facts plus opinions about those facts. Journalists and editors strive to maintain these distinctions even though the difference between news and opinion is not always clear-cut. Sometimes, for example, the best way to make news understandable is to include some clarifying or interpretive opinion.

News becomes biased (in the sense used here) when it introduces inaccuracies and unfairness caused by the writer's values. Opinions can be biased for the same reason, but they need not be. When opinions are well supported by evidence, they can be free of distortions and actually enhance the audience's understanding and awareness of complex social and political issues. Consider this passage from an opinion piece by Paul Krugman, a Nobel Prize–winning economist and a columnist for the *New York Times*:

> In one way, Donald Trump's attack on our foreign trade partners resembles his attack on immigrants. . . . In another way, however, the trade crisis is quite different from the humanitarian crisis at the border. Children ripped from their parents and put in cages can't retaliate. Furious foreign governments, many of them U.S. allies that feel betrayed, can and will.
>
> But all indications are that Trump and his advisers still don't get it. They remain blithely ignorant about what they're getting into.
>
> Back in March, as the U.S. was imposing tariffs on steel and aluminum imports—and yes, justifying its actions against Canada (!) on the grounds of national security—Peter Navarro, the White House trade czar, was asked about possible retaliation. "I don't believe any country will retaliate," he declared, basing his claim on the supposed upper hand America has because we import more than we export.
>
> On Sunday, Canada—a country that, by the way, imports about as much from us as it exports in return—announced retaliatory tariffs against $12.6 billion of U.S. products.[16]

In this article, Krugman's point of departure is the news about President Trump's levying of tariffs against America's trading partners (Canada, the European Union, and China). His opinion is that the administration doesn't know what it's doing, and the country will suffer because of this ignorance. He speaks as an expert in economics and international affairs, analyzing the situation, offering commentary, and explaining how the tariffs run counter to international trade realities and the country's best interests. The point here is not that Krugman's opinions are correct, but that they are backed by authoritative support and are free of obvious distortions. This is what we should expect from any good journalistic reporting and blogging. This kind of respectable journalism can be found on both the political left and the right.

Nowadays opinion writing is called "advocacy journalism," especially if it vigorously advocates for a cause or advances an agenda. You can find it on blogs, websites, cable TV, social media, and talk radio. It ranges in quality from the professional, literate, and insightful to the over-the-top biased, daft, and barely readable. (Krugman's piece is an example of the higher quality kind of advocacy journalism.) Larry Atkins, the author of *Skewed: A Critical Thinker's Guide to Media Bias*, notes the positive benefits of this form:

> Advocacy journalism has a long tradition and has served many purposes. Its goal is to inform people and give them information in a manner that attempts to convince the receiver of a certain viewpoint. It can validate people's views and give them information and talking points; it can shed light on issues that are not getting much attention and can educate the public to the fact that the issue needs to be addressed. The journalist takes a side on an issue, has a specific point of view, and then argues as persuasively as possible to justify it. Reporters, bloggers, and others who engage in advocacy journalism use journalistic techniques and their specific medium—be it writing, radio, or audiovisual—as a method of advancing their cause or belief. These journalists often start with a certain premise or objective and then use their reporting skills to support that premise. . . .[17]

But advocacy journalism also has downsides, Atkins says:

> Over the past fifteen years, as newspaper circulation has declined, more and more people are turning to advocacy journalism via websites, talk radio, cable TV, and blogs to get their news. These outlets are often entertaining, provocative, and thought provoking. The problem is that many of these news sources, especially those run by just one person or a handful of people, are biased, have an agenda, don't have the resources or time to do much fact-checking, aren't heavily or carefully edited, and aren't held accountable when they get their facts wrong. . . .
>
> Sometimes advocacy journalism is used to promote a narrative even if the facts don't fit. The host's bias can be shown through tone, choice of stories, opinions, and the way he or she interviews guests. . . . There is also a tendency to demonize the other side.[18]

Consider this bit of advocacy writing:

> Previous immigration policies were a fraud. They were based on the idea that the U.S. had no illegal immigration problem whatsoever. That was a ridiculous notion then and an absurd myth now, circulated by mindless liberals and know-nothing trolls. Everyone with a brain and a modest knowledge of current events knows that illegal immigrants were pouring across the border by the millions, and they still are. Illegal immigrants should get in line and wait their turn like everyone else. The U.S.–Mexican border should be sealed by ICE, and 99% of those applying for citizenship should be rejected.

This looks like a typical blog or Facebook opinion, and it is characteristically unsupported and unfair. No evidence is cited for its assertions; there is only an appeal to popularity ("Everyone . . . knows"), a logical fallacy. It puts forth false statements and makes false assumptions. Taken together, these errors help to paint an inaccurate, and therefore unfair, picture of both immigrants and immigration policy. This post is strongly biased; it is bad advocacy journalism.

Can You Tell the Difference between Fact and Opinion?

The Pew Research Center tested 5,035 U.S. adults on their ability to "recognize as factual—something that's capable of being proved or disproved by objective evidence—or as an opinion that reflects the beliefs and values of whoever expressed it."

The study found that

> [a] majority of Americans correctly identified at least three of the five statements in each set [two sets in all]. But this result is only a little better than random guesses. Far fewer Americans got all five correct, and roughly a quarter got most or all wrong. Even more revealing is that certain Americans do far better at parsing through this content than others. Those with high political awareness, those who are very digitally savvy and those who place high levels of trust in the news media are better able than others to accurately identify news-related statements as factual or opinion.

In the study, test subjects were asked to choose between

> **a factual statement** regardless of whether it was accurate or inaccurate. In other words, they were to choose this classification if they thought that the statement could be proved or disproved based on objective evidence.

and

> **an opinion statement,** regardless of whether they agreed with the statement or not. In other words, they were to choose this classification if they thought that it was based on the values and beliefs of the journalist or the source making the statement and could not definitively be proved or disproved based on objective evidence.

Take the test yourself. Here are the ten statements; decide which ones are factual statements and which ones are opinion statements. (Answers are at the end.)

1. Abortion should be legal in most cases.
2. Immigrants who are in the U.S. illegally are a very big problem for the country today.
3. Healthcare costs per person in the U.S. are the highest in the developed world.
4. President Barack Obama was born in the United States.
5. Government is almost always wasteful and inefficient.
6. Immigrants who are in the U.S. illegally have some rights under the Constitution.
7. ISIS lost a significant portion of its territory in Iraq and Syria in 2017.

Liberal and Conservative Bias

The question of partisan media bias is a hot one, with the public seeing bias everywhere in the news, conservatives and liberals trying to prove bias by citing seemingly clear-cut cases, and many commentators simply assuming widespread media bias based on the flimsiest evidence. But decades of research on the question show that charging the media with overall bias and making the charge stick is harder than most people think. Adam J. Schiffer, author of *Evaluating Media Bias*, sums up some of the relevant research:

> Political-science and mass communication scholars have spent forty years characterizing the degree of tilt in the mainstream US news media, with varying levels of quantitative sophistication and attention to crucial theoretical and definitional quandaries. The most defensible read of the literature is that the popular claim of an overall, systematic leftward tilt is unsupported.[19]

And there are many reasons why accusations of partisan bias based on less rigorous grounds may *seem* right but are probably wrong.

> Bias charges succumb to many pathologies. Among the most common are that the charge attacks journalists or owners rather than their product, the charger fails to specify a standard, the standard is ideologically loaded and thus is more of a partisan talking point than a valid media criticism, the charger expects balance between unbalanced phenomena, an alleged imbalance can be explained by factors other than media bias, the charger cherry-picks confirming evidence and ignores discontinuing content, or a charger with a vested interest in a particular conclusion makes a subjective assessment of news slant. Consumers of news criticism should also be on the lookout for blatantly dishonest argumentation such as misrepresentation of the accused content. Though rare, even the mainstream bias-watchdog organizations will occasionally stoop to this level.[20]

One of the obstacles to proving a systematic partisan bias in news coverage is what Schiffer calls "reality." In elections, there are factors besides journalistic favoritism that are known to affect election outcomes and to increase negative or positive news coverage of a candidate. These "reality" factors can undermine charges of partisan bias against the news media. Schiffer says such elements played a big role in coverage of the 2008 presidential election:

> The "reality" of presidential elections is largely set by a handful of underlying conditions that are comparable across time. These conditions include the economy and whatever factors are baked into presidential approval—war and peace, scandals, legislative success, and so forth. The fall campaign itself, with all of its twists and turns, does matter at the margins, but not nearly as much as most casual observers assume. In fact, as long as both candidates run competent campaigns, the fall events serve less as persuasion than as a way to bring voters to where we already knew they would be. . . .
>
> In addition, news-relevant reality slanted even further against Republicans than the summer forecasting models could measure. President Bush's Gallup approval rating was, by historical standards, atrocious. He bottomed out at 25% during three of the four polls taken in October 2008. His high for the whole year was 34% in January, and he mostly wallowed in the high 20s during the crucial campaign months. And then, of course, the economy crashed. The Great Recession began with a string of bank failures and ended up tanking the stock market and dragging GDP growth deep into negative territory by the election quarter.
>
> The campaign-related factors in the election only exacerbated the imbalance. Obama was the first major-party nominee of a minority ethnicity, a fact that surely would have garnered attention regardless of party. He also parlayed his youth, charisma, and a tech-savvy staff into generating enthusiasm, particularly among young voters, that was unprecedented in recent campaigns. It is tough to cover those factors, particularly in the horse-race style that dominates election news, without the measurable tone slanting in his favor. . . .[21]

Conservatives sometimes argue this way: Surveys consistently show that most American journalists are liberals; thus, the media has a liberal slant, for liberal journalists cannot help but insert their worldview into their work. Liberals make a parallel argument: Large conglomerates own all large national news organizations, and their heads (who are often conservatives) are thought to skew media coverage toward conservative positions that benefit the corporations financially and economically; therefore, the news media has an overall conservative bias.

But neither bias argument is sound. From the fact that many reporters have liberal beliefs, it does not follow that their reporting is liberal. Their biases may be restrained by professional ethics, audience expectations, conscientious editors, or owners loathe to offend large segments of their readership. Establishing that liberal reporters' personal beliefs lead to liberal reporting requires direct empirical evidence. In the same vein, from the fact that major news organizations have conservative leaders and tend toward conservative economic views of the world, it does not follow that the reporting coming out of those organizations is conservative. Such a claim requires supporting evidence.

It's not difficult to find particular instances of biased reporting in ostensibly neutral media organizations. A critical examination of a report's claims, assumptions, tone, and evidence will tell you whether it is biased and to what degree. But the sweeping accusation that mainstream news outlets consistently lean left or right is harder to prove, though not impossible.

Advertising

Advertising is the practice of calling the public's attention to something to induce them to buy products or services or otherwise change their opinions or behavior. Advertising exists because interested parties—companies, governments, organizations, political groups, and individuals—pay for it to exist. They pay to advance their own ends, agendas, and ideas. Unlike many other communicators—journalists, scholars, and serious authors, for example— advertisers are not necessarily obliged to adhere to standards of objectivity, fairness, or reliability. Advertising is motivated reasoning on stimulants and thus should be viewed through the lens of critical thinking.

Advertising is like air: It is everywhere, so pervasive and so natural that we forget it's there, yet penetrating and changing us every day. Advertising messages hit us rapid-fire and nonstop from social media, email, websites, podcasts, movie theaters, magazines, newsletters, newspapers, television, radio, book covers, junk mail, product labels, billboards, vehicle signs, T-shirts, wall posters, flyers, and who knows what else. Ads permeate all media—print, broadcasting, publishing, and the Internet. Caught in this whirl of words and sounds and images, we can easily overlook the obvious and disconcerting facts behind them: (1) All advertising is designed to influence, persuade, or manipulate us; (2) to an impressive degree and in many ways, it *does* successfully influence, persuade, or manipulate us; and (3) we are often oblivious to—or in outright denial about— how effectively advertising influences, persuades, or manipulates us.

How Advertising Works

How well advertising does its job can be measured in money. Advertising in traditional media can cost a great deal. A single full-page magazine ad can cost tens of thousands of dollars; a thirty-second TV ad can run into the millions (especially on Super Bowl Sunday). But companies are willing to pay the price because advertising works. The revenues garnered from advertising can outweigh its costs by wide margins; in the case of a magazine ad or a TV spot, the gain could easily be hundreds of thousands or millions of dollars. In addition, advertisers and advertising agencies invest heavily each year in scientific consumer research to determine how to configure ads precisely to elicit the desired response from people. Again, they make these investments because there is a sure payoff: Consumers usually respond just as the research says they will. How do your eyes track across a newspaper ad when you are looking at it? Would you respond better to a TV commercial if the voice-over came from Rihanna, Michelle Obama, Taylor Swift, or Dwayne Johnson? Would the magazine ad be more likely to sell you the cottage cheese if the headline used the word *creamy* instead of *smooth*? You may not care about any of this, but advertisers do because such seemingly trivial bits of information can help them influence you in ways you barely suspect.

Advertising online is even more powerful and pervasive. It has become the most precise, calibrated, targeted, and sneaky form of advertising in history. Pop-up ads, banner ads, display ads, click-through ads (ads that you click through to the advertiser's chosen destination), and more—these digital enticements never sleep. Digital advertising revenue rose to more than $100 billion in 2018. In a typical week of working and playing online, you are likely to encounter thousands of online ads. A single video ad can rack up millions of shares in record time. And every choice, click, or view gets logged and analyzed so advertisers can come at you again and again.

However averse we are (or think we are) to advertising or to its aims, we cannot deny its appeal. We like advertising, at least some of it. We easily can point to ads that annoy us or insult our intelligence, but most of us can also recall ones that are entertaining, funny, inspiring, even informative.

How, then, should critical thinkers think about advertising? What should our attitude be as we are exposed to countless come-ons per minute? The principle that should guide us is reasonable skepticism. Recall that this principle asks us to give up the habit of automatically accepting claims in the media, to reject the assumption that most of what's said online is true, to stop taking the word of online sources on faith. It says that we should not believe a claim unless there are legitimate reasons for doing so.

And we generally do have good reasons to doubt advertising claims and to be wary of advertising's persuasive powers. This means that usually the most reasonable response to advertising is a degree of suspicion. If we prefer truth over falsehood, if we would rather not be mistaken or bamboozled, if we want to make informed choices involving our time and money, then a general wariness toward advertising ploys is justified. This principle does not assume that all ad claims are false or that advertising cannot be genuinely informative or useful. It simply says that we should not accept uncritically an ad's message or impact on us.

The good reasons for suspicion include the obvious fact that the purpose of advertising is to sell or promote something. To put the point bluntly, though advertising can be both truthful and helpful, its primary function is *not* to provide objective and accurate information to consumers. Advertisers will tell you many good things about their products but are unlikely to mention all the bad. Their main job is *not* to help consumers make fully informed, rational choices about available options. Advertising is advertising—it is not intended to be an impartial search for facts or a program of consumer protection. We are therefore justified in maintaining the same attitude toward advertising that we would toward a complete stranger who wants to sell us a widget: His motives are obviously pecuniary while his commitment to honesty is unknown.

Another obvious reason for suspicion is that advertising has a reputation for—and a history of—misleading messages. The world is filled with ads that make dubious or false claims, use fallacious arguments (stated or implied), and employ psychological tricks to manipulate consumer responses.

Some of these methods fit neatly in our rundown of fallacies and rhetorical ploys in the previous chapter. Ads frequently employ fallacious appeals to authority ("As an Olympic gold medal winner, I can tell you that PowerVitamin 2000 really works!"), appeals to emotion ("Enjoy the goodness and warmth of Big-Brand Soup, just like mother used to make"), appeals to popularity ("CNN, America's number-one source for news"), hasty generalizations ("Mothers everywhere will love Softie Diapers—our test mothers sure did!"), and faulty analogies ("As a businessman, I saved General Motors. As president, I can save this country.").

Internet Advertising

Internet advertising is like the ocean. There may be a lot of things to see on the surface, but most of the action, power, and danger are down below. Below the surface, data scientists and computer programmers use statistics and linear algebra to optimize the impact of advertising and microtarget you as a potential prospect. A simple click-through Facebook ad sits there on your screen, enticing you to buy a new pair of running shoes. But this little enticement is not random. Beneath the digital appearance of the ad, algorithms and cookies have already identified you as someone who has an interest in running and fitness, who earns more than $45,000 per year, who votes for Democrats, who frequents dating sites, who has bought shoes online before—and who is more likely than not to buy these particular shoes right now.

Here's an explanation of how all this works by Dina Srinivasan, a former advertising executive and antitrust scholar:

> Digital advertising is automated, data-driven, and opaque in its mechanics. That 22-year-old [media buyer] has had to make way for data scientists, mathematicians, and computer programmers who, behind the scenes, use statistics, calculus, and linear algebra to optimize advertising campaigns, by micro-targeting users and constantly tweaking algorithms.
>
> Does that car manufacturer still want to reach men looking to buy a car? A data scientist may tell them the optimal target is a 39-year-old man, carrying on an extramarital affair, who's on the brink of divorce. They can model this hypothesis (and prove it works), and advertising companies like Google and Facebook can put that into execution, finding ways to home in and target those types of people online.
>
> When you go to a website and load a page, in the milliseconds that it takes for that page to load, there are real-time auctions running in the background that determine which ads to load on *your* page. Almost all online ads

are delivered in this way, where highly complex auction markets make their money by competing on who can better track users and invade their privacy more thoroughly.

The targeting begins the moment you as a reader visit any website. Typically, your IP address, your location, and the URL of the page you are on are swiped from your browser without your explicit knowledge, and shared with advertising companies that run these ad auctions. The goal, of course, is to build as specific a portrait about you as possible—by linking your device with your identity—and cookies are a common tool for doing so.[22]

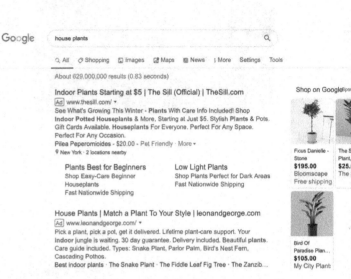

Google search results for "house plants."

Internet advertising began in 1994 with simple banner ads, which were followed over the years by a stunning proliferation of other kinds of ads, each seemingly more sophisticated and effective than the last. We can divide them into three types.

Paid search ads show up in search engine results on Google, Bing, Dogpile, Webopedia, Yahoo, and other search sites. If you search for "house plants" on any of these platforms, the first results will likely consist of ads for house plants or gardening products, usually labeled "ad" or "sponsored." The nonadvertising results—articles by plant experts, for example—will follow. That the ads appear near the top of the list is, of course, not an indication of their accuracy or reliability. Someone pays to have those ads ranked first.

Social media ads appear on—you guessed it—social media platforms, including Facebook, Instagram, YouTube, Twitter, Snapchat, TikTok, Pinterest, and LinkedIn. Advertisers pay to have their ads not just posted on social media, but also posted to a specific targeted audience defined by people's personal, demographic, and behavioral characteristics. These ads, often labeled "sponsored" or "promoted," appear as banners, display ads, click-through ads, and autoplay videos (essentially digital TV ads).

Display ads are the billboards of the online world, appearing in many guises, including static images, floating banners, sidebar ads, popups, background wallpaper, and autoplay or user-play videos. These ads are presented on websites (or topic-specific

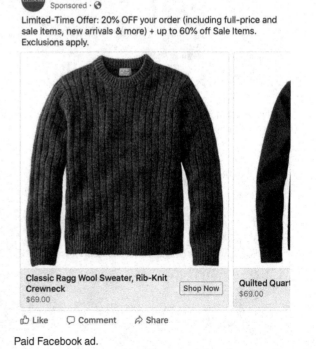

Paid Facebook ad.

Lenovo ✔ @Lenovo
Welcome to an epic global competition powered by the world's most Stylish & Savage gaming PCs. @PlayApex and @LenovoLegion present the Apex Legends Global Series.

#CES2020🖤 #LenovoCES

Apex Legends Global Series with Lenovo Legion
lenovo.com

♡ 2   ↻ 16   ♡ 115   ⬆

▣ Promoted

Paid Twitter ad.

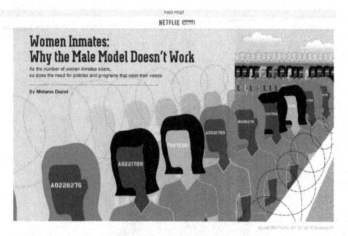

A native ad promoting the second season of Netflix's Orange Is the New Black appeared in the New York Times.

Buzzfeed's native ad "A Cat's Guide to Taking Care of Your Human," produced in partnership with Purina, the pet food company. The video begins, "Despite being huge and having the ability to open canned goods, humans are frail in both body and mind and we must care for them."

sections of websites) that are related to the product or service being touted and may or not be targeted at specific demographic or behavioral visitors.

Native advertising is paid advertising designed to imitate the tone, style, and look of a publication's editorial or journalistic content. Indeed, the effectiveness of native advertising depends on *not* looking like ads—or rather, looking like just another editorial feature. These ads attempt to persuade not by overt sales pitches but indirectly through informative and engaging stories, vignettes, and personal profiles, showing up on social media feeds and web pages as videos, slide shows, or text. The Federal Trade Commission has guidelines for ensuring that the nature of the ads is transparent, and so the ads are usually tagged as "sponsored content," "promoted," "recommended for you," or "promoted stories." But critics complain that they still mislead, for many people don't seem to be able to tell the difference between them and genuine editorial content.

Suppose you click on an article titled "The 7 Worst Financial Mistakes I Made Before I Turned 30," which takes you to the Jones Investment Company blog. You obviously will get a different kind of coverage of the subject than you might get from, say, the *Wall Street Journal*, the *Economist*, or a bestselling book by experts on the topic. Or say you click on a video about the "The 10 Best Scuba Diving Sites in the World," which takes you to the Acme Beach Travel Agency website. Maybe you were hoping for a more independent and less biased source? The point is that it does matter whether you are aware that the story you are enjoying is native advertising.

Native advertising takes many forms, ranging from simple and straightforward to sophisticated and nearly indistinguishable from editorial content.

Political Advertising

Political advertising is a far bigger challenge (or a far bigger affront) to critical thinking than most other forms of advertising. It is often difficult to tell the difference between political advertising and propaganda, for the former can be just as deliberately biased and misleading as the latter. And now that political ads have gone digital and started microtargeting us on social media feeds, they can be more insidious and potent than ever.

The Early Signs Of Type 2 Diabetes - Research Type 2 Diabetes Treatments
Yahoo Search | Sponsored

3 Warning Signs Your Dog Is Crying For Help
Dr. Marty Nature's Blend | Sponsored

$796 average savings for drivers wh switch and save? Word.
Progressive | Auto Insurance Quotes | Sponsored

Best Luxury Vehicles for Under $50k
Luxury Cars | Search Ads | Sponsored

8 Cars So Loaded It's Hard to Believe They Cost Unde
Auto Enthusiast | Search Ads | Sponsored

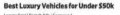

A bank of native ads hosted on CNN.com.

Back in the media stone age (the 1950s), political TV ads consisted of cartoons and videos of speeches or testimonials, all designed to portray a candidate in a positive light. Very tame stuff. But in the run-up to the 1964 presidential election, political advertising took a radical turn when a TV ad for Democratic presidential candidate Lyndon B. Johnson aired. Johnson's opponent was Barry Goldwater, a conservative Republican and militant anticommunist. The ad featured a little girl picking the petals from a daisy and counting to ten as she plucks them. When she reaches ten, the camera zooms into the girl's eye and freezes as a man's booming voice starts counting down from ten. Suddenly a nuclear bomb explodes, and a roaring, white-hot mushroom cloud fills the screen. A voiceover declares, "These are the stakes. To make a world in which all of God's children can live or to go into the dark. We must either love each other or we must die. Vote for President Johnson on November 3. The stakes are too high for you to stay home."

Barry Goldwater isn't mentioned, but the implication is that if he is elected, a nuclear holocaust will result, killing millions of children like the one in the ad.

Thus the negative political ad was born. After this, political opponents were portrayed in TV attack ads as unsavory, dangerous, untrustworthy, wishy-washy, or worse. Smearing a politician or distorting a political idea was easy. As editing technology has evolved, lying and misleading through video has become easier still. It is now possible not merely to put logical fallacies and rhetorical gimmicks to work in political videos, but also to magnify their impact a hundredfold. It is now commonplace for political videos to make someone look as if he or she is saying or doing something that is completely made up.

The sixty-second "Peace, Little Girl" ad that aired during the 1964 presidential campaign.

Reputable fact-checking organizations have been sounding the alarm about the problem for some time. According to Glenn Kessler of the *Washington Post*'s Fact Checker,

> If a picture says a thousand words, video can be even more powerful. But the Internet is increasingly populated with false and misleading videos—spread by politicians, advocacy groups and others—viewed by millions. That poses a challenge not only to fact checkers but to anyone relying on social media or web searches to get information or find the latest news.
>
> Advancements in technology make it easier for just about anyone to create convincingly falsified video. Moreover, people in today's polarized political climate seem increasingly willing to believe what they want to believe—especially when it aligns with their political values and is shown in video. This potent combination of advancements in technology, the spread of social media and an impressionable population allows video misinformation to spread rapidly.[23]

Political videos can present false or misleading messages through the words they use (lies, half-truths, exaggerations, etc.) or through technical manipulation of the videos themselves. Here are some examples of the former: political ads from the 2018 election, with comments and analysis by FactCheck.org:

Falsely Portraying a Democratic Candidate as Anti–Immigration and Customs Enforcement

TV ads in Arkansas' 2nd Congressional District falsely portray Democratic candidate Clarke Tucker as wanting to abolish the U.S. Immigration and Customs Enforcement.

Rep. French Hill, a two-term congressman, is airing a TV ad called "We Must Enforce the Law" that shows images of tattooed members of a transnational gang known as the Mara Salvatrucha, or MS-13, and warns that they are "infiltrating America." (As we have written, the MS-13 gang has had a presence in the U.S. since the early 1980s, beginning in Southern California, and currently numbers about 10,000—a figure the Department of Justice has been using since 2006.)

The announcer says, "MS-13, the most dangerous gang infiltrating America, but Washington liberals want to get rid of ICE, the police enforcing our immigration laws and protecting our border from MS-13." Photos of House Minority Leader Nancy Pelosi and Senate Minority Leader Chuck Schumer appear on the screen as the

TV attack ad directed at Democratic candidate Clarke Tucker.

announcer says "Washington liberals," even though neither Pelosi nor Schumer support abolishing ICE.

The ad then says that Tucker "attended an anti-ICE rally" and "refused to take a position" on the "abolish ICE" movement. It quotes Tucker as saying, "I don't know what it is." This is misleading. Tucker did not attend an "anti-ICE rally," and he has taken a position on ICE.[24]

TV ad accusing Senator Joe Manchin of "fighting the Trump agenda."

Misleading the Public about a Politician's Voting Record

A Republican TV ad claims Sen. Joe Manchin of West Virginia is "fighting the Trump agenda," even though he has voted with the president nearly 61% of the time.

In fact, Manchin has voted with Trump more often than any Democratic senator.

The ad was released by the National Republican Senatorial Committee on Aug. 14, and is the second in its series of commercials attacking Manchin, who is running for reelection in a state that Trump won by more than 40 percentage points in 2016.

The narrator starts by pointing out that Manchin backed Hillary Clinton for president despite her once saying that her plan for renewable energy production was "going to put a lot of coal miners and coal companies out of business." (Her full comments, however, included a promise to bring renewable energy jobs to coal country to replace those lost jobs, as we wrote during the presidential campaign.)

Manchin told Politico he threatened to pull his support for Clinton after those remarks, but her pledge to invest $20 billion in West Virginia won him over. Looking back, Manchin said, "it was a mistake politically" to endorse Clinton.

The ad's narrator, however, isn't being fully transparent when he says, "now Manchin's fighting the Trump agenda."

That is followed by a video clip of Trump saying of the senator, "But he votes against everything. And he voted against our tax cuts."

Manchin did vote against the Tax Cuts and Jobs Act, as did all Democrats in the House and Senate. He also voted against other Trump-supported legislation, including bills to repeal or replace parts of the Affordable Care Act, which even some Republicans opposed.

But Manchin has voted *with* Trump more often than against him.[25]

Democratic attack ad falsely accusing Republican Representative Martha McSally of voting "to essentially end Medicare."

Telling an Old Lie about Medicare

This ad from the Democratic Senatorial Campaign Committee dredges up an old claim we haven't heard much in recent years—saying Republican Rep. Martha McSally of Arizona "voted to essentially end Medicare." That's a reference to a budget plan, first proposed by Rep. Paul Ryan, that calls for changing Medicare—not *ending* it—to a system in which seniors would use premium-support payments to select their own plan from a Medicare exchange. . . .

Democratic Rep. Kyrsten Sinema also tweeted the claim in mid-October. Both the tweet and the ad include the words "essentially end Medicare" in quotes and refer to a *Wall Street Journal* article. But that's a truncated quote from the 2011 *Journal* article, which said Ryan's plan "would essentially end Medicare, which now pays most of the health-care bills for 48 million elderly and disabled Americans, *as a program that directly pays those bills.*" (The emphasis is ours.)

So it wouldn't terminate the Medicare program, as the ad says. Instead, it would change how the program operates.[26]

Manipulated videos have become the go-to tactic for political smearing, propaganda, and hatchet jobs. Here are some examples, examined and categorized by type of manipulation by the *Washington Post*'s Fact Checker[27]:

A video claimed by President Trump and Representative Matt Gaetz to show men giving money to women and children in Honduras to cross the U.S. border.

Paying Women and Children to Cross the U.S. Border?

Misrepresentation: Presenting unaltered video in an inaccurate manner misrepresents the footage and misleads the viewer. President Trump and Rep. Matt Gaetz (R-Fla.) claimed a video showed men giving money to women and children in Honduras to cross the U.S. border ahead of the 2018 midterm elections; Gaetz suggested that the money came from U.S. organizations and George Soros. However, the video was shot in Guatemala, not Honduras, and it was unclear why the men were handing out money to women and children.

The Mashup of Two Separate Interviews?

A spliced video showing alleged interview with Representative Alexandria Ocasio-Cortez.

Splicing: Editing together disparate videos fundamentally alters the story that is being told. CRTV took soundbites from an interview Rep. Alexandria Ocasio-Cortez conducted with another news outlet and edited together footage of its own anchor asking questions. In less than 24 hours, the video had nearly 1 million views. CRTV later said the video was satire. [The question to Rep. Ocasio-Cortez was "Do you have any knowledge whatsoever about how our political system works?" Rep. Ocasio-Cortez is shown shaking her head.]

President Trump Loves Nuclear War?

Splicing: During the 2016 presidential campaign, a pro-Clinton political ad combined President Trump's quotes over footage and excluded key context. The video plays Trump saying: "This is the Trump theory on war. I'm really good at war. I love war, in a certain way." And then after a quick dip to black, immediately plays, "Including with nukes, yes, including with nukes." But his comment about nuclear weapons was actually in reference to Japan using nuclear weapons to defend itself from North Korea.

Emma Gonzalez Tears up the U.S. Constitution?

Doctoring: Altering the frames of a video—cropping, changing speed, using Photoshop, dubbing audio, or adding or deleting visual information—can deceive the viewer. A photoshopped gif was circulated on social media showing Parkland student and gun-control advocate Emma Gonzalez tearing the U.S. Constitution in half. The original image was posted in a Teen Vogue story about teenage activists and shows Gonzalez ripping up a gun-range target.

Phillip Picardi
@pfpicardi

At left is @tyler_mitchell's photo of @Emma4Change for the cover of @TeenVogue. At right is what so-called "Gun Rights Activists" have photoshopped it into. #MarchForOurLives

A photoshopped gif showing Emma Gonzalez doing something she never did.

The most influential, beguiling, and relentless political ads on the planet may be the ones you see on Facebook. That's because they can microtarget millions of users based on their psychological and behavioral characteristics, hit those users again and again with tailored messages, and run the whole operation indefinitely and below the radar.

Consider the case of the 2016 election of Donald Trump. Brad Parscale, President Trump's former digital marketing expert, claims that his Facebook advertising campaign won the election. Whether or not this is true, his methods of precisely targeting millions of people on Facebook with political ads helped to usher in a new era of stealth political influence through social media. *The Guardian* reports on how Parscale did it and why it matters:

> Parscale claims he typically ran 50,000 to 60,000 variations of Facebook ads each day during the Trump campaign, all targeting different segments of the electorate.
>
> Understanding the meaning of a single one of those ads would require knowing what the ad actually said, who the campaign targeted to see that ad, and how that audience responded. Multiply that by 100 and you have a headache; by 50,000 and you'll start to doubt your grasp on reality. Then remember that this is 50,000 a day over the course of a campaign that lasted more than a year. . . .
>
> Any candidate using Facebook can put a campaign message promising one thing in front of one group of voters while simultaneously running an ad with a completely opposite message in front of a different group of voters. The ads themselves are not posted anywhere for the general public to see (this is what's known as "dark advertising"), and chances are, no one will ever be the wiser.
>
> That undermines the very idea of a "marketplace of ideas," says Ann Ravel, a former member of the Federal Election Commission who has long advocated stricter regulations on digital campaigning. "The way to have a robust democracy is for people to hear all these ideas and make decisions and discuss," Ravel said. "With microtargeting, that is not happening."[28]

Fortunately there are ways to take at least some of the mystery out of how we are being targeted on Facebook. On any Facebook ad, we can see (some) of the information used to target us by clicking on the dots in the upper right corner of the ad and selecting "Why am I seeing this?" Also, *ProPublica*, the independent investigative newsroom, has been compiling a searchable database of political ads—ads that are hardly ever seen outside the targeted audience of Facebook users (https://projects.propublica.org/facebook-ads/). It allows us to see what ads are being displayed to users sorted by age, gender, city or state, and political orientation (liberal, conservative, or neither liberal nor conservative). It shows us, for example, the ads targeting a forty-five-year-old woman living in California who is a liberal and the ads aimed at a sixty-five-year-old man living in Washington, D.C., who is a conservative.

KEY WORDS

advertising	objectivity	reasonable skepticism
bias	opinion	
fake news	native advertising	

SUMMARY
Fake News

- Although applying the tools of critical thinking to media fallacies and fictions is crucial, something even more important is required, something without which critical thinking is not possible: an attitude of reasonable skepticism. Reasonable skepticism means that we *do not believe a claim unless there are legitimate reasons for doing so*. Legitimate reasons are those that increase the likelihood of a claim being true. Such reasons come from reliable evidence, trustworthy sources, and critical reasoning.
- Strategies we can employ to distinguish fake from real include reading laterally, reading critically, using Google and Wikipedia carefully, and checking our own biases.
- It is reasonable to (1) accept claims that are supported independently by reliable authorities, evidence, or other claims that you know to be true; (2) accept claims that are adequately supported by the source itself through citations to other credible sources; (3) reject claims when there is good reason for believing them false; and (4) suspend judgment on claims that you are unsure of.
- The best, most reliable fact-checker organizations share certain characteristics that we can readily identify: (1) They are nonpartisan, and their funding is fully disclosed; (2) they explain their fact-checking methodology and disclose their sources; (3) they use nonpartisan and primary sources whenever possible and are appropriately skeptical of strongly biased information; (4) they employ neutral wording and minimize appeals to emotions, stereotypes, and logical fallacies; (5) they avoid partisan considerations in selecting topics to cover; (6) they promptly correct errors after publication; and (7) they have a solid track record in accurate reporting.
- Highly recommended fact-checkers include Snopes.com, PolitiFact.com, FactCheck.org, Hoax-Slayer.com, Fact Checker at the *Washington Post*, and AP Fact Check.

Media Bias

- *Accuracy* entails faithfulness to the evidence, and *incompleteness* refers to leaving out important parts of a story and thereby distorting the presentation of the facts.
- Objectivity in journalism is ensuring that the story exhibits no explicit or implicit preference for one set of values over another.
- Bias is a distorted and unfair perspective caused by the values of the writer or editor. A biased news story contains a distorted and unfair presentation of facts, *and* the distortion and unfairness is caused by the writer's or editor's values, not merely by error or oversight.
- A partisan reporter does not necessarily produce biased stories (she may control her bias while writing and reporting), a nonpartisan reporter may produce biased stories, and a story defending a partisan view is biased only if it contains distortions caused by the reporter's values.
- Evaluative terms can be used to express judgments about something, but not all evaluative language expresses bias.
- News is an account of events or situations that can be verified through objective evidence. Opinions, in the news business, are expressions of views that often cannot be verified entirely in this way—they are explanations, interpretations, judgments, speculations, and the like.
- News becomes biased when it introduces inaccuracies and unfairness caused by the writer's values. Opinions can be biased for the same reason, but they need not be. When opinions are well supported by evidence, they can be free of distortions and actually enhance the audience's understanding and awareness of complex social and political issues.
- Two common conservative and liberal arguments about news bias are unsound. Conservatives argue that surveys consistently show that most American journalists are liberals; thus, the media has a liberal slant, for liberal journalists cannot help but insert their worldview into their work. Liberals argue that large conglomerates own all large national news organizations, and their heads (who are often conservatives) are thought to skew media coverage toward conservative positions that benefit the corporations financially and economically; therefore, the news media has an overall conservative bias.
- It's not difficult to find particular instances of biased reporting in ostensibly neutral media organizations. A critical examination of a report's claims, assumptions, tone, and evidence will tell you whether it is biased and to what degree. But the sweeping accusation that mainstream news outlets consistently lean left or right is harder to prove, though not impossible.

Advertising

- Advertising runs on money, with billions of dollars spent on it every year and billions of dollars earned as a result.

- Online advertising has become the most precise, calibrated, targeted, and insidious form of advertising in history, hitting us with thousands of targeted ads per week.
- It's important to approach all advertising with an attitude of reasonable skepticism.
- Although advertising can be both truthful and helpful, its primary function is *not* to provide objective and accurate information to consumers; its purpose is *not* to help consumers make fully informed, rational choices about available options.
- Behind every ad you see online, data scientists and computer programmers are using statistics and linear algebra to optimize the impact of the ad by microtargeting you as a potential prospect.
- It's essential to distinguish between editorial content and native advertising.
- Political videos can present false or misleading messages through fallacies and rhetoric and through the manipulation of the videos themselves.
- Facebook political ads are used to target millions of users based on their psychological and behavioral characteristics.

 EXERCISES

Exercise 5.1

REVIEW QUESTIONS

*1. What is objectivity in journalism? What is bias?

2. What is connotation? How can the connotations of words introduce bias into a news story? Do connotations and evaluative language always introduce bias?

3. In journalism, what is the difference between news and opinion?

4. Does research support the idea that there is an overall, systematic leftward tilt in mainstream news media?

5. Is the mere expression of opinion in a news piece a sure sign of bias? Why or why not? What makes an expression of opinion biased?

*6. What is advertising? What is its purpose?

7. What is reasonable skepticism?

8. What is usually the most reasonable response to advertising?

9. How do data scientists and computer programmers optimize the impact of online advertising?

*10. What is native advertising?

11. In video manipulation, what is the technique of misrepresentation?

12. How can doctoring be used to create a false or misleading video?

13. How are lies different from merely false statements?

14. Is biased reporting the same thing as fake news? Why or why not?

Exercise 5.2

1. How has fake news adversely affected legitimate news, news consumers, and the idea of objective truth?

2. What is the Pizzagate incident? What does it suggest about the possible real-world consequences of fake news?

* 3. How are lies different from merely false statements?

4. Is biased reporting the same thing as fake news? Why or why not?

5. What is reasonable skepticism?

* 6. What are legitimate reasons for believing that a claim is true?

7. What are three illegitimate reasons for accepting or rejecting claims from a media source?

8. What are three questions to ask to help you determine the reliability of an online source?

9. Do you agree that it's unethical to share fake news? Why or why not?

10. In assessing the accuracy of a news story, why is it important to consult other sources?

11. When is Google most useful as a research tool?

12. What is the best way to use Wikipedia?

Exercise 5.3

Answer the following questions.

1. Consider the "paying women and children to cross the U.S. border" video mentioned in this chapter. If you were seeing this video for the first time, how would you go about checking its accuracy? Describe each step in the process.

2. Consider the "President Trump loves nuclear war" video mentioned in this chapter. If you were seeing this video for the first time, how would you go about checking its accuracy? Describe each step in the process.

Exercise 5.4

Examine the following excerpts from opinions published online and (1) identify any word connotations and other evaluative terms, (2) indicate whether the wording introduces bias, and (3) determine whether the opinions expressed are supported by evidence.

1.

One thing no liberal will ever turn down is the opportunity to get a standing ovation for accusing *someone else* of racism.

Democrats have placed their opening bid in the immigration talks on Trump's 10-yard line—a hilariously unbalanced "compromise" that is worse than their original proposal. Now, they are battering him with accusations of racism to force him into an amnesty deal that he was specifically elected to prevent.

Forced to choose, soccer moms are going with MSNBC—*and, hey, if that means we'll still have Rosa to clean the house, well, that's OK, too!*

Liberals have gotten a free ride for too long on using phony claims of "racism" to promote policies that hurt black people but help themselves. It's like spoiling a kid; by the time he's 15, it's impossible to get him to clean his room.

The virtue signalers have been out in force lately, putting in museum-quality performances ever since receiving an unsubstantiated report about Trump's alleged "s---hole countries" comment in a private meeting.

Ann Coulter, "The Left's Dirty Little Secret—Cleaned by Rosa!" Jan. 17, 2018, http://www.anncoulter.com/columns/2018-01-17.html (July 23, 2018).

*2.

Rush Limbaugh is coming for your children. Not in the flesh, thank God. But on his radio show last Thursday, the right's favorite gasbag announced that, after a two-decade hiatus, he is returning to the publishing world, this time with a history lesson for the grade-school set.

The title of his forthcoming book is *Rush Revere and the Brave Pilgrims: Time Travel Adventures with Exceptional Americans*. As befitting an author of such extraordinary narcissism, the book's hero is "a fearless middle-school history teacher named Rush Revere, who travels back in time and experiences American history as it happens," and the book's cover features the colonial-themed caricature of Limbaugh that also serves as the logo of his patriot-themed brand of iced tea.

Michelle Cottle, "Rush Limbaugh Has No Business Teaching History to Our Kids," *Daily Beast*, Sept. 10, 2013, https://www.thedailybeast.com/rush-limbaugh-has-no-business-teaching-history-to-our-kids (July 23, 2018).

3.

The great myth of many is that the left cares about people, that the compassion in American politics is almost exclusively found in the Democrat Party.

It's the exact opposite. Look at the people that vote for 'em. They're all angry. They're all miserable. They all feel left out in one way. They all need therapy. They're all constantly enraged. And you know why? Because nothing the Democrat Party ever promises 'em happens. Their lives do not get better. They've allowed themselves to become victims, thereby waiting for everybody else to do something for them because they've been convinced they can't do anything on their own because they're a victim, the deck's stacked against them.

So they're waiting for the Democrat Party, they're waiting for the Democrats and the American left to make things better. How do they define that? Making things better is punishing their enemies, not really making things better for them. I defy anybody, other than the wealthy Hollywood tech sector and the Wall Street sector, [to] go out and find your average radical leftist Democrat voter, and you will not find a happy person. And you will not find a person satisfied with what the Democrat Party has done to improve life for those people.

Rush Limbaugh, transcript, April 5, 2018, rushlimbaugh.com, https://www.rushlimbaugh.com/daily/2018/04/05/myth-liberals-care-people/(July 23, 2018).

 FIELD PROBLEM

Answer the following questions after reading the report by FactCheck.org assessing whether the polio vaccine in the 1950s and 1960s caused people to develop cancer: "Did the Polio Vaccine Cause Cancer?" (https://www.factcheck.org/2018/04/did-the-polio-vaccine-cause-cancer/).

1. What is FactCheck.org's verdict on the vaccine–cancer claim?
2. What sources does FactCheck.org use to discover the facts?
3. How confident are you that FactCheck.org has arrived at the correct answer? Give reasons for your answer.

 SELF-ASSESSMENT QUIZ

Answers appear in "Answers to Self-Assessment Quizzes" (Appendix D).

1. What are the ways that bias can be manifested in news stories?
2. In journalism, what is the difference between news and opinion?
3. According to Pew Research, what is the difference between factual statements and opinion statements?
4. What is the factor that Schiffer says can lead someone to think that a news report is biased when in fact it is not?
5. Does research support the idea that there is an overall, systematic leftward tilt in mainstream news media?
6. Is the mere expression of opinion in a news piece a sure sign of bias? Why or why not? What makes an expression of opinion biased?
7. What is usually the best response to advertising?
8. What are paid search ads? What are display ads?

9. With what famous TV ad did negative political advertising begin?

10. How is the success of advertising measured?

11. What has become the most precise, calibrated, targeted, and sneaky form of advertising in history?

12. What is the most obvious reason for being suspicious of advertising?

Answer the following questions after reading the report by Snopes.com assessing whether "... 700-Plus Undocumented People, Including Sex Offenders, [Were] Caught in El Paso Overnight" (https://www.snopes.com/fact-check/700-arrests-el-paso-border/).

13. What exactly did Snopes.com discover about this claim? For example, were there really seven hundred plus migrants involved? Were there sex offenders in this group? If so, how many? Did most of the migrants present themselves peacefully while seeking asylum? What was the makeup of the seven hundred—were they mostly families, juveniles, adult men? Why were they seeking asylum?

14. Where did the initial media report about the migrants appear? Were there discrepancies between this report and the later fully researched report done by Snopes? If so, what were the differences?

15. What sources did Snopes.com use to confirm the facts?

16. How could the initial report have been used for political purposes?

Read the following news story and then answer questions 17–20.

Soldiers Sweep up Saddam's Hit Goons

July 1, 2003—WASHINGTON—U.S. troops captured 319 suspected Ba'ath Party murderers as part of a tough new crackdown on regime diehards yesterday, as Defense Secretary Donald Rumsfeld forcefully denied that the United States is getting into a "quagmire" in Iraq.

Military officials said U.S. forces carried out 27 raids and also seized more than $9 million in cash as well as hundreds of machine guns and grenade launchers over the past two days as part of Operation Sidewinder.

The military offensive is a get-tough display of American power aimed at defeating Saddam Hussein's loyalists and outside terrorists responsible for hit-and-run attacks on U.S. troops and sabotage of Iraq's power and water services. But the Iraqi goon squads continued their guerrilla-style campaign yesterday, ambushing a U.S. Avenger air-defense vehicle in the ultra-tense town of Fallujah, wounding Jeremy Little, an Australian-born sound man for NBC news.

The Pentagon says 65 soldiers have been killed and scores more wounded in a series of ambushes and attacks by Saddam loyalists since the war was declared over May 1.

But at a Pentagon briefing, Rumsfeld tried to counter growing criticism in Congress and in the media over the U.S. policy toward Iraq and angrily denied that the U.S. is getting into another Vietnam War quagmire. . . .

Rumsfeld admitted that fighting in Iraq "will go on for some time," but said "more and more Iraqis" are starting to cooperate with coalition forces in their hunt for Saddam's goon squads.[29]

17. Is the story slanted toward or against a particular group mentioned in the story? How?

18. Are there instances of loaded or biased language or emotional appeals in the story or headline? If so, give examples.

19. What is the main source for this story?

20. Is this story lacking another perspective on the events? Is there more to the story that isn't mentioned? If so, explain.

 ## INTEGRATIVE EXERCISES

These exercises pertain to material in Chapters 1–5.

For each of the following passages, indicate whether it contains an argument. If it does, specify the conclusion and premises, whether it is deductive or inductive, and whether it is a good argument (sound or cogent). Some passages may contain no argument.

1. Andrea denies that she is an atheist, so she must be a theist.

2. You say that there are no such things as ghosts, but can you prove that they don't exist?

3. "Didn't Tom Cruise make a stock-car movie in which he destroyed thirty-five cars, burned thousands of gallons of gasoline, and wasted dozens of tires? If I were given the opportunity, I'd say to Tom Cruise, 'Tom, most people don't own thirty-five cars in their *life*, and you just trashed thirty-five cars for a movie. Now you're telling other people not to pollute the planet? Shut up, sir.'" [Rush Limbaugh]

4. "The large number of female voters for Arnold Schwarzenegger in California announces one thing: the death of feminism. That so many women would ignore his sexual misconduct and vote for him bespeaks the re-emergence of the reckless phallus." [Letter to the editor, *Newsday*]

5. Hillary Clinton supports gun-control legislation. As you know, all fascist regimes of the twentieth century passed gun-control legislation. We are forced to conclude that Hillary Clinton is a fascist.

6. If Congress bans automatic weapons, America will slide down a slippery slope leading to the banning of all guns, the shredding of the Bill of Rights, and a totalitarian police state.

7. Affirmative action makes for a better society. Everybody knows that, even if they won't admit it.

8. Thinking is like swimming. Just as in swimming it's easy to float on the top but hard to dive deep, it's easy in thinking to float along on the surface of an issue but difficult to use your intellect to delve down into the layers.

9. "If a cell, under appropriate conditions, becomes a person in the space of a few years, there can surely be no difficulty in understanding how, under appropriate conditions, a cell may, in the course of untold millions of years, give origin to the human race." [Herbert Spencer]

10. The chancellor is either a crook or a nut. He is a crook. Thus, he is no nut.

11. Everything must either happen by random accident or by divine intervention. Nothing happens by pure accident, so everything must happen because of divine intervention.

12. Children should never be spanked. Spanking is harmful. I've talked to three mothers about this issue, and they all agree that spanking harms a child's self-esteem and development.

13. The Eagles are the most popular rock group in history because they have sold the most records.

14. My professor says that telling a lie is never morally permissible. But that's ridiculous. The other day I heard him tell a bald-faced one to one of his students.

15. "Not all forms of gender discrimination are unethical. There are a number of exclusively male or female fitness clubs around the country utilized by religious individuals who shun the meat market scene. If a woman wants to spare herself the embarrassment of being ogled in her sports bra while doing thigh-thrusts, it is her right to work out with women only. Similarly, if a man wants to spare himself the temptation of working out with lingerie models, he should be allowed membership to strictly male fitness clubs. It would be unreasonable to require nondiscrimination of these private clubs, or to make them build separate facilities to accommodate everyone." [Letter to the editor, *Arizona Daily Wildcat*]

16. "Highway checkpoints, drug testing, ubiquitous security cameras and now the government's insistence on the use of sophisticated software tools to spy on the American people all point to a single vision. This vision was shared with us years ago, in George Orwell's book *1984*. Big Brother is indeed watching." [Letter to the editor, *Buffalo News*]

17. There are those on campus who would defend a student's right to display a Confederate flag on his or her dorm room door. But there is no such right. Slavery was wrong, is wrong, and always will be wrong.

18. "It is impossible to make people understand their ignorance; for it requires knowledge to perceive it and therefore he that can perceive it hath it not." [Jeremy Taylor]

19. If you give that homeless guy fifty cents today, tomorrow he will want a dollar, then five dollars, then ten, and where will it stop? Before you know it, *you're* homeless.

20. The biblical story of Adam and Eve in the garden of Eden is true. If it weren't true, it would not be in the Bible.

✎ WRITING ASSIGNMENTS

Choose an online news source from the list below, review its latest online reporting, and read the assessment of the site's accuracy and bias by the website mediabiasfactcheck.com. Then write three paragraphs answering these questions: Do you agree with the website's judgment about the source's bias? Do you agree with the rating for factual accuracy? Give reasons for your answers.

CNN
Blue Dot Daily
Fox News
USA Today
Breitbart

11

Judging Scientific Theories

CHAPTER OBJECTIVES

SCIENCE AND NOT SCIENCE
- Understand why science is not the same thing as technology, ideology, and scientism.

THE SCIENTIFIC METHOD
- Know the five steps of the scientific method.
- Understand the logic of scientific testing.
- Learn why no scientific hypothesis can be conclusively confirmed or conclusively confuted.

TESTING SCIENTIFIC THEORIES
- Using the steps of the scientific method, be able to explain how a scientist would go about testing a simple hypothesis in medical science.
- Understand why scientists use control groups, make studies double-blind, include placebos in testing, and seek replication of their work.

JUDGING SCIENTIFIC THEORIES
- Be able to list the five criteria of adequacy and explain what they mean.
- Understand how to apply the criteria of adequacy to the theories of evolution and creationism and why the text says that evolution is the better theory.

SCIENCE AND WEIRD THEORIES
- Be able to explain why evaluating weird claims might be worthwhile.

MAKING WEIRD MISTAKES
- Understand why it can be so easy to err when trying to evaluate weird theories.
- Be prepared to explain three major errors that people often make when they are trying to assess extraordinary experiences and theories.
- Learn the distinction between logical and physical possibility.

153

- Be able to use the TEST formula to evaluate extraordinary theories.
- Understand why eyewitness testimony is often unreliable.

THE WORLD IS CHOCKABLOCK WITH CLAIMS IN THE FORM OF EXPLANATIONS— *theoretical explanations*, to be more precise, about why something is the case or why something happens. An overwhelming number of such theories are offered to explain the cause of events: why the window broke, why the moon looks so pale, why Ralph stole the bike, why the stock market tanked. As critical thinkers, we do the best we can in evaluating these theories that come our way, testing them if possible, looking for alternative theories, and applying the criteria of adequacy. As it turns out, science is in the same line of work.

Science seeks to acquire knowledge and understanding of reality, and it does so through the formulation, testing, and evaluation of theories. When this kind of search for answers is both systematic and careful, science is being done. And when we ourselves search for answers by scrutinizing possible theories—and we do so systematically and carefully—we are searching scientifically.

Let's examine the scientific process more closely.

> "The aim of science is not to open the door to infinite wisdom, but to set a limit to infinite error."
>
> —**Bertolt Brecht**

Science and Not Science

First, let's explore what science is *not*.[1]

Science is not technology. Science is a way of searching for truth—a way that uses what's often referred to as *the scientific method*. Technology is not a search for truth; it's the production of products—DVDs, cell phones, wireless computers, robots that sweep the carpet, better mousetraps. Technology applies knowledge acquired through science to practical problems that science generally doesn't care about, such as the creation of electronic gadgets. Technology seeks facts to use in producing stuff. Science tries to understand how the world works not by merely cataloging specific facts but by identifying general principles that both explain and predict phenomena.

This nice distinction gets blurry sometimes when technologists do scientific research in order to build a better product or scientists create gadgets in order to do better scientific research. But, in general, science pursues knowledge; technology makes things.

Science is not ideology. Some people say that science is not a way of finding out how the world works, but a worldview affirming how the world is, just as Catholicism or socialism affirms a view of things. To some, science is not only an ideology, but also a most objectionable one—one that posits a universe that is entirely material, mechanistic, and deterministic. On this "scientific view," the world—including us—is nothing more than bits of matter forming a big machine that turns and whirs in predetermined ways. This mechanistic notion is thought to demean humans and human endeavors by reducing us to the role of cogs and sprockets.

Seven Warning Signs of Bogus Science

What would a distinguished scientist tell trial judges who must try to discern whether scientific testimony by an expert is credible? Robert L. Park is that scientist (as well as an author and professor of physics), and he has identified the following clues "that a scientific claim lies well outside the bounds of rational scientific discourse." He cautions, though, that "they are only warning signs—even a claim with several of the signs could be legitimate."

Claims for the existence of Bigfoot rest largely on the shaky underpinning of anecdotal evidence.

1. **The discoverer pitches the claim directly to the media.** The integrity of science rests on the willingness of scientists to expose new ideas and findings to the scrutiny of other scientists. Thus, scientists expect their colleagues to reveal new findings to them initially. An attempt to bypass peer review by taking a new result directly to the media, and then to the public, suggests that the work is unlikely to stand up to close examination by other scientists.

2. **The discoverer says that a powerful establishment is trying to suppress his or her work.** The idea is that the establishment will presumably stop at nothing to suppress discoveries that might shift the balance of wealth and power in society. Often, the discoverer describes mainstream science as part of a larger conspiracy that includes industry and government. Claims that the oil companies are frustrating the invention of an automobile that runs on water, for instance, are a sure sign that the idea of such a car is baloney.

3. **The scientific effect involved is always at the very limit of detection.** Alas, there is never a clear photograph of a flying saucer or the Loch Ness monster. All scientific measurements must contend with some level of background noise or statistical fluctuation. But if the signal-to-noise ratio cannot be improved, even in principle, the effect is probably not real and the work is not science.

   Thousands of published papers in parapsychology, for example, claim to report verified instances of telepathy, psychokinesis, or precognition. But those effects show up only in tortured analyses of statistics. The researchers can find no way to boost the signal, which suggests that it isn't really there.

4. **Evidence for a discovery is anecdotal.** If modern science has learned anything in the past century, it is to distrust anecdotal evidence. Because

anecdotes have a very strong emotional impact, they serve to keep superstitious beliefs alive in an age of science. The most important discovery of modern medicine is not vaccines or antibiotics; it is the randomized double-blind test, by means of which we know what works and what doesn't. Contrary to the saying, the word "data" is not the plural of "anecdote."

5. **The discoverer says a belief is credible because it has endured for centuries.** There is a persistent myth that hundreds or even thousands of years ago, long before anyone knew that blood circulates throughout the body or that germs cause disease, our ancestors possessed miraculous remedies that modern science cannot understand. Much of what is termed "alternative medicine" is part of that myth.

6. **The discoverer has worked in isolation.** The image of a lone genius who struggles in secrecy in an attic laboratory and ends up making a revolutionary breakthrough is a staple of Hollywood's science-fiction films, but it is hard to find examples in real life. Scientific breakthroughs nowadays are almost always syntheses of the work of many scientists.

7. **The discoverer must propose new laws of nature to explain an observation.** A new law of nature, invoked to explain some extraordinary result, must not conflict with what is already known. If we must change existing laws of nature or propose new laws to account for an observation, it is almost certainly wrong.[2]

But we can't identify science with a specific worldview. At any given time, a particular worldview may predominate in the scientific community, but this fact doesn't mean that the worldview is what science is all about. Predominant worldviews among scientists have changed over the centuries, but the general nature of science as a way of searching for truth has not. For example, the mechanistic view of the universe, so common among scientists in the seventeenth century, has now given way to other views. Discoveries in quantum mechanics (the study of subatomic particles) have shown that the old mechanistic perspective is incorrect.

Science is not scientism. One definition of *scientism* is the view that science is the only reliable way to acquire knowledge. Put another way, science is the only reliable road to truth. But in light of the reliability of our sense experience under standard, unhindered conditions (see Chapter 4), this claim is dubious. We obviously do know many things without the aid of scientific methodology.

But there is a related point that is not so dubious. Science may not be the only road to truth, but it is an extremely reliable way of acquiring knowledge about the empirical world. (Many philosophers of science would go a step further and say that science is our *most reliable* source of knowledge about the world.) Why is science so reliable? Science embodies to a high degree what is essential to

"Science is not gadgetry. The desirable adjuncts of modern living, although in many instances made possible by science, certainly do not constitute science."
—**Warren Weaver**

reliable knowing of empirical facts: systematic consideration of alternative solutions or theories, rigorous testing of them, and careful checking and rechecking of the conclusions.

Some would say that science is reliable because it is self-correcting. Science does not grab hold of an explanation and never let go. Instead, it looks at alternative ways to explain a phenomenon, tests these alternatives, and opens up the conclusions to criticism from scientists everywhere. Eventually, the conclusions may turn out to be false, and scientists will have to abandon the answers they thought were solid. But usually, after much testing and thinking, scientists hit upon a theory that does hold up under scrutiny. They are then justified in believing that the theory is true, even though there is some chance that it is flawed.

The Scientific Method

The scientific method cannot be identified with any particular set of experimental or observational procedures because there are many different methods to evaluate the worth of a hypothesis. In some sciences such as physics and biology, hypotheses can be assessed through controlled experimental tests. In other sciences such as astronomy and geology, hypotheses usually must be tested through observations. For example, an astronomical hypothesis may predict the existence of certain gases in a part of the Milky Way, and astronomers can use their telescopes to check whether those gases exist as predicted.

The scientific method, however, does involve several steps, regardless of the specific procedures involved:

1. Identify the problem or pose a question.
2. Devise a hypothesis to explain the event or phenomenon.
3. Derive a test implication or prediction.
4. Perform the test.
5. Accept or reject the hypothesis.

Scientific inquiry begins with a problem to solve or a question to answer. So in step 1 scientists may ask: What causes X? Why did Y happen? Does hormone therapy cause breast cancer? Does aspirin lower the risk of stroke? How is it possible for whales to navigate over long distances? How did early hominids communicate with one another? Was the Big Bang an uncaused event?

In step 2 scientists formulate a hypothesis that will constitute an answer to their question. In every case there are facts to explain, and the hypothesis is an explanation for them. The hypothesis guides the research, suggesting what kinds of observations or data would be relevant to the problem at hand. Without a hypothesis, scientists couldn't tell which data are important and which are worthless.

Where do hypotheses come from? One notion is that hypotheses are generated through induction—by collecting the data and drawing a generalization from them to get a hypothesis. But this can't be the way that most hypotheses are formulated because they often contain concepts that aren't in the data. (Remember, theories generally reach beyond the known data to posit the existence of things unknown.) The construction of hypotheses is not usually based

"The essence of science: ask an impertinent question, and you are on the way to a pertinent answer."
—Jacob Bronowski

on any such mechanical procedure. In many ways, they are created just as works of art are created. Scientists dream them up. They, however, are guided in hypothesis creation by certain criteria—namely, the criteria of adequacy we examined in the last chapter. With testability, fruitfulness, scope, simplicity, and conservatism as their guide, they devise hypotheses from the raw material of the imagination.

Remember, though, that scientists must consider not just their favorite hypothesis, but also alternative hypotheses. The scientific method calls for consideration of competing explanations and for their examination or testing at some point in the process. Sometimes applying the criteria of adequacy can immediately eliminate some theories from the running, and sometimes theories must be tested along with the original hypothesis.

In step 3 scientists derive implications, or consequences, of the hypothesis to test. As we've seen, sometimes we can test a theory directly, as when we simply check the lawnmower's gas tank to confirm the theory that it won't run because it's out of gas. But often theories cannot be tested directly. How would we directly test, for example, the hypothesis that chemical X is causing leukemia in menopausal women? We can't.

So scientists test indirectly by first deriving a test implication from a hypothesis and then putting that implication to the test. Deriving such an observational consequence involves figuring out what a hypothesis implies or predicts. Scientists ask, "If this hypothesis were true, what consequences would follow? What phenomena or events would have to obtain?"

Recall that we derived test implications in the problem of the car that wouldn't start in Chapter 10. One hypothesis was that the car wouldn't start because a vandal had sabotaged it. We reasoned that if a vandal had indeed sabotaged the car, there would be tracks in the snow around it. But there were no tracks, disconfirming the sabotage hypothesis.

The logic of hypothesis testing, then, works like this. When we derive a test implication, we know that if the hypothesis to be tested (H) is true, then there is a specific predicted consequence (C). If the consequence turns out to be false (it does not obtain as predicted), then the hypothesis is probably false, and we can reject it. The hypothesis, in other words, is disconfirmed. We can represent this outcome in a conditional, or hypothetical, argument:

If H, then C.
not-C.
Therefore, not-H.

This is, remember, an instance of modus tollens, a valid argument form. In this case, H would be false even if only one of several of its consequences (test implications) turned out to be false.

However, we would get a very different situation if C turned out to be true:

If H, then C.
C.
Therefore, H.

Are You Scientifically Literate?

Surveys conducted by the National Science Foundation (NSF) have consistently shown that Americans' understanding of science and the scientific process is limited and that belief in such things as psychic powers and UFOs is more widespread than we might expect in a scientifi-

cally advanced culture. For years the NSF has been gauging public understanding of science using a nine-question knowledge survey. In 2012 Americans scored a 5.8 out of the 9 questions (65 percent). Here's the survey so you can test your own scientific literacy. Answers are at the end. (*Note:* More than 25 percent of respondents got question 3 wrong!)

1. The center of the Earth is very hot. True or false?
2. The continents have been moving their location for millions of years and will continue to move. True or false?
3. Does the Earth go around the sun, or does the sun go around the Earth?
4. All radioactivity is man-made. True or false?
5. Electrons are smaller than atoms. True or false?
6. Lasers work by focusing sound waves. True or false?
7. It is the father's gene that decides whether the baby is a boy or a girl. True or false?
8. Antibiotics kill viruses as well as bacteria. True or false?
9. Human beings, as we know them today, developed from earlier species of animals. True or false?

Answers: 1. True; 2. True; 3. The Earth goes around the sun; 4. False; 5. True; 6. False; 7. True; 8. False; 9. True.

Notice that this is an instance of affirming the consequent, an invalid argument form. So just because C is true, that doesn't necessarily mean that H is true. If a consequence turns out to be true, that doesn't *prove* that the hypothesis is correct. In such a result, the hypothesis is confirmed, and the test provides at least some evidence that the hypothesis is true. But the hypothesis isn't then established. If other consequences for the hypothesis are tested, and all the results are again positive, then there is more evidence that the hypothesis is correct. As more and more consequences are tested, and they are shown to be true, we can have increasing confidence that the hypothesis is in fact true. As this evidence accumulates, the likelihood that the hypothesis is actually false decreases—and the probability that it's true increases.

In step 4 scientists carry out the testing. Usually this experimentation is not as simple as testing one implication and calling it quits. Scientists may test many consequences of several competing hypotheses. As the testing proceeds, some hypotheses are found wanting, and they're dropped. If all goes well, eventually one hypothesis remains, with considerable evidence in its favor. Then step 5 can happen, as the hypothesis or hypotheses are accepted or rejected.

Because scientists want to quickly eliminate unworthy hypotheses and zero in on the best one, they try to devise the most telling tests. This means that they are on the lookout for situations in which competing hypotheses have different test consequences. If hypothesis 1 says that C is true, and hypothesis 2 says that C is false, a test of C can then help eliminate one of the hypotheses from further consideration.

As we've seen, implicit in all this is the fact that no hypothesis can ever be *conclusively* confirmed. It's always possible that we will someday find evidence that undermines or conflicts with the evidence we have now.

Likewise, no hypothesis can ever be *conclusively* confuted. When scientists test hypotheses, they never really test a single hypothesis—they test a hypothesis together with a variety of background assumptions and theories. So a hypothesis can always be saved from refutation by making changes in the background claims. (As we detailed in the previous chapter, sometimes these changes are made by constructing ad hoc hypotheses—by postulating unverifiable entities or properties.) In such situations, no amount of evidence logically compels us to conclusively reject a hypothesis.

But our inability to conclusively confirm or confute a hypothesis does not mean that all hypotheses are equally acceptable. Maintaining a hypothesis in the face of mounting negative evidence is unreasonable, and so is refusing to accept a hypothesis despite accumulating confirming evidence. Through the use of carefully controlled experiments, scientists can often affirm or deny a hypothesis with a high degree of confidence.

 REVIEW NOTES

Steps in the Scientific Method

1. Identify the problem or pose a question.
2. Devise a hypothesis to explain the event or phenomenon.
3. Derive a test implication or prediction.
4. Perform the test.
5. Accept or reject the hypothesis.

Testing Scientific Theories

Let's see how we might use the five-step procedure to test a fairly simple hypothesis. Suppose you hear reports that some terminal cancer patients have lived longer than expected because they received high doses of vitamin C. And say that the favored hypothesis among many observers is that the best explanation for the patients' surviving longer is that vitamin C is an effective treatment against cancer. So you decide to test this hypothesis: High doses of vitamin C can increase the survival time of people with terminal cancer. (Years ago, this hypothesis was actually proposed and tested in three well-controlled clinical trials.[3]) An obvious alternative hypothesis is that vitamin C actually has no effect on the survival of terminal cancer patients and that any apparent benefits are due mainly to the placebo effect (the tendency for people to temporarily feel better after they're treated, even if the treatment is a fake). The placebo effect could be leading observers to believe that people taking vitamin C are being cured of cancer and are thus living longer. Or the placebo effect could be making patients feel better, enabling them to take better care of themselves (by eating right or complying with standard medical treatment, for example), increasing survival time.

Now, if your hypothesis is true, what would you expect to happen? That is, what test implication could you derive? If your hypothesis is true, you would expect that terminal cancer patients given high doses of vitamin C would live longer than terminal cancer patients who didn't receive the vitamin (or anything else).

How would you conduct such a test? To begin with, you could prescribe vitamin C to a group of terminal cancer patients (called the experimental group) but not to another group of similar cancer patients (called the control group) and keep track of their survival times. Then you could compare the survival rates of the two groups. But many people who knowingly receive a treatment will report feeling better—even if the treatment is an inactive placebo. So any positive results you see in the treated group might be due not to vitamin C but to the placebo effect.

To get around this problem, you would need to treat both groups, one with vitamin C and the other with a placebo. That way, if most of the people getting the vitamin C live longer than expected and fewer of those in the placebo group do, you can have slightly better reason for believing that vitamin C works as advertised.

But even this study design is not good enough. It's possible for the people conducting the experiment, the experimenters, to unknowingly bias the results. Through subtle behavioral cues, they can unconsciously inform the test subjects which treatments are real and which ones are placebos—and this, of course, would allow the placebo effect to have full rein. Also, if the experimenters know which treatment is the real one, they can unintentionally misinterpret or skew the study results in line with their own expectations.

This problem can be solved by making the study *double-blind*. In double-blind experiments, neither the subjects nor the experimenters know who receives the

> "The grand aim of all science is to cover the greatest number of empirical facts by logical deduction from the smallest number of hypotheses or axioms."
>
> **—Albert Einstein**

> "Science is an edged tool, with which men play like children, and cut their fingers."
>
> **—Arthur Eddington**

Nonintervention (Population) Studies

Not all medical hypotheses are tested by treating (or not treating) groups of patients and analyzing the results (as in the vitamin C example). Many are tested without such direct intervention in people's lives. The former type of study is known as an intervention, or controlled, trial, while the latter is called, not surprisingly, a *nonintervention* study (also an *observational* or *population* study). The basic idea in a nonintervention study is to track the interplay of disease and related factors in a specified population, uncovering associations among these that might lead to better understanding or control of the disease process.

A typical nonintervention study might go like this: For seven years scientists monitor the vitamin E intake (from food and supplements) and the incidence of heart disease of ninety thousand women. Evaluation of these data shows that the women with the highest amounts of vitamin E in their diets have a 40 percent lower incidence of heart disease. That is, for reasons unknown, a lower risk of heart disease is associated with a higher intake of vitamin E in women. This study does not show that higher intakes of vitamin E *cause* less heart disease, only that there is a link between them. Perhaps some other factor merely associated with vitamin E is the true protector of hearts, or maybe women who take vitamin E are more likely to do other things (such as exercise) that lower their risk of heart disease.

Generally, nonintervention studies cannot establish cause-and-effect relationships, though they may hint that a causal relationship is present. And sometimes multiple nonintervention studies yielding the same results can make a strong case for a causal connection. Intervention trials, however, *can* establish cause and effect.

Nonintervention studies have led scientists to some of the most important findings in preventive health. It was a series of such studies done over decades, coupled with other kinds of scientific data, that revealed that cigarette smoking caused cancer. And it was such investigations that showed that high blood pressure, high cholesterol, overweight, and smoking are risk factors for heart disease.

Note to critical thinkers: Very often the media misreport the results of nonintervention studies, reading cause and effect into a mere association. For example, if a single nonintervention study finds a link between chewing gum and better eyesight, a headline in the morning paper (or a TV newscaster) may proclaim that "gum-chewing improves your eyesight!" Maybe, maybe not—but the study would not justify that conclusion.

real treatment and who the inactive one. A double-blind protocol for your vitamin study would ensure that none of the subjects would know who's getting vitamin C, and neither would the experimenters.

What if you have a double-blind setup but most of the subjects in the vitamin C group were sicker to begin with than those in the placebo control group? Obviously, this would bias the results, making the vitamin C treatment look less effective—even if it *is* effective. To avoid this skewing, you would need to ensure that each group is as much alike as possible to start—with all subjects being around the same age, same physical condition, same stage of cancer, and so on.

Finally, you would need to run some statistical tests to ensure that your results are not a fluke. Even in the most tightly controlled studies, it's possible that the outcome is the result of random factors that cannot be controlled. Statisticians have standard methods for determining when experiment results are likely, or not likely, to be due to chance.

Suppose you design your study well and you conduct it. The results: The patients receiving the high doses of vitamin C did not live longer than the placebo group. In fact, all the subjects lived about the same length of time. Therefore, your hypothesis is disconfirmed. However, the alternative hypothesis—that vitamin C has no measurable effect on the survival of terminal cancer patients—is confirmed.

Should you now reject the vitamin C theory? Not yet. Even apparently well-conducted studies can have hidden mistakes in them, or there can be factors that the experimenters fail to take into account. This is why scientists insist on study *replication*—the repeating of an experiment by different groups of scientists. If the study is replicated by other scientists, and the study results hold up, then you can be more confident that the results are solid. In such a case, you could safely reject the vitamin C hypothesis. (This is, in fact, what scientists did in the real-life studies of vitamin C and cancer survival.)

At this point, when evidence has been gathered that can bear on the truth of the hypothesis in question, good scientific judgment is crucial. It's here that consideration of other competing hypotheses and the criteria of adequacy again come into play. At this stage, scientists need to decide whether to reject or accept a hypothesis—or modify it to improve it.

Judging Scientific Theories

As you can see, theory testing is part of the broader effort to assess the merits of one theory against a field of alternatives. And as you know by now, this broader effort will always involve, explicitly or implicitly, the application of the criteria of adequacy to the theories in question:

- Testability: Whether there's some way to determine if a theory is true
- Fruitfulness: The number of novel predictions made
- Scope: The number of diverse phenomena explained
- Simplicity: The number of assumptions made
- Conservatism: How well a theory fits with existing knowledge

"When, however, the lay public rallies around an idea that is denounced by distinguished but elderly scientists and supports that idea with great fervour and emotion—the distinguished but elderly scientists are then, after all, probably right."

—Isaac Asimov

Let's study two important examples to see how scientists manage this task: The first is a classic case from the history of science; the second, a contemporary tale of what many perceive as a battle between science and religion. Notice that the steps itemized by the TEST formula are implicit in the evaluation process.

Copernicus versus Ptolemy

Consider the historic clash between the geocentric (Earth-centered) and the heliocentric (sun-centered) theories of planetary motion. It's difficult to imagine two rival theories that have more profoundly influenced how humanity views itself and its place in the universe.

In the beginning was the geocentric view. Aristotle got things going by putting forth the theory that a spherical Earth was at the center of a spherical universe consisting of a series of concentric, transparent spheres. On one celestial sphere we see the sun, the moon, and the known planets. On the outermost sphere we behold the stars. All the heavenly bodies rotate in perfect circles around the stationary Earth. The heavenly bodies are pure, incorruptible, and unchanging; the Earth is impure, corruptible, and transient.

Then came the great astronomer and mathematician Ptolemy, who flourished in Alexandria between 127 and 148 C.E. He discovered inconsistencies

 FURTHER THOUGHT

Copernicus on Ptolemy's System

Copernicus was shocked at how complex and seemingly arbitrary Ptolemy's revered system was. He thought that Ptolemy, through countless revisions and additions, had created not a beautiful model—but a kind of monster. As Copernicus put it,

> It is as though an artist were to gather the hands, feet, head and other members for his images from diverse models, each part excellently drawn, but not related to a single body, and since they in no way match each other, the result would be a monster rather than a man.

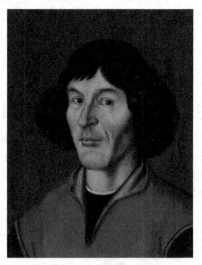

Nicolaus Copernicus (1473–1543).

"IT'S BLACK, AND IT LOOKS LIKE A HOLE.
I'D SAY IT'S A BLACK HOLE."

in the traditional geocentric system between the predicted and observed motions of the planets. He found, in other words, that Aristotle's theory was not conservative, a crucial failing. So he fine-tuned the old view, adding little circular motions (called epicycles) along the planet orbits and many other minor adjustments. He also allowed for an odd asymmetry in which the center of planet orbits was not exactly the center of Earth—all this so the theory would match up to astronomical observations. By the time Ptolemy finished tinkering, he had posited eighty circles and epicycles—eighty different planetary motions—to explain the movements of the sun, moon, and five known planets.

The result was a system far more complex than Aristotle's was. But the revised theory worked well enough for the times, and it agreed better than the earlier theory did with observational data. Despite the complications, learned people could use Ptolemy's system to calculate the positions of the planets with enough accuracy to effectively manage calendars and astrological charts. So for fifteen centuries astronomers used Ptolemy's unwieldy, complex theory to predict celestial events and locations. In the West, at least, Earth stood still in the center of everything as the rest of the universe circled around it.

The chief virtue of the Ptolemaic system, then, was conservatism. It fit, mostly, with what astronomers knew about celestial goings-on. It was also testable, as any scientific theory should be. Its biggest failing was simplicity—or the lack thereof. The theory was propped up by numerous assumptions for the purpose of making the theory fit the data.

Enter Nicolaus Copernicus (1473–1543). He was disturbed by the complexity of Ptolemy's system. It was a far cry from the simple theory that Aristotle bequeathed to the West. Copernicus proposed a heliocentric theory in which Earth and the other planets orbit the sun, the true center of the universe. In doing so, he greatly simplified both the picture of the heavens and the calculations required to predict the positions of planets.

"[Natural selection] has no vision, no foresight, no sight at all. If it can be said to play the role of watchmaker in nature, it is the blind watchmaker."
—Richard Dawkins

Copernicus's theory was simpler than Ptolemy's on many counts, but one of the most impressive was retrograde motion, a phenomenon that had stumped astronomers for centuries. From time to time, certain planets seem to reverse their customary direction of travel across the skies—to move backward! Ptolemy explained this retrograde motion by positing yet more epicycles, asserting that planets orbiting Earth will often orbit around a point on the larger orbital path.

Seeing these orbits within orbits from Earth, an observer would naturally see the planets sometimes backing up.

But the Copernican theory could easily explain retrograde motion without all those complicated epicycles. As the outer planets (Mars, Jupiter, Saturn) orbit the sun, so does Earth, one of the inner planets. The outer planets, though, move much slower than Earth does. On its own orbital track, Earth sometimes passes the outer planets as they lumber along on their orbital track, just as a train passes a slower train on a parallel track. When this happens, the planets appear to move backward, just as the slower train seems to reverse course when the faster train overtakes it.

Copernicus's theory, however, was not superior on every count. It explained a great many astronomical observations, but Ptolemy's theory did too, so they were about even in scope. It had no big advantage in fruitfulness over the Ptolemaic system. It made no impressive predictions of unknown phenomena. Much more troubling, it seemed to conflict with some observational data.

One test implication of the Copernican theory is the phenomenon known as *parallax*. Critics of the heliocentric view claimed that if the theory were true, then as Earth moved through its orbit, stars closest to it should seem to shift their position relative to stars farther away. There should, in other words, be parallax. But no one had observed parallax.

Copernicus and his followers responded to this criticism by saying that stars were too far away for parallax to occur. As it turned out, they were right about this, but confirmation didn't come until 1832 when parallax was observed with more powerful telescopes.

Another test implication seemed to conflict with the heliocentric model. Copernicus reasoned that if the planets rotate around the sun, then they should show phases just as the moon shows phases due to the light of the sun falling on it at different times. But in Copernicus's day, no one could see any such planetary phases. Fifty years later, though, Galileo used his new telescope to confirm that Venus had phases.

Ultimately, scientists accepted the Copernican model over Ptolemy's because of its simplicity—despite what seemed at the time like evidence against the theory. As Copernicus said, "I think it is easier to believe this [sun-centered view] than to confuse the issue by assuming a vast number of Spheres, which those who keep the Earth at the center must do."[4]

Evolution versus Creationism

Few scientific theories have been more hotly debated among nonscientists than evolution and its rival, creationism (or creation science). Both theories purport to explain the origin and existence of biological life on Earth, and each claims to be a better explanation than the other. Can science decide this contest? Yes. Despite the complexity of the issues involved and the mixing of religious themes with the nonreligious, good science can figure out which theory is best. Remember that the best theory is the one that explains the phenomenon and measures up to the criteria of adequacy better than any of its competitors. There is no reason that the scientific approach cannot provide an answer here—even in this thorniest of thorny issues.

"Science is an integral part of culture. It's not this foreign thing, done by an arcane priesthood. It's one of the glories of human intellectual tradition."
—**Stephen Jay Gould**

Can You See Evolution?

Critics of the theory of evolution often ask, "If evolution occurs, why can't we see it?" Here's how the National Academy of Sciences responds to this objection (http://books.nap.edu/html/creationism/evidence.html):

> Special creationists argue that "no one has ever seen evolution occur." This misses the point about how science tests hypotheses. We don't see Earth going around the sun or the atoms that make up matter. We "see" their consequences. Scientists infer that atoms exist and Earth revolves because they have tested predictions derived from these concepts by extensive observation and experimentation.
>
> Furthermore, on a minor scale, we "experience" evolution occurring every day. The annual changes in influenza viruses and the emergence of antibiotic-resistant bacteria are both products of evolutionary forces. . . . On a larger scale, the evolution of mosquitoes resistant to insecticides is another example of the tenacity and adaptability of organisms under environmental stress. Similarly, malaria parasites have become resistant to the drugs that were used extensively to combat them for many years. As a consequence, malaria is on the increase, with more than 300 million clinical cases of malaria occurring every year.

Neither the term "evolution" nor the concept began with Charles Darwin (1809–1882), the father of evolutionary theory. The word showed up in English as early as 1647. The ancient Greek philosopher Anaximander (c. 611–547 B.C.E.) was actually the first evolutionary theorist, inferring from some simple observations that humans must have evolved from an animal and that this evolution must have begun in the sea. But in his famous book *On the Origin of Species* (1859), Darwin distilled the theory of evolution into its most influential statement.

Scientists have been fine-tuning the theory ever since, as new evidence and new insights pour in from many different fields, such as biochemistry and genetics. But the basic idea has not changed: Living organisms adapt to their environments through inherited characteristics, which results in changes in succeeding generations. Specifically, the offspring of organisms differ physically from their parents in various ways, and these differences can be passed on genetically to their offspring. If an offspring has an inherited trait (such as sharper vision or a larger brain) that increases its chances of surviving long enough to reproduce, the individual is more likely to survive and pass the trait on to the next generation. After several generations, this useful trait, or adaptation, spreads throughout a whole population of individuals, differentiating the population from its ancestors. *Natural selection* is the name that Darwin gave to this process.

"It is a good morning exercise for a research scientist to discard a pet hypothesis every day before breakfast. It keeps him young."
—**Konrad Lorenz**

Creation science, in contrast, maintains that (1) the universe and all life was created suddenly, out of nothing, only a few thousand years ago (six thousand to ten thousand is the usual range); (2) natural selection could not have produced living things from a single organism; (3) species change very little over time; (4) man and apes have a separate ancestry; and (5) the Earth's geology can be explained by catastrophism, including a worldwide flood.[5]

The first thing we should ask about these two theories is whether they're testable. The answer is yes. Recall that a theory is testable if it predicts or explains something other than what it was introduced to explain. On this criterion, evolution is surely testable. It explains, among other things, why bacteria develop resistance to antibiotics, why there are so many similarities between humans and other primates, why new infectious diseases emerge, why the chromosomes of closely related species are so similar, why the fossil record shows the peculiar progression of fossils that it does, and why the embryos of related species have such similar structure and appearance.

Creationism is also testable. It too explains something other than what it was introduced to explain. It claims that Earth's geology was changed in a worldwide flood, that the universe is only a few thousand years old, that all species were created at the same time, and that species change very little over time.

Innumerable test implications have been derived from evolutionary theory, and innumerable experiments have been conducted, confirming the theory. For example, if evolution is true, then we would expect to see systematic change in the fossil record from simple creatures at the earlier levels to more complex individuals at the more recent levels. We would expect not to see a reversal of this configuration. And this sequence is exactly what scientists see time and time again.

Creationism, however, has not fared as well. Its claims have not been borne out by evidence. In fact, they have consistently conflicted with well-established scientific findings.

This latter point means that creationism fails the criterion of conservatism—it conflicts with what we already know. For example, the scientific evidence shows that Earth is not six thousand to ten thousand years old—but billions of years old. According to the National Academy of Sciences,

> There are no valid scientific data or calculations to substantiate the belief that Earth was created just a few thousand years ago. [There is a] vast amount of evidence for the great age of the universe, our galaxy, the Solar system, and Earth from astronomy, astrophysics, nuclear physics, geology, geochemistry, and geophysics. Independent scientific methods consistently give an age for Earth and the Solar system of about 5 billion years, and an age for our galaxy and the universe that is two to three times greater.[6]

CHARLES DARWIN SLIDING INTO THIRD WITH HIS REALIZATION THAT THE FITTEST SURVIVE

© 2002 by Sidney Harris. www.ScienceCartoonsPlus.com

Creationism also fails the criterion of conservatism on the issue of a geology-transforming universal flood. Again, the National Academy of Sciences:

> Nor is there any evidence that the entire geological record, with its orderly succession of fossils, is the product of a single universal flood that occurred a few thousand years ago, lasted a little longer than a year, and covered the highest mountains to a depth of several meters. On the contrary, intertidal and terrestrial deposits demonstrate that at no recorded time in the past has the entire planet been under water. . . . The belief that Earth's sediments, with their fossils, were deposited in an orderly sequence in a year's time defies all geological observations and physical principles concerning sedimentation rates and possible quantities of suspended solid matter.[7]

Has either theory yielded any novel predictions? Evolution has. It has predicted, for example, that new species should still be evolving today; that the fossil record should show a movement from older, simpler organisms to younger, more complex ones; that proteins and chromosomes of related species should be similar; and that organisms should adapt to changing environments. These and many other novel predictions have been confirmed. Creationism has made some novel claims, as we saw earlier, but none of these has been supported by good evidence. Creationism is not a fruitful theory.

The criterion of simplicity also draws a sharp contrast between the two theories. Simplicity is a measure of the number of assumptions that a theory makes. Both theories make assumptions, but creationism assumes much more. Creationism assumes the existence of a creator and unknown forces. Proponents of creationism readily admit that we do not know how the creator created or what creative processes were used.

In this contest of theories, the criterion of scope—the number of diverse phenomena explained—is probably more telling than any of the others. Biological evolution explains a vast array of phenomena in many fields of science. In fact, a great deal of the content of numerous scientific fields—genetics, physiology, biochemistry, neurobiology, and more—would be deeply perplexing without the theory of evolution. As the eminent geneticist Theodosius Dobzhansky put it, "Nothing in biology makes sense except in the light of evolution."[9]

Virtually all scientists would agree—and go much further:

> It helps to explain the emergence of new infectious diseases, the development of antibiotic resistance in bacteria, the agricultural relationships among wild and domestic plants and animals, the composition of Earth's atmosphere, the molecular machinery of the cell, the similarities between human beings and other primates, and countless other features of the biological and physical world.[10]

Creationism, however, can explain none of this. And it provokes, not solves, innumerable mysteries: What caused the worldwide flood? Where did all that water come from? Where did it all go? Why does Earth seem so ancient (when it's said to be so young)? How did the creator create the entire universe suddenly—out of nothing? Why does the fossil record seem to suggest evolution

Gaps in the Fossil Record?

Creationists hold that if evolution were true, then there should be fossil remains of transitional organisms. But, they insist, there are gaps where transitional fossils should be, so evolution didn't happen. But this claim is incorrect. There are transitional fossils:

> Gaps in the fossil record are not even a critical test of evolution vs. progressive creation, as evolution also predicts gaps. There are some 2 million described species of living animals, but only 200,000 described fossil species. Thus, it is impossible to provide a minutely detailed history for every living species. This is because, first, the fossil record has not been completely explored. It is pretty hard to overlook a dinosaur bone! Yet, though dinosaurs have been excavated for over 150 years, 40% of the known species were found in the last 20 years or so (*Discover*, March 1987, p. 46). It is likely many more dinosaur species remain to be found. Second, sedimentary rocks were formed locally in lakes, oceans, and river deltas, so many upland species were never fossilized. Third, many deposits that were formed have been lost to erosion. Thus, a complete record is impossible.

In 2006 scientists discovered this 375-million-year-old fossil of a species that spans the gap between fish and land animals.

> However, there is a critical test. Evolution predicts that some complete series should be found, while [creationists predict] that none should ever be found. In fact, many excellent series exist. The evolution of the horse is known in exquisite detail from *Hyracotherium* (*Eohippus*) to the modern horse (G. G. Simpson, *Horses*, 2nd ed. Oxford, 1961). Scientific creationists have been forced to claim that the series is but an allowed variation within a created "kind." If so, then rhinoceroses, tapirs, and horses are all the same "kind," as they can be traced to ancestors nearly identical to *Hyracotherium*! All of these fossils lie in the correct order by both stratigraphic and radioisotope dating.
>
> Another critical test is Darwin's prediction that ". . . our early ancestors lived on the African continent. . . ." (*The Descent of Man*, p. 158). An excellent, detailed series of skulls and some nearly complete skeletons now connect modern man to African australopithecines. Some of the extinct australopithecines had brains about the size and shape of those of chimpanzees.[8]

and not creation? So many questions are an indication of diminished scope and decreased understanding.

Good scientists must be prepared to admit this much: If creationism meets the criteria of adequacy as well as evolution does, then creationism must be as good a theory as evolution. But creationism fails to measure up to the criteria of adequacy. On every count it shows itself to be inferior. Scientists then are justified in rejecting creationism in favor of evolution. And this is exactly what they do.

 FURTHER THOUGHT

The Clash over "Intelligent Design"

A controversial view known as intelligent design is the latest conceptual challenge to evolution, maintaining that biological life is much too complex to be fully explained by evolutionary processes. Take a moment to reflect on this synopsis of part of the debate:

> The proponents of intelligent design, a school of thought that some have argued should be taught alongside evolution in the nation's schools, say that the complexity and diversity of life go beyond what evolution can explain.
>
> Biological marvels like the optical precision of an eye, the little spinning motors that propel bacteria and the cascade of proteins that cause blood to clot, they say, point to the hand of a higher being at work in the world.
>
> In one often-cited argument, Michael J. Behe, a professor of biochemistry at Lehigh University and a leading design theorist, compares complex biological phenomena like blood clotting to a mousetrap: Take away any one piece—the spring, the baseboard, the metal piece that snags the mouse—and the mousetrap stops being able to catch mice.
>
> Similarly, Dr. Behe argues, if any one of the more than 20 proteins involved in blood clotting is missing or deficient, as happens in hemophilia, for instance, clots will not form properly.
>
> Such all-or-none systems, Dr. Behe and other design proponents say, could not have arisen through the incremental changes that evolution says allowed life to progress to the big brains and the sophisticated abilities of humans from primitive bacteria.
>
> These complex systems are "always associated with design," Dr. Behe, the author of the 1996 book *Darwin's Black Box*, said in an interview. "We find such systems in biology, and since we know of no other way that these things can be produced, Darwinian claims notwithstanding, then we are rational to conclude they were indeed designed."
>
> It is an argument that appeals to many Americans of faith.
>
> But mainstream scientists say that the claims of intelligent design run counter to a century of research supporting the explanatory and predictive

power of Darwinian evolution, and that the design approach suffers from fundamental problems that place it outside the realm of science. For one thing, these scientists say, invoking a higher being as an explanation is unscientific.

"One of the rules of science is, no miracles allowed," said Douglas H. Erwin, a paleobiologist at the Smithsonian Institution. "That's a fundamental presumption of what we do."

That does not mean that scientists do not believe in God. Many do. But they see science as an effort to find out how the material world works, with nothing to say about why we are here or how we should live.

And in that quest, they say, there is no need to resort to otherworldly explanations. So much evidence has been provided by evolutionary studies that biologists are able to explain even the most complex natural phenomena and to fill in whatever blanks remain with solid theories.

This is possible, in large part, because evolution leaves tracks like the fossil remains of early animals or the chemical footprints in DNA that have been revealed by genetic research.

For example, while Dr. Behe and other leading design proponents see the blood-clotting system as a product of design, mainstream scientists see it as a result of a coherent sequence of evolutionary events.

Early vertebrates like jawless fish had a simple clotting system, scientists believe, involving a few proteins that made blood stick together, said Russell F. Doolittle, a professor of molecular biology at the University of California, San Diego.

Scientists hypothesize that at some point, a mistake during the copying of DNA resulted in the duplication of a gene, increasing the amount of protein produced by cells.

Most often, such a change would be useless. But in this case the extra protein helped blood clot, and animals with the extra protein were more likely to survive and reproduce. Over time, as higher-order species evolved, other proteins joined the clotting system. For instance, several proteins involved in the clotting of blood appear to have started as digestive enzymes.

By studying the evolutionary tree and the genetics and biochemistry of living organisms, Dr. Doolittle said, scientists have largely been able to determine the order in which different proteins became involved in helping blood clot, eventually producing the sophisticated clotting mechanisms of humans and other higher animals. The sequencing of animal genomes has provided evidence to support this view.

For example, scientists had predicted that more primitive animals such as fish would be missing certain blood-clotting proteins. In fact, the recent sequencing of the fish genome has shown just this.

"The evidence is rock solid," Dr. Doolittle said. . . .

Dr. Behe, however, said he might find it compelling if scientists were to observe evolutionary leaps in the laboratory. He pointed to an experiment by Richard E. Lenski, a professor of microbial ecology at Michigan State University, who has been observing the evolution of *E. coli* bacteria for more than 15 years. "If anything cool came out of that," Dr. Behe said, "that would be one way to convince me."

Dr. Behe said that if he was correct, then the *E. coli* in Dr. Lenski's lab would evolve in small ways but never change in such a way that the bacteria would develop entirely new abilities.

In fact, such an ability seems to have developed. Dr. Lenski said his experiment was not intended to explore this aspect of evolution, but nonetheless, "We have recently discovered a pretty dramatic exception, one where a new and surprising function has evolved," he said.

Dr. Lenski declined to give any details until the research is published. But, he said, "If anyone is resting his or her faith in God on the outcome that our experiment will not produce some major biological innovation, then I humbly suggest they should rethink the distinction between science and religion."

Dr. Behe said, "I'll wait and see."[11]

As it turned out, Dr. Lenski's experiment showed that the bacteria did indeed evolve, acquiring many significant mutations and new abilities.

 EXERCISES

Exercise 11.1

REVIEW QUESTIONS

1. How does science differ from technology?
2. What is the scientific method?
3. Can science be identified with a particular worldview?
4. According to the text, what is scientism?
5. According to the text, why is science such a reliable way of knowing?
* 6. What are the five steps of the scientific method?
7. Can hypotheses be generated through induction? Why or why not?
8. What does it mean to derive a test implication from a theory?
* 9. What is the conditional argument reflecting the fact that a theory is disconfirmed?

10. What is the conditional argument reflecting the fact that a theory is confirmed?

11. Can theories be conclusively confirmed? Why or why not?

* 12. Can theories be conclusively disconfirmed? Why or why not?

13. According to the text, is creationism as good a scientific theory as evolution? Why or why not?

Exercise 11.2

For each of the following phenomena, devise a hypothesis to explain it and derive a test implication to test the hypothesis.

1. In a recent study of scientific literacy, women performed better than men in understanding the scientific process and in answering questions about basic scientific facts and concepts.

* 2. Jamal found giant footprints in his backyard and mysterious tufts of brown fur clinging to bushes in the area. Rumors persist that Bigfoot, the giant primate unknown to science, is frequenting the area. Two guys living nearby also claim to be perpetrating a hoax about the existence of the creature.

3. A man with a gun entered a mall in Chicago and began shooting randomly at shoppers, shouting something about demons using his body to commit horrible acts.

4. For years after the tragedy of September 11, 2001, there were no major terrorist attacks in the United States.

5. The CIA reviewed the president's State of the Union speech before he made it and verified that the intelligence information in the speech was correct. Later it was found that some of the information was erroneous and based on dubious sources.

* 6. Weight trainers swear that the supplement creatine dramatically increases their performance.

7. Many people who take B vitamins for their headaches report a lower incidence of headaches.

8. Recent research confirms a link between diets high in saturated fat and a higher risk of coronary artery disease.

9. When John got home, he found that the lock on his door had been broken and his TV was missing.

10. The economic gap between the very rich and the very poor widened considerably in 2014.

Exercise 11.3

Using your background knowledge and any other information you may have about the subject, devise a competing theory for each of the following and then apply the criteria of adequacy to both of them—that is, ascertain how well each theory does in relation to its competitor on the criteria of testability, fruitfulness, scope, simplicity, and conservatism.

1. Phenomenon: People report feeling less pain after trying acupuncture.

   Theory: Treatment with acupuncture needles can alleviate pain.

2. Phenomenon: In the United States in 2014, a few people contracted the Ebola virus even though none of them had traveled recently to places in Africa known to be the source of the virus.

   Theory: The virus was carried from Africa to the United States by trade winds in the Atlantic Ocean.

*3. Phenomenon: The unexpected melting of massive chunks of the world's glaciers.

   Theory: Local climate changes.

4. Phenomenon: A rare species of fungus grows in only one place in the world—the wing tips of a beetle that inhabits caves in France.

   Theory: Evolution.

5. Phenomenon: As the job market worsens, BLACKS lose jobs faster than WHITES.

   Theory: Racial prejudice.

6. Phenomenon: The psychic was able to recount a number of personal details about a recently deceased person he never met.

   Theory: Psychic ability.

*7. Phenomenon: Almost all of the terrorist attacks in the world in the past five years have been perpetrated by religious fanatics.

   Theory: Religion fosters terrorism.

8. Phenomenon: Twenty patients with severe arthritis pain were prayed for by fifty people, and fourteen out of those twenty reported a significant lessening of pain.

   Theory: Prayer heals.

9. Phenomenon: Over the past year, two terminally ill cancer patients in Broderick Hospital were found to be cancer free.

   Theory: Treatment with a new type of chemotherapy works.

10. Phenomenon: Air pollution levels in San Francisco are at their highest levels in years.

   Theory: Increased numbers of SUVs being driven in the San Francisco area.

Exercise 11.4

For each of the following theories, derive a test implication and indicate whether you believe that such a test would likely confirm or disconfirm the theory.

1. Elise has the power to move physical objects with her mind alone.

*2. Ever since the city installed brighter streetlights, the crime rate has been declining steadily.

3. The Ultra-Sonic 2000 pest-control device can rid a house of roaches by emitting a particular sound frequency that humans can't hear.

4. The Dodge Intrepid is a more fuel-efficient car than any other on the road.

5. Practitioners of transcendental meditation can levitate—actually ascend unaided off the ground without physical means of propulsion.

* 6. Eating foods high in fat contributes more to overweight than eating foods high in carbohydrates.

7. Lemmings often commit mass suicide.

8. The English sparrow will build nests only in trees.

Exercise 11.5

Read the following passages and answer the following questions for each one:

1. What is the phenomenon being explained?

2. What theories are advanced to explain the phenomenon? (Some theories may be unstated.)

3. Which theory seems the most plausible and why? (Use the criteria of adequacy.)

4. Regarding the most credible theory, is there a test implication mentioned? If so, what is it? If not, what would be a good test implication for the theory?

5. What test results would convince you to change your mind about your preferred theory?

PASSAGE 1

"In the past several years, a researcher named David Oates has been advocating his discovery of a most interesting phenomenon. Oates claims that backward messages are hidden unintentionally in all human speech. The messages can be understood by recording normal speech and playing it in reverse. . . . [According to Oates] 'Any thought, any emotion, any motive that any person has can appear backwards in human speech. The implications are mind boggling because reverse speech opens up the Truth.' . . . To our knowledge there is not one empirical investigation of reverse speech in any peer-reviewed journal. If reverse speech did exist it would be, at the very least, a noteworthy scientific discovery. However, there are no data to support the existence of reverse speech or Oates's theories about its implications."[12]

PASSAGE 2

"Michael Behe, a Lehigh University biochemist, claims that a light-sensitive cell, for example, couldn't have arisen through evolution because it is 'irreducibly complex.' Unlike the scientific creationists, however, he doesn't deny that the universe is billions of years old. Nor does he deny that evolution has occurred. He only denies that every biological system arose through natural selection.

"Behe's favorite example of an irreducibly complex mechanism is a mouse trap. A mouse trap consists of five parts: (1) a wooden platform, (2) a metal hammer, (3) a spring, (4) a catch, and (5) a metal bar that holds the hammer down when the trap is set. What makes this mechanism irreducibly complex is that if any one of the parts were removed, it would no longer work. Behe claims that many biological systems, such as cilia, vision, and blood clotting, are also irreducibly complex because each of these systems would cease to function if any of their parts were removed.

"Irreducibly complex biochemical systems pose a problem for evolutionary theory because it seems that they could not have arisen through natural selection. A trait such as vision can improve an organism's ability to survive only if it works. And it works only if all the parts of the visual system are present. So, Behe concludes, vision couldn't have arisen through slight modifications of a previous system. It must have been created all at once by some intelligent designer. . . .

"Most biologists do not believe that Behe's argument is sound, however, because they reject the notion that the parts of an irreducibly complex system could not have evolved independently of that system. As Nobel Prize–winning biologist H. J. Muller noted in 1939, a genetic sequence that is, at first, inessential to a system may later become essential to it. Biologist H. Allen Orr describes the processes as follows: 'Some part (A) initially does some job (and not very well, perhaps). Another part (B) later gets added because it helps A. This new part isn't essential, it merely improves things. But later on A (or something else) may change in such a way that B now becomes indispensable.' For example, air bladders—primitive lungs—made it possible for certain fish to acquire new sources of food. But the air bladders were not necessary to the survival of the fish. As the fish acquired additional features, however, such as legs and arms, lungs became essential. So, contrary to what Behe would have us believe, the parts of an irreducibly complex system need not have come into existence all at once."[13]

Exercise 11.6

Read the following passage about a study conducted on the use of vitamin C to treat cancer. Identify the hypothesis being tested, the consequences (test implication) used to test it, and whether the hypothesis was confirmed or disconfirmed.

PASSAGE 1

"In 1978, the Mayo Clinic embarked on a prospective, controlled, double-blind study designed to test Pauling and Cameron's claims [for the effectiveness of vitamin C]. Each patient in this study had biopsy-proven cancer that was considered incurable and unsuitable for further chemotherapy, surgery, or radiation. The patients were randomized to receive 10 grams of vitamin C per day or a comparably flavored lactose placebo. All patients took a glycerin-coated capsule four times a day.

"The patients were carefully selected so that those vitamin C and placebo groups were equally matched. There were 60 patients in the vitamin C group and 63 in the placebo group. The age distributions were similar. There was a slight predominance of males, but the ratio of males to females was virtually identical. Performance status was measured using the Eastern Cooperative Oncology Group Scale, a clinical scale well recognized by cancer researchers. Most study patients had some disability from their disease, but only a small proportion were bedridden. Most patients had advanced gastrointestinal or lung cancer. Almost all had received chemotherapy, and a smaller proportion had undergone radiation therapy.

"The results were noteworthy. About 25% of patients in both groups showed some improvement in appetite. Forty-two percent of the patients on placebo alone experienced enhancement of their level of activity. About 40% of the patients experienced mild nausea and vomiting, but the two groups had no statistically significant differences in the number of episodes. There were no survival differences between patients receiving vitamin C and those receiving the placebo. The median survival time was approximately seven weeks from the onset of therapy. The longest surviving patient in this trial had received the placebo. Overall, the study showed no benefit from vitamin C."[14]

Science and Weird Theories

What good is science and inference to the best explanation in the realm that seems to lie *beyond* common sense and scientific inquiry—the zone of the extraordinary, the paranormal, and the supernatural? In this land of the wonderfully weird—the interesting and mysterious domain of UFOs, ESP, ghosts, psychic predictions, tarot card readings, and the like—exactly what work can science do?

From reading Chapter 10, you probably have already guessed that science and critical reasoning can be as useful in assessing weird claims as they are in sizing up mundane ones. Inference to the best explanation—whether wielded in science or everyday life—can be successfully applied to extraordinary theories of all kinds. Fortunately for critical thinkers, the TEST formula outlined in Chapter 10 for finding the best theoretical explanation is not afraid of ghosts, monsters, or space aliens. In the next few pages, we will get a good demonstration of these points by examining some extraordinary theories in much greater detail than we have previously.

Science has always been interested in the mysterious, and from time to time it has also ventured into the weird. In the past 150 years, scientists have tested spiritualism, clairvoyance, telepathy, telekinesis (moving physical objects with the mind alone), astrology, dowsing, the Loch Ness monster, faith healing, fire walking, and more. Among these we should also count some bizarre phenomena that scientists never tire of studying—black holes, alternative dimensions of space, and the microworld of subatomic particles (the weirdest of the weird) where the laws of physics are crazy enough to make Alice in Wonderland scream.

But why should anyone bother to learn how to evaluate weird claims in the first place? Well, for one thing, they are widely believed (see accompanying box) and often difficult to ignore. They are, after all, heavily promoted in countless television programs, movies, books, magazines, and tabloids. And—like claims in politics, medicine, and many other fields—they can dramatically affect people's lives, for better or worse. It's important then for anyone confronted with such popular and influential claims to be able to assess them carefully.

In addition, if you really care whether an extraordinary claim is true or false, there is no substitute for the kind of critical evaluation discussed here. Accepting (or rejecting) a weird claim solely because it's weird will not do. A horselaugh is not an argument, and neither is a sneer. Weird claims often turn out to be false, and, as the history of science shows, they sometimes surprise everyone by being true.

Making Weird Mistakes

So in science and in our own lives, the critical assessment of weird theories is possible—but that doesn't mean the process is without risks. It's easy for a scientist or anyone else to err when thinking about extraordinary claims. Weird claims and experiences have a way of provoking strong emotions, preconceived attitudes, and long-held biases. In the world of the weird, people (including scientists and other experts) are often prone to the kinds of errors in reasoning we discussed in Chapter 4, including resisting contrary evidence, looking for confirming evidence, and preferring available evidence. Those who contemplate extraordinary things also seem to be especially susceptible to the following errors.

Leaping to the Weirdest Theory

When people have an extraordinary experience, they usually try to make sense of it. They may have a seemingly prophetic dream, see a ghostly shape in the dark, watch their astrologer's prediction come true, think that they've witnessed a miracle, or feel that they have somehow lived another life centuries ago. Then they cast about for an explanation for such experiences. And when they cannot think of a natural explanation, they often conclude that the explanation must be paranormal or supernatural. This line of reasoning is common but fallacious. *Just because you can't think of a natural explanation doesn't mean that there isn't one.* You may just be ignorant of the correct explanation. Throughout history, scientists have often been confronted with astonishing phenomena that they could not explain in natural terms at the time. But they didn't assume that the phenomena must be paranormal or supernatural. They simply kept investigating—and they eventually found natural explanations. Comets, solar eclipses, meteors, mental illness, infectious diseases, and epilepsy were all once thought to be supernatural or paranormal but were later found through scientific investigation to have natural explanations. When confronted then with a phenomenon that you don't understand, the most reasonable response is to search for a natural explanation.

The fallacious leap to a nonnatural explanation is an example of the appeal to ignorance discussed in Chapter 6. People think that since a paranormal or supernatural explanation has not been shown to be false, it must be true. This line, though logically fallacious, can be very persuasive.

The failure to consider alternative explanations is probably the most common error in assessing paranormal claims. As we've seen, this failure can be willful: People can refuse to consider

"TELL THEM ABOUT YOUR PSORIASIS, BETTY. MAYBE THEY CAN CURE IT."

Harley Schwadron.

seriously a viable alternative. But honest and intelligent people can also simply be unaware of possible natural explanations. Looking for alternative explanations requires imagination and a deliberate attempt to "think outside the box."

Mixing What Seems with What Is

Sometimes people leap prematurely to an extraordinary theory by ignoring this elementary principle: *Just because something seems real doesn't mean that it is.* Because of the nature of our perceptual equipment and processes, we humans are bound to have many experiences in which something appears to be real but

 REVIEW NOTES

Common Errors in Evaluating Extraordinary Theories

1. Believing that just because you can't think of a natural explanation, a phenomenon must be paranormal.
2. Thinking that just because something *seems* real, it *is* real. (A better principle: It's reasonable to accept the evidence provided by personal experience only if there's no good reason to doubt it.)
3. Misunderstanding logical possibility and physical possibility. Also, believing that if something is logically possible, it must be actual.

is not. The corrective for mistaking the unreal for the real is applying another important principle that we discussed in Chapter 4: It's reasonable to accept the evidence provided by personal experience only if there's no good reason to doubt it. We have reason to doubt if our perceptual abilities are impaired (we are under stress, drugged, afraid, excited, etc.), we have strong expectations about a particular experience (we strongly expect to see a UFO or hear spooky noises, for example), and observations are made under poor conditions (the stimuli are vague and ambiguous or the environment is too dark, too noisy, too hazy, etc.). Scientists can falter here just as anyone else can, which is why they try to use research methods that minimize reasons for doubt.

Misunderstanding the Possibilities

Debates about weird theories often turn on the ideas of possibility and impossibility. Skeptics may dismiss a weird theory by saying, "That's impossible!" Believers may insist that a state of affairs is indeed possible, or they may proclaim, *"Anything* is possible!" Such protestations, however, are often based on misunderstandings.

The experts on the subject of possibility (namely, philosophers) often talk about *logical possibility* and *logical impossibility*. Something is logically impossible if it violates a principle of logic (that is, it involves a logical contradiction). Something is logically possible if it does not violate a principle of logic (does not involve a logical contradiction). Anything that is logically impossible can't exist. We know, for example, that there are no married bachelors because these things involve logical contradictions (male humans who are both married and not married). Likewise we know that there are no square circles because they involve logical contradictions (things that are both circles and not circles). We must conclude from all this that, despite what some people sincerely believe, it is not the case that anything is possible. If a weird phenomenon is logically impossible, we needn't investigate it further because it can't exist. Most alleged paranormal phenomena, however, are not logically impossible. ESP, UFOs, reincarnation, dowsing, spontaneous human combustion, out-of-body experiences, and many more generally do not involve any logical contradiction.

Philosophers also refer to *physical possibility* and *physical impossibility*. Something is said to be physically impossible if it violates a law of science. We know that traveling faster than the speed of light is physically impossible because such an occurrence violates a law of science. Perpetual motion machines are physically impossible because they violate the law of science known as the conservation of mass-energy. Thus, scientists are skeptical of any extraordinary phenomenon that is said to be physically impossible.

Yet whether an event violates a law of nature is very difficult—perhaps impossible—to prove. The philosopher of science Theodore Schick Jr. explains why:

> No event . . . can provide sufficient grounds for believing that a miracle [a violation of scientific law] has occurred, because its seeming impossibility may simply be due to our ignorance of the operative laws. . . . We would be justified in believing that an apparent violation of a natural law was a

miracle only if we were justified in believing that no natural law would ever be discovered to explain the occurrence. But we can never be justified in believing that, because no one can be sure what the future will bring. We can't rule out the possibility that a natural explanation will be found for an event, no matter how incredible.[15]

Some things that are logically possible are physically impossible. It's logically possible for Vaughn's dog to fly to another galaxy in sixty seconds. This astounding performance does not violate a principle of logic. But it does violate laws of science pertaining to speed-of-light travel and gravitation. It is therefore physically impossible. The upshot of all this is that, contrary to what some people would have us believe, if something is logically possible, that doesn't mean it's physically possible. That is, if something is logically possible, that doesn't mean it's actual. Many logically possible things may not be real.

Judging Weird Theories

Now let's do a detailed evaluation of two extraordinary theories using the TEST formula from Chapter 10. Recall the procedure's four steps:

Step 1. State the theory and check for consistency.
Step 2. Assess the evidence for the theory.
Step 3. Scrutinize alternative theories.
Step 4. Test the theories with the criteria of adequacy.

Science uses such a procedure to assess all manner of extraordinary explanations, and—by proceeding carefully and systematically—so can you.

Crop Circles

Crop circles are large-scale geometric designs pressed or stamped into fields of grain. They are often circular but can be almost any shape, ranging from simple patterns to complex pictograms or symbols. They can measure a few feet

People have been faking UFO photos for decades, insisting the pictures showed the genuine article and attracting a lot of publicity and true believers. This, despite the ease of making fakes. Astronomer Tom Callen created these two with a camera, some UFO models, and Paint Shop Pro. Do these images look as authentic as those you've seen in TV documentaries purporting to have photographic proof of UFOs?

in diameter or span the length of several football fields. Interest in crop circles began in the 1970s when they started mysteriously appearing overnight in the grain fields of southern England. The crops would be neatly flattened with the stalks pressed together and sometimes impressively interlaced. In the 1980s and 1990s, interest in the phenomenon grew as crop circles proliferated throughout the world, showing up in Europe, Africa, Australia, the United States, and elsewhere. In 2002 Hollywood got into the act by releasing the movie *Signs* starring Mel Gibson. He plays a Pennsylvania farmer who discovers massive crop circles in his fields and is soon drawn into encounters with extraterrestrial beings.

From the beginning, crop circles have been both intriguing and controversial. The controversy has centered mostly on one question: What theory best explains the existence of crop circles? Many explanations for the cause of the phenomenon have been offered and debated, with plenty of people making the case for their favorite theory through books, magazine articles, and, of course, the Internet. Let's examine some of these theories and see if we can separate the good from the bad.

Step 1. We begin with a theory that has gotten a great deal of attention from skeptics and believers alike.

Theory 1: Crop circles are created by small whirlwinds of electrified air (a.k.a. wind vortices). The idea here is that crop circles are made by columns of whirling, charged air similar to dust devils or miniature tornadoes. These vortices form above grain fields and then plunge to the ground, discharging the electricity and flattening the grain in swirled patterns. But unlike tornadoes, wind vortices leave the stalks of grain undamaged.

Step 2. What is the evidence for this theory? The evidence is indirect. Natural crop-circle vortices are unknown to science, but similar vortices are reported to have been produced artificially in laboratories. A few people claim to have seen the vortices in open fields. An electrified vortex might produce light during discharge, and sure enough, eyewitnesses have reported seeing "balls of light" and other light phenomena in or near crop circles. Many crop-circle enthusiasts (known as "cereologists" or "croppies") have photographed what they claim are mysterious lights near crop circles, and the photographs show impressive balls of light and strange glowing arcs. Some croppies also report hearing strange sounds near crop circles (humming noises, for example). Finally, some cereologists have reported that the plants in crop circles differ anatomically from those outside the circles. The joints in stalks, for example, may be bigger in crop-circle plants than in plants growing elsewhere.

The Art of Crop Circles

To many people, crop circles are the work of space aliens, or the result of natural processes, or the mischievous doings of pranksters. But to some, crop circles are an art form. Every year in Britain, serious artists hit the fields and, under cover of darkness, create crop-circle formations that are elegant enough to hang in a museum—if they would fit. John Lundberg, a graphic design artist, is one of these artistic circle makers.

Who—or what—is the artist?

[Lundberg's] group, known as the Circlemakers, considers their practice an art. Lundberg estimates that there are three or four dedicated crop circle art groups operating in the United Kingdom today, and numerous other small groups that make one or two circles a year more or less as a lark.

Circlemakers [www.circlemakers.org] now does quite a bit of commercial work; in early July, the group created a giant crop formation 140 feet (46 meters) in diameter for the History Channel. But they also still do covert work in the dead of night.

Formulating a design and a plan, from original concept to finished product, can take up to a week. "It has to be more than a pretty picture. You have to have construction diagrams providing the measurements, marking the center, and so on," said Lundberg. Creating the art is the work of a night. . . .

"You think about art in terms of authorship and signature," he said. But circle makers never claim credit for specific formations they created. "To do so would drain the mystery of crop circles," he explained. "The art form isn't just about the pattern making. The myths and folklore and energy [that] people give them are part of the art."

Over the last 25 years, the formations have evolved from simple, relatively small circles to huge designs with multiple circles, elaborate pictograms, and shapes that invoke complex non-linear mathematical principles. A formation that appeared in August 2001 at Milk Hill in Wiltshire contained 409 circles, covered about five hectares, and was more than 800 feet (243 meters) across.[16]

This evidence, however, is weak. Producing a vortex in a laboratory does not prove that it exists "in the wild." In fact, there is no good evidence that crop-circle vortices exist in nature. As with most unfamiliar and provocative phenomena, eyewitness accounts of vortices are generally unreliable, especially since people generally don't know what a true crop-circle vortex looks like. Sightings of various light phenomena are not direct evidence for the existence of vortices because they can be explained in alternative ways. The lights could come from many other sources, including ball lightning (a documented phenomenon), commercial aircraft, military aircraft, the parachute flares of pranksters, and the flashlights of people making crop circles (there are plenty of people who make crop circles as hoaxes or works of art). The photographs of light phenomena also have alternative explanations. The arcs and balls of light in these photos can be easily produced when the flash reflects off of the camera strap, insects, droplets of water, and the like. Photos of weird lights are also easily faked. Reports of strange sounds, like the reports of weird lights, are not good evidence of vortices at work because the sounds could have several alternative causes (farm machinery, wind, etc.). And even if there are anatomical differences between crop-circle plants and noncircle plants, this would not show that crop circles are made by vortices. At most, it would suggest only that crop-circle plants are different, however the circles are made. (This same point applies to claims about other kinds of differences between crop-circle areas and noncircle locations, including alleged magnetic or soil anomalies. The anomalies, if they exist, do not confirm that crop circles are made in any particular way.)

The biggest problem for the crop-circle vortex theory is that it doesn't explain the evidence. The theory seems adequate to explain circular crop-circle designs (a whirlwind would seem to be just the thing to make a circle on the ground), but not all crop circles are circular. Many are incredibly complex amalgams of squares, triangles, straight lines, and shapes that have no names.

Step 3. Now let's examine a popular alternative theory.

Theory 2: Crop circles are made by extraterrestrial beings (space aliens). This explanation asserts only that crop circles are the work of aliens; it does not specify how the aliens do it. The circles could be created by alien spacecraft, energy beams from space, or "thought energy" from places unknown. This theory has seemed plausible to some people in light of the intricacy and beauty of crop-circle pictograms, with a few croppies insisting that aliens must be communicating in geometrical language. To some, the circles have seemed much too complicated and elegant to be the result of human ingenuity.

The evidence for this alien explanation? The elegant complexity of crop circles has been thought to be pretty good support for the theory. Who else but aliens would create such brilliant masterpieces on such a large scale—masterpieces that are best viewed from the air or space

"Bloody hell! Crap circles."

I Confess: I'm a Crop-Circle Prankster

Other than to make great art, why would anyone want to go skulking around in the night to make crop circles in someone's wheat field? Maybe this confession from an unrepentant circle-maker will clear things up:

I made my first crop circle in 1991. My motive was to prove how easy they were to create, because I was convinced that all crop circles were man-made. It was the only explanation nobody seemed interested in testing. Late one August night, with one accomplice—my brother-in-law from Texas—I stepped into a field of nearly ripe wheat in northern England, anchored a rope into the ground with a spike and began walking in a circle with the rope held near the ground. It did not work very well: the rope rode up over the plants. But with a bit of help from our feet to hold down the rope, we soon had a respectable circle of flattened wheat.

Two days later there was an excited call to the authorities from the local farmer: I had fooled my first victim. I subsequently made two more crop circles using far superior techniques. A light garden roller, designed to be filled with water, proved helpful. Next, I hit on the "plank walking" technique that was used by the original circle makers, Doug Bower and the late Dave Chorley, who started it all in 1978. It's done by pushing down the crop with a plank suspended from two ropes. To render the depression circular is a simple matter of keeping an anchored rope taut. I soon found that I could make a sophisticated pattern with very neat edges in less than an hour.

Getting into the field without leaving traces is a lot easier than is usually claimed. In dry weather, and if you step carefully, you can leave no footprints or tracks at all. There are other, even stealthier ways of getting into the crop. One group of circle makers uses two tall bar stools, jumping from one to another.

But to my astonishment, throughout the early 1990s the media continued to report that it was impossible that all crop circles could be man-made. They cited "cereologists"—those who study crop circles—and never checked for themselves. There were said to be too many circles to be the work of a few "hoaxers" (but this assumed that each circle took many hours to make), or that circles appeared in well-watched crops (simply not true), or that circle creation was accompanied by unearthly noises (when these sounds were played back, even I recognized the nocturnal song of the grasshopper warbler).[17]

itself? A few people have announced that they found very intricate mathematics in the more elaborate crop-circle designs. Also, some have reported seeing odd lights in the vicinity of crop circles, and others have claimed that they saw actual alien craft in the night sky not far from the crop-circle fields. A few cereologists have even claimed that they caught sight of UFOs in the process of making crop circles.

This evidence, however, is problematic and has some of the same weaknesses as the wind vortex evidence. The complexity and beauty of crop circles do not lend support to the alien theory because the artistry of the crop formations has an obvious alternative explanation: Humans made them. There are numerous documented cases of humans—either hoaxers or artists—creating stunningly exquisite and elaborate crop circles, some with plenty of mathematics built in. Because the human artist explanation is at least as plausible as the alien artist one, the artistic or intellectual impressiveness of crop circles can give no weight to the alien theory. As mentioned earlier, light phenomena near crop circles also have alternative explanations. Nighttime UFO sightings might seem to be good evidence that aliens are up to something. But they are susceptible to many of the doubt-producing factors that we discussed in Chapter 4: darkness, ambiguous stimuli, lack of cues to the true position and size of moving objects, perceptual construction, stress, strong emotions, expectancy, and more. Eyewitness reports of aliens actually constructing crop circles constitute very weak evidence for theory 2. Such extraordinary reports require reliable corroborating evidence, but no alien activity of any kind has ever been scientifically documented, despite allegations to the contrary.

Many people favor a more down-to-earth theory.

Theory 3: Crop circles are made by humans using ordinary means. This explanation encompasses the creation of crop circles by hoaxers, artists, or any other humans. The relevant evidence suggests that many crop circles have indeed been produced by humans. In 1991 two English artists with a sense of humor, Doug Bower and Dave Chorley, declared that they had been making crop circles for years to fool gullible people who believed in UFOs. They demonstrated their circle-making skills for reporters and television audiences, easily producing very elaborate crop circles in a short time. To create their designs, they used only ropes and planks. They showed that crop circles thought to be way beyond human ability were in fact made by humans using incredibly simple techniques. Their formations fooled many people including at least one prominent cereologist. Many circle-watchers conceded that human hoaxers were making crop circles and that distinguishing "true" circles from fake ones is no cinch. A leading cereologist admitted that 80 percent of crop circles in Britain were made by humans.

It is clear, however, that Bower and Chorley could not have created all the known crop circles. From southern England, crop-circle creation spread all over the globe, appearing in increasing numbers. This spread of the phenomenon, though, seemed to correlate with increased international media coverage of crop circles, suggesting that other humans may have been inspired to

"It is easier to attribute UFO sightings to the known irrationalities of terrestrials than to the unknown efforts of extraterrestrials."
—**Richard Feynman**

copy English circle-making. In addition, many artists have been fascinated by the aesthetics of crop circles and have generated their own masterpieces in grain.

Croppies have argued that humans can't be responsible for some crop circles because there are often no signs of human activity at formation sites (no footprints, paths through the grain, etc.). But as the circle-building of hoaxers suggests, crop circles can be produced by humans without leaving evidence of human activity behind. Hoaxers, for example, can often avoid leaving footprints in a grain field by walking along tramlines, the narrow footpaths created by farm machinery.

Also, as suggested earlier, physical anomalies in crop-circle plants or soil do not prove that crop circles are made in any particular way. It's possible that anomalies are produced by the techniques used in human circle-making. Some have suggested, for example, that enlarged joints in grain stalks are the result of the bent stalks baking in the hot sun.

Step 4. Now let's see what happens when we apply the criteria of adequacy to these three theories. Theories 1 and 3 seem equal in terms of testability. Both predict something other than what they were introduced to explain. Theory 1, for example, predicts that in the creation of a crop circle, an electrified vortex forms above the formation area—something that should be detectable by the right kind of scientific instruments. Theory 3 is certainly testable because human activity is detectable and measurable. Theory 2 (aliens) may or may not be testable, depending on how alien activity is construed. We will give the theory the benefit of the doubt and say that it too is testable.

Theories 1 and 2 are not fruitful, for they have yielded no surprising predictions. We could argue, though, that theory 3 is fruitful because the creation of specific crop circles at designated times and places has been successfully predicted by hoaxers (the ones who created the circles).

In terms of scope, on the one hand, neither theory 1 nor 2 gets any points. The vortex theory does not explain anything other than the creation of crop circles. Theory 2 could be construed as explaining many things in which aliens are involved (UFO sightings, abductions, UFO crashes, etc.). But positing the existence of mysterious beings that act in mysterious ways for mysterious reasons does not seem to explain much of anything. Theory 3, on the other hand, can be used to explain many strange phenomena because humans, after all, are responsible for many hoaxes and bizarre happenings.

As far as simplicity is concerned, theories 1 and 2 are in deep trouble. Like most paranormal explanations, they both posit the existence of unknown entities (charged, naturally occurring vortices and space aliens). Theory 3 sticks with known entities and processes.

On the criterion of conservatism, theories 1 and 2 are again in trouble. There is no good evidence that the hypothesized vortex has ever occurred anywhere. And we have no good reason to believe that either space aliens or alien technology has ever visited Earth, let alone created some nice designs in a wheat field.

Eyewitness Testimony and Extraordinary Things

A great deal of the evidence for paranormal phenomena is eyewitness testimony. Unfortunately, research suggests that eyewitness testimony generally can't be trusted—especially when the testimony concerns the paranormal. For example, in some studies people who had participated in seances later gave wildly inaccurate descriptions of what had transpired. Researchers have found that people's beliefs and expectations seem to play a big role in the unreliability of testimony about the paranormal.

> Different people clearly have different beliefs and expectations prior to observing a supposed psychic—skeptics might expect to see some kind of trickery; believers may expect a display of genuine psi [parapsychological phenomena]. Some seventy years ago Eric Dingwall in Britain speculated that such expectations may distort eyewitness testimony: The frame of mind in which a person goes to see magic and to a medium cannot be compared. In one case he goes either purely for amusement or possibly with the idea of discovering "how it was done," whilst in the other he usually goes with the thought that it is possible that he will come into direct contact with the other world.
>
> Recent experimental evidence suggests that Dingwall's speculations are correct.
>
> Wiseman and Morris in Britain carried out two studies investigating the effect that belief in the paranormal has on the observation of conjuring tricks. Individuals taking part in the experiment were first asked several questions concerning their belief in the paranormal. On the basis of their answers they were classified as either believers (labeled "sheep") or skeptics (labeled "goats").
>
> In both experiments individuals were first shown a film containing fake psychic demonstrations. In the first demonstration the "psychic" apparently bent a key by concentrating on it; in the second demonstration he supposedly bent a spoon simply by rubbing it.
>
> After they watched the film, witnesses were asked to rate the "paranormal" content of the demonstrations and complete a set of recall questions. Wiseman and Morris wanted to discover if, as Hodgson and Dingwall had suggested, sheep really did tend to misremember those parts of the demonstrations that were central to solving the tricks. For this reason, half of the questions concerned the methods used to fake the phenomena. For example, the psychic faked the key-bending demonstration by secretly switching the straight key for a pre-bent duplicate by passing the straight key from

one hand to the other. During the switch the straight key could not be seen. This was clearly central to the trick's method; and one of the "important" questions asked was whether the straight key had always remained in sight. A second set of "unimportant" questions asked about parts of the demonstration that were not related to the tricks' methods. Overall, the results suggested that sheep rated the demonstrations as more "paranormal" than goats did, and that goats did indeed recall significantly more "important" information than sheep. There was no such difference for the recall of the "unimportant" information.[18]

We can summarize these judgments as in the following table:

Criteria	Vortices	Aliens	Humans
Testable	Yes	Yes	Yes
Fruitful	No	No	Yes
Scope	No	No	Yes
Simple	No	No	Yes
Conservative	No	No	Yes

We can see immediately that the three theories are equal in testability, but theory 3 wins on all other counts. It is clearly the superior theory. Both the vortex theory and the alien theory fail the test of fruitfulness, scope, simplicity, and conservatism. Of these four criteria, simplicity and conservatism carry the most weight here. In general, the plausibility of a theory is weakened considerably when it posits unknown entities and processes. Likewise, a theory that doesn't fit with what we already know takes a hit in credibility. An unconservative theory, of course, can acquire some credibility if it excels in the other criteria of adequacy. But theories 1 and 2 fall short in all the criteria except testability. We can see then that theories 1 and 2 are not good explanations for crop circles. They are most likely false. Theory 3—human creation of crop circles—is a much better theory.

There are other crop-circle theories that we haven't examined. None of them seems to measure up to the criteria of adequacy as well as theory 3 does. If this is the case, then we can give an even stronger endorsement of theory 3: Crop circles are probably human-made.

Talking with the Dead

Some people claim that they can communicate with the dead, providing impressive and seemingly accurate information about a person's dead loved ones. They are called psychics (a century ago they were called mediums), and they have gained the respect of many who have come to them in search of messages from the deceased. They have appeared on television programs, published books, and offered seminars to thousands. The most famous among these modern-day mediums are psychics James Van Praagh and John Edward. Their performances assure many people that their loved ones who "have passed over" are fine and that any unsettled issues of guilt and forgiveness can be resolved.

What is the best explanation for these otherworldly performances in which the psychics appear to be in contact with the dead? Several theories have been proposed. One is that the psychics are getting information about the dead and their loved ones ahead of time (before the performances begin). Another is that the psychics are using telepathy to read the minds of the living to discover facts about the dead. But for simplicity's sake let's narrow the list of theories down to the two leading ones.

Step 1. Here's the psychics' theory.

Theory 1: The psychics are communicating information or messages to and from the disembodied spirits of people who have died. In other words, the psychics are doing exactly what they claim to be doing. They are somehow identifying the appropriate deceased spirit, receiving and decoding transmissions from that spirit, conveying the information to the living, and sending messages back to the dead.

Step 2. The main evidence in support of this theory is the psychics' performance. They typically perform before an audience and talk to audience members who have lost loved ones. The psychics appear to know facts about the dead that they could only know if they were actually communicating with the dead. They also seem to inexplicably know things about members of the audience. Often they also provide incorrect information (such as saying that a member of the audience has lost her mother when in fact the mother is very much alive). But their "hits" (times when they produce correct information) occur often enough and seem to be specific enough to impress.

Psychics have rarely been tested scientifically. The few experiments conducted to date have been severely criticized for sloppy methodology. So there is no good scientific evidence to support theory 1. Investigators who have seen the psychics' live performances (not just the edited versions of the TV programs) report that the hit rates (the percentage of hits out of the total number of statements or questions) are actually much lower than most people realize. They have found hit rates as low as 5 percent, with the highest being well under 50 percent. The low hit rate, though, may not be apparent on TV shows because misses are often edited out. Psychics tend to explain their misses with ad hoc hypotheses (explanations that cannot be verified).

Step 3. Here's the main alternative to the psychics' theory.

Theory 2: The psychics are doing "cold reading." Cold reading is a very old skill practiced by fortune-tellers, tarot-card readers, and mentalists (performers who pretend to read minds). When done well, cold reading can astonish and appear to be paranormal. In cold reading, the psychic reader surreptitiously acquires information from people (the subjects) by asking them questions, making

> ". . . we [psychics] are here to heal people and to help people grow . . . skeptics . . . they're just here to destroy people. They're not here to encourage people, to enlighten people. They're here to destroy people."
> **—James Van Praagh**

Psychic John Edward.

Why People Believe Psychic Readings

Ray Hyman was professor emeritus of psychology at the University of Oregon and an expert on the scientific investigation of paranormal claims, including psychic readings. Years of research led him to be skeptical of the validity of psychic readings, but he used to be a true believer. He explained why he went from believer to skeptic:

> Now it so happens that I have devoted more than half a century to the study of psychic and cold readings. I have been especially concerned with why such readings can seem so concrete and compelling, even to skeptics. As a way to earn extra income, I began reading palms when I was in my teens. At first, I was skeptical. I thought that people believed in palmistry and other divination procedures because they could easily fit very general statements to their particular situation. To establish credibility with my clients, I read books on palmistry and gave readings according to the accepted interpretations for the lines, shape of the fingers, mounds, and other indicators. I was astonished by the reactions of my clients. My clients consistently praised me for my accuracy even when I told them very specific things about problems with their health and other personal matters. I even would get phone calls from clients telling me that a prediction that I had made for them had come true. Within months of my entry into palm reading, I became a staunch believer in its validity. My conviction was so strong that I convinced my skeptical high school English teacher by giving him readings and arguing with him. I later also convinced the head of the psychology department where I was an undergraduate.
>
> When I was a sophomore, majoring in journalism, a well-known mentalist and trusted friend persuaded me to try an experiment in which I would deliberately read a client's hand opposite to what the signs in her hand indicated. I was shocked to discover that this client insisted that this was the most accurate reading she had ever experienced. As a result, I carried out more experiments with the same outcome. It dawned on me that something important was going on. Whatever it was, it had nothing to do with the lines in the

HEART

HEAD

LIFE

What is this palm saying? Psychologists think they know.

"Death is a part of life, and pretending that the dead are gathering in a television studio in New York to talk twaddle with a former ballroom-dance instructor is an insult to the intelligence and humanity of the living."

—Michael Shermer

hand. I changed my major from journalism to psychology so that I could learn why not only other people, but also I, could be so badly led astray. My subsequent career has focused on the reasons why cold readings can appear to be so compelling and seemingly specific. Psychologists have uncovered a number of factors that can make an ambiguous reading seem highly specific, unique, and uncannily accurate. And once the observer or client has been struck with the apparent accuracy of the reading, it becomes virtually impossible to dislodge the belief in the uniqueness and specificity of the reading. Research from many areas demonstrates this finding. The principles go under such names as the fallacy of personal validation, subjective validation, confirmation bias, belief perseverance, the illusion of invulnerability, compliance, demand characteristics, false uniqueness effect, foot-in-the-door phenomenon, illusory correlation, integrative agreements, self-reference effect, the principle of individuation, and many, many others. Much of this is facilitated by the illusion of specificity that surrounds language. All language is inherently ambiguous and depends much more than we realize upon the context and nonlinguistic cues to fix its meaning in a given situation.[19]

"Ahh.. I see your future. Get up, go to work go to bed. Get up, go to work, go to bed. Get..."

www.CartoonStock.com

statements, observing how people behave, and listening to what they say. Good cold readers always give the impression that the information actually comes from some mysterious source such as the spirits of the departed. Anyone can learn to do cold reading. It doesn't require any exotic skills or special powers. All that's needed is the practiced ability to deftly manipulate a conversation to elicit information from the subject.

Note that theory 2 does not say that the cold reading is necessarily done to deliberately deceive an audience. Cold reading can be done either consciously or unconsciously. It's possible for people to do cold reading while believing that they are getting information via their psychic powers.

To get the relevant information (or appear to have it), a psychic reader can use several cold-reading techniques. These include the following.

1. The reader encourages the subject to fill in the blanks.

   READER: I'm sensing something about the face or head or brow.
   SUBJECT: You're right, my father used to have terrible headaches.

READER: I'm feeling something about money or finances.

SUBJECT: Yes, my mother always struggled to pay the bills.

2. The reader makes statements with multiple variables so that a hit is very likely.

READER: I'm feeling that your father was dealing with a lot of frustration, anguish, or anger.

SUBJECT: Yes, he was always arguing with my brother.

3. The reader makes accurate and obvious inferences from information given by the subject.

READER: Why was your father in the hospital?

SUBJECT: He had had a heart attack.

READER: Yes, he struggled with heart disease for years and had to take heart medication for a long time. You were really worried that he would have another heart attack.

4. The reader asks many questions and treats answers as though they confirmed the reader's insight.

READER: Who was the person who got a divorce?

SUBJECT: That was my daughter. She divorced her husband in 1992.

READER: Because I feel that the divorce was very painful for her, that she was sad and depressed for a while.

5. The reader makes statements that could apply to almost anyone.

READER: I'm sensing something about a cat or a small animal.

SUBJECT: Yes, my mother owned a poodle.

With such cold-reading techniques a reader can appear to read minds. Theory 2 is bolstered by the fact that the psychics' amazing performances can be duplicated by anyone skilled in the use of cold reading. In fact, magicians, mentalists, and other nonpsychic entertainers have used cold-reading techniques to give performances that rival those of the top psychics. Regardless of their authenticity, the performances of Van Praagh, Edward, and other psychics seem to be indistinguishable from those based on cold reading. The psychics may indeed be communicating with the dead, but they look like they're using cold-reading techniques.

Step 4. Now we can apply the criteria of adequacy to these two competing explanations. Both theories are testable, and neither has yielded any novel predictions. So we must judge the theories in terms of scope, simplicity, and conservatism. And on each of these criteria, theory 2 is clearly superior. Theory 1 explains only the psychics' performances as described earlier, but theory 2 explains these performances plus other kinds of seemingly psychic readings, including tarot-card reading, fortune-telling, mentalist acts, and old-fashioned spiritualist seances. Theory 1, of course, fails the criterion of simplicity because it assumes unknown entities (disembodied spirits with certain abilities) and unknown processes (communication to and from the dead). Theory 2 makes no such assumptions. Finally, theory 1 is not conservative. It conflicts with everything we know about death, the mind, and communication. Theory 2, though, fits with existing knowledge just fine.

Here are these judgments in table form:

Criteria	Theory 1	Theory 2
Testable	Yes	Yes
Fruitful	No	No
Scope	No	Yes
Simple	No	Yes
Conservative	No	Yes

We must conclude that theory 1 is a seriously defective theory. It is unlikely to be true. Theory 2, however, is strong. It is not only superior to theory 1, but also a better explanation than other competing theories we haven't discussed in that it can explain most or all of the psychics' hits. If the cold-reading theory really is better than all these others, then we have good reasons to believe that Van Praagh, Edward, and other psychics perform their amazing feats through simple cold reading.

EXERCISES

Exercise 11.7

1. Is it reasonable to accept or reject an extraordinary claim solely because of its weirdness?
2. What are the five steps of the scientific method?
3. Is it reasonable to conclude that a phenomenon is paranormal just because you cannot think of a natural explanation?
* 4. The fallacious leap to a nonnatural explanation is an example of what logical fallacy?
5. According to the text, what is the critical thinking principle that can help you avoid mistaking how something seems for how something is?
* 6. What is logical possibility? Logical impossibility?
7. What is physical possibility? Physical impossibility?
8. Are dogs that lay eggs logically possible?
9. Is anything possible? If not, why not?
10. What is the four-step method for evaluating a theory?
11. What is the difference between science and technology?
12. What is scientism?
13. What is a placebo, and how is it used in scientific experiments?
14. What is the Copernican theory of planetary motion?
15. How reliable is eyewitness testimony? Under what circumstance are eyewitness accounts most likely to be inaccurate?

Exercise 11.8

In each of the following examples, a state of affairs is described. Devise three theories to explain each one. Include two plausible theories that are natural explanations and one competing theory that is paranormal.

1. Jack spent the night in a hotel that had a reputation for being haunted. He slept in the very room (number 666) in which a horrible murder had been committed in the 1930s. He fell asleep thinking about the crime. At 3:00 a.m. he awoke to see the apparition of a man sitting at the foot of his bed.

*2. Jacques lived in a house built back in the 1940s which was now in disrepair. As he sat reading in the parlor, he heard creaking sounds coming from upstairs.

3. Selena found herself thinking about the camping trip that she went on in Pennsylvania. She was remembering the morning she woke up to find her tent crawling with ladybugs. As she was pondering the ladybugs, she suddenly noticed a ladybug on the windowsill near her chair.

4. Some people report that in the past when they needed help in a risky situation (for example, when they were in a car accident or when they were lost in a crime-ridden neighborhood), they were aided by a stranger who never gave his or her name and who left the scene quickly after rendering assistance. They claim that the stranger must have been their guardian angel.

5. According to a recent survey, 38 percent of Americans believe in ghosts or spirits of the dead.

6. Lil's horoscope said that she would meet someone interesting. Three days after reading it, she did.

*7. Leroy dreamed that his uncle was killed in Iraq when he stepped on a land mine. When Leroy woke up, he got a call from his mother saying that his uncle had been injured in a car accident in Baghdad.

8. Eleanor has a reputation for acting strangely. Recently when her priest came to visit her in her home, she fell to the floor writhing with convulsions.

9. Nelly made a fresh batch of tortillas. On one of them she noticed that the scorch marks were unusual. She was sure that she could see the face of Jesus in the design made by the scorch marks.

10. Ali was not feeling well. He heard that a crazy woman in his village had put a curse on him because he called her a witch. The next day Ali broke his arm when he slipped and fell against some rocks.

Exercise 11.9

Using your background knowledge and any other information you may have about the subject, devise a competing, naturalistic theory for each paranormal theory that follows, and then apply the criteria of adequacy to both of them—that is, ascertain how well each theory does in relation to its competitor on the criteria of testability, fruitfulness, scope, simplicity, and conservatism.

1. Phenomenon: George and Jan have been married for twenty years. Many times George seems to know exactly what Jan is thinking, as though he could read her mind.

   Theory: George is telepathic.

2. Phenomenon: Yolanda awoke one morning and remembered having a strange dream. She dreamed that space aliens came into her bedroom while she was sleeping and abducted her. The dream seemed extremely vivid. Later in the day, she noticed some scratches on her ankle. She didn't know how they got there.

   Theory: Yolanda was abducted by aliens.

* 3. Phenomenon: In 1917 in Cottingley, England, three girls claimed to have taken photos of fairies who played with them in the garden. The photos showed the girls in the garden with what appeared to be tiny fairies dancing around them. (The 1997 movie *Fairy Tale* was about the girls and their story.)

   Theory: Fairies really do exist, and the girls photographed them.

4. Phenomenon: The Loch Ness monster is alleged to be a large aquatic creature that inhabits one of Scotland's lochs. The creature is unknown to science. People have been reporting sightings of Nessie for hundreds of years. There is no hard evidence proving the existence of the monster.

   Theory: The Loch Ness monster actually exists.

5. Phenomenon: The famous Israeli psychic Uri Geller seems to be able to bend spoons and keys with his mind. He has been performing this feat for audiences for years. Magicians claim that Geller is a fraud and that they can also bend spoons and keys with simple sleight-of-hand magic tricks.

   Theory: Geller's psychic powers enable him to bend metal with his mind.

6. Phenomenon: When there's a full moon, people seem to act weird. All you have to do to confirm this is to go downtown and observe people when there's a full moon.

   Theory: Through some unknown force, the moon exerts influence on people's behavior.

7. Phenomenon: Some people claim to be psychic detectives, psychics who help law enforcement agencies solve crimes. The psychics sometimes mention the police departments that they have assisted. This psychic detective work is hard to verify, and skeptics claim that either the psychics lie about their successes or they hit upon a solution to a crime by chance.

   Theory: The psychic abilities of psychic detectives enable them to solve crimes.

Exercise 11.10

Read the following passages and answer these questions for each one:

1. What is the phenomenon being explained?
2. What theories—stated or implied—are used to explain the phenomenon?

3. Which theory seems the most plausible and why? (Base your judgment on the evidence cited in the passage as well as any other information you might have on the subject, and use the criteria of adequacy.)

4. What kind of evidence would convince you to change your mind about your preferred theory?

PASSAGE 1

"A Ouija board is used in divination and spiritualism. The board usually has the letters of the alphabet inscribed on it, along with words such as "yes," "no," "goodbye" and "maybe." A planchette (a slidable 3-legged device) or pointer of some sort is manipulated by those using the board. The users ask the board a question and together or one of them singly moves the pointer or the board until a letter is "selected" by the pointer. The selections "spell" out an answer to the question asked.

"Some users believe that paranormal or supernatural forces are at work in spelling out Ouija board answers. Skeptics believe that those using the board either consciously or unconsciously select what is read. To prove this, simply try it blindfolded for some time, having an innocent bystander take notes on what letters are selected. Usually, the result will be unintelligible nonsense.

"The movement of the planchette is not due to paranormal forces but to unnoticeable movements by those controlling the pointer, known as the *ideomotor effect*. The same kind of unnoticeable movement is at work in dowsing.

"The Ouija board was first introduced to the American public in 1890 as a parlor game sold in novelty shops."[20]

PASSAGE 2

"Most scientists discount the existence of Bigfoot because the evidence supporting belief in the survival of a prehistoric bipedal apelike creature of such dimensions is scant. The only notable exception is Grover S. Krantz (1931–2002), an anthropologist at Washington State University. For nearly forty years, Krantz argued for the probable existence of Bigfoot, but was unable to convince the majority of scientists. The evidence for Bigfoot's existence consists mainly of testimony from Bigfoot enthusiasts, footprints of questionable origin, and pictures that could easily have been of apes or humans in ape suits. There are no bones, no scat, no artifacts, no dead bodies, no mothers with babies, no adolescents, no fur, no nothing. There is no evidence that any individual or community of such creatures dwells anywhere near any of the 'sightings.' In short, the evidence points more towards hoaxing and delusion than real discovery. Some believers dismiss all such criticism and claim that Bigfoot exists in another dimension and travels by astral projection. Such claims reinforce the skeptic's view that the Bigfoot legend is a function of passionate fans of the paranormal, aided greatly by the mass media's eagerness to cater to such enthusiasm."[21]

PASSAGE 3

"Trickery aside, what about reports of apparent animal ESP? Anecdotal evidence suggests some animals may have precognitive awareness of various types of natural catastrophes, becoming agitated before earthquakes, volcanic eruptions, cyclones, and other events. However, the creatures may actually be responding to subtle sensory factors—like variations in air pressure and tremors in the ground—that are beyond the range of human perception.

"Something of the sort may explain some instances of apparent animal prescience. For example, a Kentucky friend of mine insists that his dogs seem to know when he has decided to go hunting, exhibiting a marked excitement even though they are lodged some distance away from the house. However, it seems possible that they are either responding to some unintended signal (such as recognizing certain noises associated with his getting ready for a hunting trip) or that he is selectively remembering those occasions when the dogs' excitement happens to coincide with his intentions. Another friend says he once had dogs who seemed to know when he was going to take them for a walk, but he decided he must have unconsciously signaled them (such as by glancing in the direction of their hanging leashes)."[22]

PASSAGE 4

"Ever since humans gained the ability to look down at the Earth from airplanes, space shuttles, and satellites, we've discovered a number of unusual markings. We know very little about them. [There are some] mysterious lines that are found on the Nazca Desert of Peru. They stretch for several miles, crossing over cliffs and hills. A Swiss author named Erich von Daniken claims in his book, *Chariots of the Gods*, that these lines were made by aliens who visited the Earth long ago. A German scientist, Maria Reicher, says that von Daniken's idea is ridiculous, and she has her own theory. . . .

"Von Daniken claims that aliens landed in the Nazca Desert back when humans were still evolving from primitive beings. When the alien vehicles touched down, they gouged tracks into the desert plain. According to his theory, the ancient Nazcan natives would have believed that these lines were made by the 'fiery chariots of the sky gods.' They carefully preserved the tracks the 'gods' chariots' had made and even extended them in all directions.

"Maria Reicher believes that the Nazca lines were created by ancient Peruvians to form a kind of calendar. She found that the lines aren't formed by marks in the earth, but by dark, purplish rocks that form borders and rows. The Nazcan people separated these rocks, which litter the desert, from the yellowish sand. Ancient Peruvians depended on the annual spring rains for their very existence. Since they needed time to prepare their fields before rainy season began, they made a point of learning when the seasons changed. Reicher noticed that the lines of rocks point to a place on the horizon where the sun rose and set during the winter and summer solstice—the times when the seasons change. Her theory is that the Nazcans used these lines as a sort of grand astronomical calendar, to help them get ready for the all-important change of seasons."[23]

PASSAGE 5

The renowned prophet Michel Nostradamus (1503–1566) composed a thousand verses that foretold historical events. Here's proof. Verse XXVII reads like this:

Underneath the cord, Guien struck from the sky,
Near where is hid a great treasure,

Which has been many years a gathering,
Being found, he shall die, the eye put out by a spring.[24]

This is a clear reference to World War II. It means "paratroopers alight near the Nazi's plunder hoard and, captured, they are executed." Some people think that the verses are so vague that anyone can read anything they want into them. But they're not ambiguous at all.

Summary
Science and Not Science

- Science seeks knowledge and understanding of reality, and it does so through the formulation, testing, and evaluation of theories. Science is a way of searching for truth.
- Science is not a worldview, and we can't identify it with a particular ideology. Science is also not scientism—it is not the only way to acquire knowledge. It is, however, a highly reliable way of acquiring knowledge of empirical facts.

The Scientific Method

- The scientific method cannot be identified with any particular set of experimental or observational procedures. But it does involve several general steps: (1) identifying the problem, (2) devising a hypothesis, (3) deriving a test implication, (4) performing the test, and (5) accepting or rejecting the hypothesis.
- No hypothesis can be *conclusively* confirmed or confuted. But this fact does not mean that all hypotheses are equally acceptable.

Testing Scientific Theories

- Following the steps of the scientific method, scientists test hypotheses in many fields, including medical science. One example is the testing of the hypothesis that taking high doses of vitamin C can cure cancer.
- To minimize errors in testing, scientists use control groups, make studies double-blind, include placebos in testing, and seek replication of their work.

Judging Scientific Theories

- Theory testing is part of a broader effort to evaluate a theory against its competitors. This kind of evaluation always involves, implicitly or explicitly, the criteria of adequacy.

- The criteria are testability, fruitfulness, scope, simplicity, and conservatism.
- The criteria of adequacy played a major role in settling the historic debate about planetary motion, and they are used today to effectively judge the relative merits of the theories of evolution and creationism.

Science and Weird Theories

- Inference to the best explanation can be used to assess weird theories as well as more commonplace explanations in science and everyday life.
- Scientifically evaluating offbeat theories can often be worthwhile in determining their truth or falsity and (sometimes) in discovering new phenomena.

Making Weird Mistakes

- When people try to evaluate extraordinary theories, they often make certain typical mistakes. They may believe that because they can't think of a natural explanation, a paranormal explanation must be correct. They may mistake what *seems* for what *is*, forgetting that we shouldn't accept the evidence provided by personal experience if we have good reason to doubt it. And they may not fully understand the concepts of logical and physical possibility.
- The distinction between logical and physical possibility is crucial. Some things that are logically possible may not be physically possible, and things that are physically possible may not be actual.

Judging Weird Theories

- In both science and everyday life, the TEST formula enables us to fairly appraise the worth of all sorts of weird theories, including those about crop circles and communication with the dead, the two cases examined in this chapter.

 Field Problems

1. Find a controversial health or medical theory on the Internet and design a study to test it. Indicate the makeup and characteristics of any group in the study, whether a placebo group is used, whether the study is double-blind, and what study results would confirm and disconfirm the theory.

2. Find a controversial theory in the social sciences on the Internet and design a study to test it. Indicate the makeup and characteristics of any group in the study, whether a placebo group is used, whether the study is

double-blind, and what study results would confirm and disconfirm the theory. If the theory is one that you strongly believe, indicate the kind and level of evidence that could convince you to change your mind about it.

3. Do research on the Internet to find information on spontaneous human combustion, the theory that a human body can catch on fire due to an unknown internal chemical or biological process. Apply the TEST formula to evaluate the theory. Consider at least one plausible alternative theory. Look for background information at the Skeptic's Dictionary (http://skepdic.com), the Committee for the Scientific Investigation of Claims of the Paranormal (www.csicop.org), or *Skeptic Magazine* (www.skeptic.com).

 ## Self-Assessment Quiz

Answers appear in "Answers to Self-Assessment Quizzes" (Appendix D).

1. What is a test implication?
2. Are hypotheses generated purely through induction? Why or why not?
3. When a test implication is disconfirmed, what conditional argument is exemplified?
4. When a test implication is confirmed, what conditional argument is exemplified?
5. Why can't scientific hypotheses be conclusively confirmed?
6. Why can't scientific hypotheses be conclusively disconfirmed?

For each of the following phenomena, devise a hypothesis to explain it and derive a test implication to test the hypothesis.

7. Automobile accidents on Blind Man's Curve have increased lately, especially since the streetlight was broken and not replaced.
8. Juan was found two hours after the fatal stabbing, sitting in Central Park with blood on his shirt.
9. Mysterious lights appeared in the night sky. They looked like alien spacecraft.

For each of the following phenomena, indicate (1) a possible hypothesis to explain it, (2) a possible competing hypothesis, (3) a test implication for each hypothesis, and (4) what testing results would confirm and disconfirm the hypothesis.

10. While camping in the state park, Maria came down with a gastrointestinal illness.
11. The students who were put in a class with two teachers instead of one showed an improvement in their grades.
12. Public health officials report a significant increase in levels of stress in people who live or work in New York City.
13. Since the Vaughn family started using Super Cold-Stopper With Beta-Carotene they have suffered 50 percent fewer colds.

For each of the following hypotheses, specify a test implication and indicate what evidence would convince you to accept the hypothesis.

14. Esther stole the book from the library.
15. Most people—both white and black—are economically better off now than their parents were thirty years ago.
16. The healthcare system in this country is worse now than it was when Bill Clinton was president.

Each of the theories that follow is offered to explain why an astrological reading by a famous astrologer turned out to be wildly inaccurate. Based on a person's horoscope, he had predicted that the person was a nice man who could work with other people very well. The person turned out to be Josef Mengele, the Nazi mass murderer. Indicate which theory (a) lacks simplicity, (b) is not conservative, (c) is untestable, and (d) has the most scope. (Some theories may merit more than one of these designations.)

17. Theory: Astrology—the notion that the position of the stars and planets at your birth controls your destiny—has no basis in fact.
18. Theory: Astrology works, but the astrologer read the horoscope wrong.
19. Theory: An unknown planetary force interfered with the astrological factors that normally determine a person's destiny.

Evaluate the following theory using the TEST formula. Indicate what phenomenon is being explained. Use your background knowledge to assess the evidence. Specify one alternative theory, use the criteria of adequacy to assess the two theories, and determine which one is more plausible.

20. Joseph has acted strangely for years—always wearing black clothes and sometimes having seizures in public. He's possessed.

 Integrative Exercises

These exercises pertain to material in Chapters 3–5 and 8–11.

1. What is an enumerative induction?
2. What is an analogical induction?
3. What is a necessary condition? A sufficient condition?
4. What is the appeal to ignorance?

For each of the following arguments, specify the conclusion and premises. If necessary, add implicit premises and conclusions.

5. "While the time may be right for more privacy in our bedrooms and civil rights protection for gays in the workplace, we don't think most people want our laws rewritten to accommodate same-sex marriage. Instead, they probably agree with *Boston Globe* columnist Jeff Jacoby, who wrote, 'Sometimes, change destroys. No structure can stand for long when its bearing wall is removed. The bearing wall of marriage—its central and universal characteristic—is its heterosexuality. Knock that down and what is left is ruin.'" [Editorial, *The Tribune–Star*, Terre Haute, IN]

6. "Today in Western New York, more than 46,000 people suffer from Alzheimer's disease or a related dementia. Without a research breakthrough or the development of new treatments in the next few years, 14 million baby boomers nationwide will be victims of the disease, and the cost of their care alone will bankrupt both Medicaid and Medicare. We urge voters to call their senators and representatives to ask them to commit more funding for Alzheimer's research." [Letter to the editor, *Buffalo News*]

7. "OK, I've been shilly-shallying around here, hesitant to come right out and say what I think, but I'm becoming convinced that our president, the man with his finger on the nuclear trigger, is a bona fide nutcase. I really do. For him to say God told him to strike al-Qaida is just nutso. For him to say God told him to strike at Saddam, ditto. This guy is not dealing with a full deck." [Editorial, SFGate.com]

8. "As to his [Braxton's] reasoning that 'perhaps there is a public-health basis for anti-sodomy laws' since '. . . scores of thousands of American homosexuals died from engaging in same sexual acts,' there is a bit of a problem. Since heterosexuals also have died from diseases that have directly resulted from sex, then, by Braxton's logic, the Supreme Court would have to ban heterosexual unions as well. With all the conservatives' carping about the intrusiveness of government, one would think that the elimination of laws concerning one's private life would be cause for celebration for a conservative like Braxton." [Letter to the editor, *Newsday*]

For each of the following phenomena, indicate (1) a possible hypothesis to explain it, (2) a possible competing hypothesis, and (3) a test implication for each hypothesis.

9. The accident rate on I-295 has been very high but was reduced considerably after the speed limit was lowered to 60 mph and billboards urged drivers to obey the law.

10. In stressful situations, women appear to adapt better and quicker to the emotional demands of the situation than men do.

11. The percentage of high school seniors engaging in sexual intercourse has risen dramatically in the past six years.

12. The mosquito population in the county has decreased drastically in the past year even though county workers have curtailed the use of insecticides and have stopped urging residents to get rid of standing water on their property, which is a breeding ground for the insects.

Evaluate each of the following theories and indicate whether it is plausible or implausible.

13. Treatment for HIV/AIDS is much more effective than it used to be because of global warming.

14. Six thousand years ago a worldwide flood devastated Earth, killing all but a handful of human beings, who survived by building an ark.

15. The universe is so vast, with billions of stars that could have planets that will sustain life, that it is probable that intelligent life exists in other places besides Earth.

16. Transcendental meditation shows us that if enough people meditate together on the prevention of crime, the crime rate in an area will decrease.

Evaluate each of the following theories using the TEST formula. Use your background knowledge to assess the evidence. Specify one alternative theory, use the criteria of adequacy to assess the two theories, and determine which one is more plausible.

17. The United States lost the Vietnam War because the Americans' weapons were inferior to those of the North Vietnamese.
18. The federal deficit is astronomically high because of accounting errors.
19. The conflict between the Israelis and Palestinians is caused by the meddling of the United States and Britain.
20. Everyone who has ever beaten cancer—that is, been cured—has done so because of a wholesome diet.

 ## Writing Assignments

1. In a one-page essay evaluate the following theories using the TEST formula:

   a. **Phenomenon:** People report feeling less arthritis pain after taking fish oil capsules.
      Theory 1: Fish oil relieves joint pain.
      Theory 2: The placebo effect.
   b. **Phenomenon:** A temporary drop in the crime rate in Des Moines, Iowa, just after a transcendental meditation group meditated for three days on a lower crime rate.
      Theory 1: Transcendental meditation lowers crime rates.
      Theory 2: Normal fluctuations in Des Moines crime rate.
   c. **Phenomenon:** Fifty patients with severe arthritis pain were prayed for by one hundred people, and twenty-five out of those fifty patients reported a significant lessening of pain.
      Theory 1: Prayer heals.
      Theory 2: Normal pain remission that is characteristic of arthritis.

2. Read Essay 14 ("Fighting Islamic Terrorists Who Stifle Free Speech") in Appendix B and write a two-page essay assessing the strength or validity of its argument.
3. Devise two theories to explain the low test scores of most of the students in your calculus course, and then write a two-page paper evaluating the worth of the two theories.
4. Write a three-page essay evaluating the arguments in Essay 19 ("Freedom of Expression: Policy Reflects Common Sense") and Essay 18 ("Freedom of Expression: Protect Student Speech—Even 'Unwise' Bong Banner"). Explain which essay contains the stronger argument and why.

Index